D1738851

The Rhetorical Career of César Chávez

The Rhetorical Career of César Chávez

John C. Hammerback
and
Richard J. Jensen

TEXAS A&M UNIVERSITY PRESS
COLLEGE STATION

The paper used in this book meets the minimum requirements
of the American National Standard for Permanence
of Paper for Printed Library Materials, Z39.48-1984.
Binding materials have been chosen for durability.

Library of Congress Cataloging-in-Publication Data

Hammerback, John C.
    The rhetorical career of César Chávez / John C. Hammerback and
Richard J. Jensen. — 1st ed.
        p.   cm.
    Includes bibliographical references and index.
    ISBN 0-89096-808-X (alk. paper)
    1. Chavez, Cesar, 1927–   —Oratory.   2. Discourse analysis.
3. Persuasion (Rhetoric)   4. Labor leaders—United States.
5. Mexican American migrant agricultural laborers.   6. Trade-unions—Migrant
agricultural laborers—United States.   7. Trade-unions—Mexican American
Membership.   8. United Farm Workers.   I. Jensen, Richard J. (Richard Jay),
1943–   . II. Title.
HD6509.C48H36   1998
331.88'13'092—dc21   97-32794
                                                                        CIP

Contents

Acknowledgments

For assistance in our rhetorical analysis, we owe a debt to many scholars, some cited in our footnotes and text and others who are invisible yet influential in our thinking about matters rhetorical. Particularly important to us have been Frederick J. Antczak and a literary giant upon whom Antczak relied, Kenneth Burke. Among the many others who taught us through their writings are Martha (Solomon) Watson, Kathleen Hall Jamieson, Karlyn Kohrs Campbell, Edwin B. Black, Walter R. Fisher, Maurice Charland, and the other literary giant who informed Antczak, Wayne C. Booth.

Although our book is not voluminous, we accrued many debts while writing it. Our understanding of Chávez's thinking about and practice of discourse was deepened by our study of his handwritten comments on drafts, outlines, and notes of speeches provided by his press secretary for many years, Marc Grossman. Our warm thanks to Marc for generously sharing his expertise and experiences, along with the texts, in a lengthy and enlightening meeting in Sacramento. Filmmaker and professor Rick Tejada-Flores could scarcely have been more generous or helpful: He gave us the transcripts of his valuable collection of some fifty films that captured crucial moments in Chávez's career and public address, a collection that Tejada-Flores and his associates spent two years collecting. Among others to whom we owe gratitude are: our teachers at Indiana University for the personalized and inspirational education they offered; our respective wives, Jean and Carol, for their usual good cheer, love, and understanding; our daughters Mary Kay, Kristen, and Karen, who by attending their respective universities and working at their respective jobs let us concentrate on our work; Professor Richard A. Garcia, for generously sharing an unpublished interview with Chávez; Ronald J. Mahoney, of the Special Collections at California State University, Fresno, and Kathy Schmeling, of the Archives of Labor and Urban Affairs at Wayne State University in Detroit, for hospitality during our visits and for generously providing documents of all kinds; and professors Bernard Duffy, Andrew King, William Starosta, and David Zarefsky, each of whom read the manuscript in either its very early or nearly completed stage and made useful suggestions for revision. Several members of the United Farm Workers (UFW) were generous in responding to questions and furnishing documents: Magdaleno M. Rose-Avila and Abe Bonowitz of the César E. Chávez Foundation, Julie Chávez Rodríguez, Arturo Rodríguez, and Linda Chávez at UFW headquarters at La Paz, in Keene, California.

The authors also wish to acknowledge the vital assistance of California State University, Hayward, for a sabbatical leave during the winter and spring quarters of 1996; Cal State's School of Arts, Letters, and Social Sciences for a faculty development grant to help with travel and duplicating; and the Greenspun School of Communication, University of Nevada, Las Vegas, for generous funding of travel, copying, typing, and translating of Chávez's discourse. Thanks to Beth Macom for her superb work as an editor.

The Rhetorical Career of César Chávez

Introduction

"Time accomplishes for the poor what money does for the rich," wrote César Chávez in a 1969 public letter that reflected his belief that the lives of farm workers would improve in the future. "While we do not belittle or underestimate our adversaries, for they are the rich and powerful and possess the land, we are not afraid nor do we cringe from the confrontation. We welcome it! We have planned for it. We know that our cause is just, that history is a story of social revolution, and that the poor shall inherit the land."[1]

As early as 1966, a CBS news documentary called Chávez "the most persuasive union leader to come along in a generation."[2] Over the years close observers would note his skill with words and reliance on discourse; many called him charismatic; others marveled at his "messianic ability."[3] Chávez employed rhetorical discourse—herein defined as communication that influences audiences varying in size from huge to a single person—indefatigably in the service of his union and movement; and he rhetorically extended his vision and influence far past the workers whom he led, addressing a wide variety of audiences including congressional committees, television viewers, college gatherings, and many others.

This book presents the story of Chávez's career from a rhetorical perspective. Such a perspective adds to an understanding of his career, for Chávez himself—as we demonstrate—consciously gave discourse a central place in his worldview, painstakingly developed principles and techniques of communication that would be effective for him and his coworkers, consistently told supporters of the crucial importance of discourse to achieve his movement's goals, and exhaustively engaged in a career-long rhetorical campaign for his cause. He was an extraordinarily skilled communicator who placed his discourse at the very heart of his career.

Despite the vital place of public address in Chávez's life as a leader, historians and other scholars who have written his story have not carefully examined his rhetorical campaigns, presented in detail—or at all—Chávez's view of the workings and function of his discourse, explained his extraordinary urge to speak and write, or attempted a detailed accounting of how and why he succeeded as a rhetor. Recent books have begun to focus on Chávez's use of public discourse. In *The Fight in the Fields: César Chávez and the Farmworkers Movement* (1997), journalists Susan Ferriss and Ricardo Sandoval provide a carefully researched and clearly written biography of Chávez's life and history of the United Farm Workers (UFW). The book was created to accompany "The Fight in the Fields," a documentary on Chávez and his union shown on U.S. public television in April of 1997. Although Ferriss and Sandoval often use Chávez's own words from interviews, articles, and speeches to tell his life story, they do not analyze Chávez's rhetoric or examine his public discourse in detail.

The other recent study, *César Chávez: A Triumph of Spirit* (1995), by historians Richard Griswold del Castillo and Richard A. Garcia, shows more interest in and understanding of rhetorical matters than do other writers on Chávez. Along with providing valuable historical and ideological context in their recounting of Chávez's life and career, they offer an insightful and illuminating interpretation based on Chávez's life as "text" for the liberal authors who created Chávez's public persona. Yet the irony is heavy: These authors who carefully treat the man as text ignore the texts of the man. Their postmodern analysis places Chávez in the position of object, though Chávez himself always acted as a subject, convinced that his writing, speaking, and other forms of communication made a difference.

Indeed, we present ample evidence that Chávez's discourse did make a difference. Initially lacking financial wealth, political power, family influence, or even an education past the eighth grade, he had little else but his discourse to convince farm workers to join his organizing movement and then to generate public support for it. So why does Chávez's rhetorical career remain a mystery? The largest of questions remain unanswered: What motivated him to speak and write incessantly and across a lifetime? Why did he select his particular and in some cases peculiar rhetorical goals and tactics? What *were* those goals, means, and the other rhetorical qualities that comprised his rhetorical profile? What rhetorical dynamics accounted for his effects on audiences, allowing a quiet communicator to be a charismatic leader? Smaller but still important questions also remain unanswered: How did Chávez adapt to audiences based on their ethnic compositions or interests? Indeed, did he adapt at all? How did his discourse change during his career? What themes endured throughout his career? What addresses commanded his greatest attention and preparation?

Our book attempts to answer these and other questions and will eliminate some of the mystery surrounding the man and his career by adding this vital rhetorical dimension to the story of César Chávez.[4] Indeed this dimension dominates his career; Chávez consciously placed rhetorical discourse at the center of his life's work.

César Chávez rose from the ranks of the poorest and least powerful segment of American society to achieve a status rare in contemporary times: He was a genuine hero. His accomplishments and commitment astounded friend and foe alike. Against almost insurmountable odds he overcame the vast strength of California's agribusiness to create the nation's first permanent union of farm workers, then led that union to a series of remarkable triumphs. He also became a leading civil-rights advocate for Mexican Americans and indeed for many marginalized groups in the nation, a quiet yet charismatic speaker and effective writer who persuaded and inspired many to support his cause.

The unpretentious, soft-spoken, and modest Chávez, a child of migrant work-ers and himself a former crop-picker who had little formal education, seemed an unlikely candidate for such success as a rhetor and leader. His achievements would rest upon a fortuitous combination of the historical situation he confronted and the personal qualities, rhetorical skills, experiences, and worldview he possessed. Chávez began his career in the 1960s, a time when minorities throughout the United States were demanding their shares of the American Dream. In the South-west and in California, Mexican Americans were creating numerous activist or-ganizations to fight for their rights. In central California, Mexican Americans comprised the majority of farm workers and possessed a history of militant, al-beit unsuccessful, attempts to unionize. These conditions invited the changes that Chávez would initiate as he formed and furthered a labor union and a social movement. An invitation to change, however, does not itself produce changes; and conditions alone could not ensure his success. It would take the man to alter the material world. And of Chávez, in turn, would be required the particular outlook, skills, and qualities necessary both to create a powerful rhetorical mes-sage and to preach it incessantly in a sustained and at times exhausting lifelong campaign as an activist union leader.

By the end of his life César Chávez had personal stature achieved by few Americans in recent history. He transcended his own movement, ethnic group, and the issues he addressed. Moreover, as Griswold del Castillo and García ob-served, Chávez was the only Mexican-American leader whose appeal was suc-cessful across "class and generational as well as regional lines."[5]

Reactions to his death in 1993 constituted one measure of his esteem and influence. One Hispanic leader observed that, "If you ask any Hispanic of my generation . . . the first name that comes to mind is César Chávez."[6] To Califor-nia state senator Art Torres, "He was our Gandhi . . . our Martin Luther King"; former California governor Jerry Brown called him a visionary who sought "a more cooperative society and a more caring society"; and U.S. President Bill Clinton spoke of Chávez as "an authentic hero to millions of people throughout the world" and "an inspiring fighter for the cause to which he dedicated his life." A survey of fifty articles reporting Chávez's death found the following words and phrases commonly used to describe him: saint, heroic figure, man of vision, tireless champion, and champion of the poor. Richard A. García wrote upon Chávez's death that many individuals "had already started to see him as a national metaphor of justice, humanity, equality, and freedom."[7] Griswold del Castillo and García added that "Until César Chávez emerged in the mid-1960s, there was no Martin Luther King Jr. in Mexican-American politics."[8]

Such accolades had become the norm long before Chávez died. His fight for the poor and downtrodden captured the imagination of many Americans in the 1960s, and his public image continued to grow throughout his life. That image is featured in the following sample of descriptions of him during his career: "He is a guerrilla leader, in the tradition of [Emiliano] Zapata, who has advocated the aggressive nonviolent philosophy of Gandhi to the farm-worker cause"; "Mr. Chávez has been called a 'Mexican Martin Luther King' and 'the most charismatic union leader in the country'"; "an idealist . . . an activist with a near-mystic vision, a militant with a dedication to nonviolence"; an individual with "a great deal of personal magnetism"; "a folk legend among Hispanics and labor activists"; "a modern prophet sent by God to declare justice and equity for farm workers"; and "a small man with a soothing, spiritual presence"; an individual who is nonviolent "in the spirit of Mohandas Gandhi and Martin Luther King"; and "one of the heroic figures of our time."[9] Richard Rodríguez wrote in 1991 that Chávez "wielded a spiritual authority" for Chicanos that made him a "folk hero," a status, according to Griswold del Castillo and García, that made him "synonymous with La Causa [the cause]" throughout the Southwest.[10] One writer proposed that Chávez had created a "minor miracle" because of the "70 percent increase in real wages [for farm workers] from 1964 to 1980, pension plans, disability insurance, health-care benefits, and the creation of a credit union." But beyond those tangible benefits the UFW "has guaranteed migrants the right to bargain and given them a political voice in California, Arizona, and Texas."[11] A 1985 article in the *New Republic* summarized his image: "César Chávez is one of the last representatives of a dying breed—the charismatic 1960s hero."[12] Such recognition for his heroism was not confined to the United States: Chávez received prestigious awards from Mexico and other countries and was admired throughout the world.[13]

In a 1968 statement that typified his own modesty, Chávez downplayed his elevated reputation: "There is a great need for heroes in this country. . . . Frequently I am heralded as the savior of the farm worker when I do less work than most of the people who are involved." He abhorred the tendency of the press and others to "pick on one human being" and ignore others. He requested that he not be made a hero until he ultimately succeeded or failed in building the union; history alone, he said, should be allowed to judge his actions.[14]

Although he was revered by many people, Chávez had powerful enemies. Historians Matt Meier and Feliciano Rivera wrote that he could be viewed "as messiah or devil" depending upon your perspective.[15] His opponents labeled him as a "'Communist,' 'Alinsky-dupe' [after organizer Saul Alinsky], 'opportunist' [who was plotting to collect union dues to be used for his personal gratification], 'gangster,' 'phony civil-rights worker,' 'outsider,' and 'colossal fraud.'"[16] After his death, however, even his longtime critics acknowledged his rhetorical abilities and profound impact. One such critic offered this mixed view of his life: "He was a worthy advocate for his cause. . . . He was no saint, but he certainly changed the face of California agriculture."[17]

Whether Chávez was praised or damned, his heavy reliance on public discourse to reach his goals is indisputable and remarkable. In an interview he quantified the extraordinary frequency of his speaking during one of his particularly active campaigns: "In 1969 I did three months where I spoke an average of eight speeches a day. For three months. Every single day. I think I got off maybe two Sundays, three Sundays in three months. And sometimes I'd be speaking at eleven o'clock at night."[18] His rhetorical means and medium went beyond public speaking to include numerous articles and public letters, many well-publicized fasts, and a variety of other nonverbal tactics. Chávez's commitment to public address emerges graphically in a single incident during one of his lengthy speaking tours. While giving a speech he was "actually pelted with eggs and tomatoes, but . . . he was so exhausted that he scarcely noticed. He kept right on with his speech." Because he was so controlled, many members of the audience began to cheer. Chávez later recalled: "I made a lot of friends there."[19] His dedication to discourse sometimes exasperated those close to him, as when in 1972 a coworker complained that Chávez enjoyed organizing farm workers but "can't do it right now because he has to go around speaking."[20]

Despite Chávez's frequent public speaking, he did not fit into the typical mold of the charismatic orator. Communication scholars often describe a charismatic orator as one who has the "superior ability to communicate orally," one whose fiery, confident, and high-voltage style and manner stands out incandescently from that of everyday speakers.[21] Chávez clearly did not meet that description. Winthrop Yinger, a Chávez biographer who observed the organizer speaking numerous times over a ten-year period in the 1960s and 1970s, reported that Chávez remained "reticent, shy. He still blends into crowds and often goes unnoticed by many." Another biographer described Chávez in these words: "The Messianic quality about him is suggested by his voice, which is mesmerizing—soft, perfectly modulated, pleasantly accented. More than anything else he seems to impart what Fred

Ross [Chávez's mentor in organizing] calls 'a sense of quiet power.'"[22] Chávez himself acknowledged the anxiety that soft-spoken and modest people often feel when speaking in public: "I don't like public speaking. Not at all. . . . And I still get butterflies in my stomach. . . . Once it's over I say, 'Oh thank God, it's over. I can rest now.'" "No, I am not fiery," he would add, "I am not a speaker. I am a listener."[23]

Just as Chávez remained modest and quiet throughout a life filled with public acclaim, to a large degree his goals, means, and manner as an orator and leader remained largely unaltered throughout his career. "I haven't changed," he explained; "My goal has always been very simple. Don't preach to people; try to involve people. . . . I want to make it simple, just very simple."[24] Noting in 1975 that Chávez's oratory had changed little over the years, Yinger contrasted Chávez's simple style to that of other Chicano leaders of the 1960s such as Rodolfo "Corky" Gonzales and Reies López Tijerina "who . . . employ flamboyance and fiery oratory."[25] Chávez's simplicity surfaced in many aspects of his discourse, perhaps most obviously in his conversational tone: "He does not punctuate his ideas with shouts; indeed, he seldom raises his voice at all." His quiet tone "makes the speaking situation more intimate, personal."[26]

In reference to Chávez's consistency in both life and rhetoric, a Chávez biographer quoted Tennessee Williams's statement that a person couldn't help being changed by fame and publicity. "It is difficult not to agree with [Williams]," he added, "but in the case of César Chávez the signs have not become evident. If this is an act, it is a magnificent one." Another writer agreed: "To this day, Chávez remains unchanged." The Reverend James Drake, a Protestant minister who worked intimately with Chávez during his early years of protest, pointed to the origins of Chávez's consistency: "The pains taken by César were never part of an act. They were a very real extension of his philosophy that human beings are subjects to be taken seriously."[27]

This book traces that rhetorical and biographical consistency, far surpassing the only other scholarly analysis of Chávez's discourse (our own previous writings), which drew largely from a sample in the 1960s and early 1970s of three speeches he delivered and one plan he helped to write. In this study we base our conclusions on a much deeper and broader study of Chávez's public address, from the beginning of his career in Delano, California, in the early and middle 1960s to the end of his life in 1993. We examine Chávez's speeches, represented by complete texts, audiotapes, partial texts, outlines, and notes he used; his essays and complete interviews, which appeared in newspapers, journals, and on television; and his recorded, published, televised, and filmed responses to reporters' questions. We analyze speeches and essays he gave in Spanish, in Spanish and English, and in English, before audiences differing widely in interests and composition.

Some of these addresses went through several carefully written drafts; others represented a standard set of themes, arguments, and explanations during a particular period; still others were designed for a single audience and occasion.

In our prior attempts to illuminate Chávez's rhetorical career, we constructed a model based on his worldview, a set of beliefs that directed him to his rhetorical strategies and qualities and provided his motivation to keep speaking regardless of immediate effects. To reach our goals in this book, we construct a second model to help explain Chávez's startling transformation of some audiences and persuasion of others. Our application of the model to Chávez's public address not only illuminates his rhetorical dynamics, it allows us to challenge and perhaps change the boundaries of both rhetorical and social-movement theory and principles and thus offer theoretical contributions that transcend Chávez and his movement.

Although it is true that one of our goals is to present a history of Chávez's public address—to give a sense of the sheer volume of his speeches and writings, to identify the themes, arguments, and explanations that formed his substantive message, and to make clear how this message addressed and adapted to the issues he faced—we believe that our study has much more to offer than a mere chronicle and reconstruction of his practice and theory of words. We argue that our vantage point is indispensable to answer essential questions and to resolve apparent contradictions raised by the life of this leader who was shy but sought publicity, who was consistent in ideas and manner yet adaptable in tactics and strategies, who began with no noticeable resources and ended with spectacular accomplishments, who was quiet and calm by nature and as a speaker yet charismatic and inspirational in his oratory, and who professed to dislike speaking in public but enacted an extraordinary commitment to public address. Just as Chávez positioned his discourse at the very center of his career, so we rely on a rhetorical analysis to tell an indispensable part of the story of that career. Through this analysis we hope to unravel the puzzle of how, as one writer put it, Chávez through his characteristically "less than fiery speeches and his flat and monotonous tone" established "an aura" of greatness and how, as a professor of Chicano Studies put it, Chávez's "spirit existed in all of his followers."[28] In contrast to prior studies of Chávez, we approach him on his own terms by starting with his own view of and expectations for his life, career, and discourse.

The scope and depth of Chávez's persuasion is too vast to be covered completely in a book of this size. Accordingly, we focus on a select and representative group of his public speeches, writings, interviews, and, to a lesser extent, nondiscursive and largely nonverbal rhetorical events such as marches, fasts, and strikes. We do not concentrate on Chávez's place as a leader in the Mexican-

American protest movement, because his lifetime of work was dedicated primarily to the farm-labor movement.[29]

In each chapter we seek to provide readers with a sense and feel for Chávez's discourse by letting him tell much of his story in his own words. Consequently, we quote generously from his texts. We realize that on occasion rhetorical works under his name were not his creation alone. Some texts, for example, were the work of Chávez and his press aide Marc Grossman, although the ideas, form, and style remained Chávez's. On one of his most significant documents, "The Plan of Delano," Chávez worked with a team of writers; we do not thus base our overall analysis of Chávez's rhetoric on the content, style, or form of the "Plan," although we do quote from it.[30] Whether Chávez alone composed the discourse attributed to him is less important to us, however, than are the causes and consequences of his rhetorical effectiveness and influence. Whenever audiences attributed a text to Chávez, we focus on the rhetorical qualities of that text and on Chávez's rhetorical dynamics with that audience. Although in some cases Chávez shared composition of the texts we study, his ideas and techniques dominated the public address attributed to him and thereby indicate—as we have also been told by the speechwriter who most worked with him—that he was the primary or exclusive author.[31]

Chapter 1 chronicles Chávez's life from his birth to the point in 1962 when he first began to organize a group that would become a union, tracing his preparation as a rhetor/leader and exploring the roots of his worldview. Chapter 2 presents the theoretical and practical sources of Chávez's theory and practice of discourse, placing his view of rhetorical communication into a broad backdrop of his intertwined conceptions of union leadership, religion, and related topics, and giving special attention to his Christian millennialism and its influence on his rhetorical career. Chapter 3 provides an introduction to our approach to Chávez's discourse and a model for its analysis; it also relates our approach to rhetorical and social-movement theories. Chapter 4 focuses on Chávez's rhetorical career from 1963 through 1970, the period when he established his union and developed and tested his rhetorical means and message; Chapter 5 covers his career from 1970 through 1975, when he achieved great personal and professional success yet faced sizeable and persistent obstacles. Chapter 6 identifies the rhetorical tactics, techniques, and manner that made up important components of his rhetorical profile and synthesizes its various elements. Chapter 7 spans his period of transition as a leader and rhetor from 1976 to 1983; and Chapter 8, which surveys the last decade of his life, discusses several of his most carefully constructed addresses and examines his written rhetoric. Chapter 9, the conclusion, summarizes and synthesizes the major findings, interpretations, and implications of our book.

Chapter 1

The Making of a
Rhetor and a Movement

In 1962 César Chávez arrived in the small town of Delano, California, with an ambitious goal: He wanted to create a union among farm workers. Although he was already an experienced community organizer, Chávez faced a formidable task. As writer Peter Matthiessen observed, "Until Chávez appeared, union leaders had considered it impossible to organize seasonal farm labor, which is in large part illiterate and indigent, and for which even mild protest may mean virtual starvation."[1] Lacking the political power and financial resources ordinarily thought necessary for such an undertaking, Chávez took on a powerful industry that had never been successfully unionized.

To accomplish this herculean task, Chávez would need to inform, persuade, and/or change the self-perceived identities of various audiences. And for this rhetorical feat he would draw upon two powerful sets of resources: his knowledge, understanding, commitment, and rhetorical abilities; and his heritage, life, and appearance. Some of Chávez's resources resulted from providence or good fortune; others were hard-earned and the result of conscious effort. This chapter identifies the origin and traces the development of these varied resources as we recount the story of Chávez's life from birth to his arrival in Delano.

César Estrada Chávez was born on March 31, 1927, in Yuma, Arizona. During the first years of César's life, the Chávez family lived on a small farm near the town. Chávez remembered those years with great affection: ". . . we had a big adobe ranch house, with lots and lots of space. We . . . had a special place [where] we would play, by this tree that was our own. And [where] we built things—playhouses, bridges, barns. . . ."[2]

Chávez's father, Librado, owned several businesses, "running a grocery store, an auto-repair shop, and a poolroom about twenty miles north of Yuma."[3] When the family could not pay its property taxes during the depression of the 1930s, it lost the land and businesses. Chávez sadly remembered the day a deputy sheriff came to the farm and ordered the family to leave: "He had the papers that told us we had to leave, or go to jail. My mother came out of the house crying, we children knew there was trouble, but we were confused, worried. For two or three days the deputy came back, every day . . . and we had to leave. When we left the farm, our whole life was upset, turned upside down. We had been part of a very stable community, and we were about to become migrant workers. We had been uprooted." When the Chávezes left, the family had to abandon most of its possessions. Adding to eleven-year-old César's emotional pain, the new owners lacked his affection for the property. "We had these corrals," Chávez recalled, "made of rails and those rails were our swings, that was where we would play after we had watered the horses and cows. . . . Before we left, [a] big tractor came and started knocking down those corrals. That crushed me. I really didn't know what was happening. . . ."[4]

Chávez described how his family had acquired and then lost its farm:

There was a law in the United States . . . it's been like a hundred years now when you could get a piece of land. They used to call it in English the Homestead Act, like the public land that you know about. Well to that little valley it's where they came, that is my grandfather who had 15 kids—9 daughters and 6 sons. And they positioned themselves in that valley, a very rich valley. That's where they cultivated lettuce and well in 1937 the ranchers with one thing or another forced us out; we lost our land. We had a small ranch, my dad had eighty acres, but we lost everything.[5]

The experience left an indelible imprint on Chávez. Years later he looked back fondly to the time when his family had owned land, when they had possessed roots and stability: "Land ownership is very important, and my dad had very strong feelings about the land. If we had stayed there, possibly I would have been a grower. God writes in exceedingly crooked lines." On another occasion he stated, "I bitterly missed the ranch. Maybe that is when the rebellion started. Some had been born into the migrant stream. But we had been on the land, and I knew a different way of life. We were poor, but we had liberty. The migrant is poor, and he has no freedom."[6]

Upon leaving its farm, the family packed what it owned in its old Studebaker and joined other migrants who were driving north and west, working the harvests through Arizona and California. Chávez described the hardships of those early years:

That winter of 1938 I had to walk to school barefoot through the mud, we were so poor. . . . After school we fished in the canal and cut wild mustard greens—otherwise we would have starved. Everyone else left the camp we were living in, but we had no money for transportation. When everyone else left, they shut off the lights, so we sat around in the dark. We finally got a few dollars from some relatives in Arizona and bought enough gas . . . to get us to Los Angeles. Our car broke down in L.A. and my mother sold crocheting in the street to raise the money for enough gas to get to Brawley. We lived three days in our car in Brawley before we found a house we could afford to rent.[7]

In Brawley, California, the family found work tying carrots into bunches using raffia twine. Workers were paid by the number of bunches they tied each day, and were forced to furnish their own twine—an added hardship. Chávez recalled buying the raffia and soaking it overnight so that it could be split in three ways to save money, a precious savings to families who earned no more than a dollar each day. "It was bad," he said, "I don't know what kept those workers from revolting. . . ."[8]

Chávez remembered his early years in California as an innocent period in which he and his family naively believed the promises of labor contractors. Eventually, however, the Chávezes learned the harsh lessons and corresponding conventions of itinerant farm-working. They discovered "little tricks like living under bridges and things like that. Once we learned the ropes, we began helping other green families . . . so they wouldn't have it as rough as we did." One winter the family was stranded in Oxnard, California, and forced to live in a tent. When his parents could not earn money, Chávez and one of his brothers searched beside a highway for the tinfoil in empty cigarette packages. They collected enough to form an eighteen-pound ball that they sold to purchase tennis shoes and sweatshirts.[9] These experiences taught young César the value of leadership and would help him later embody his cause through his discourse, for "he knew firsthand the taste, feel, smell, and touch of its agony and injustices."[10]

The family's poverty and migratory lifestyle severely limited young César's formal education. Because he moved so often, he never attended one school for an extended period of time, and left school for the last time after the eighth grade to help support his family.[11] Later he calculated that he had attended thirty-seven separate schools and learned little from many of them. "We were really pushed back, beaten back," he said; "education had nothing to do with our way of life."[12]

Many of the schools he and his siblings attended were segregated by race; at others, the Chávez children were treated badly by Anglo students. Nor were the teachers necessarily better. Chávez carried painful memories of teachers who treated him like he "didn't exist" and punished him and other Mexican-American children for speaking Spanish: "Once a teacher hung a sign on [students] that said 'I am a clown, I speak Spanish.'"[13]

Segregation extended beyond the classroom. One incident, early in his life, that held great symbolic import for Chávez is cited in many writings about him:

> We went this one time to a diner, it had a sign on the door "White Trade Only" but we went in anyway. We had heard that they had these big hamburgers, and we wanted one. There was a blonde, a blue-eyed girl behind the counter, a beauty. She asked what we wanted—real tough you know?—and when we ordered a hamburger, she said, "We don't sell to Mexicans," and she laughed when she said it. She enjoyed doing that, laughing at us. We went out, but I was real mad, enraged. It had to do with my manhood.[14]

Decades later Chávez could still hear the young woman laughing. "For twenty years," he concluded, "it seemed to cut us out of the human race." Such vivid memories remained with him; and as an adult he confided: "I still feel the prejudice, whenever I go through a door. I expect to be rejected, even when I know there is no prejudice there."[15]

His experiences as a migrant supplied Chávez with justification for his later actions because, as labor historian Cletus E. Daniel writes, he "instinctively understood that farm workers would cease to be victims only when they discovered the means to take control of their own lives."[16] Chávez believed that a strong union that could achieve fair wages and adequate working conditions could partially help "settle a personal score" for the treatment he had once endured.[17]

Chávez's mother, Juana, kept the family unified through painful and degrading times. She taught the children through the traditional knowledge contained in *dichos* (proverbs or sayings) such as "What you do to others, others do to you"; "He who holds the cow, sins as much as he who kills her"; and "If you're in the honey, some of it will stick to you." She also offered *consejos* (advice), often contained in stories with a moral lesson *(cuentos)*, and was fond of saying, "He who never listens to consejos will never grow to be old." Chávez recounted an example of such advice: "I remember her story of the stone freezing in the boy's hand . . . a very disobedient son who came home drunk and got real mad at his mother. He picked up a rock and was about to throw it at her when it froze to his hand."[18] The stories of Chávez's mother ranged widely, some promoting obedience and honesty, others telling of miracles. Such sayings and stories, an integral part of Mexican-American culture, reappeared years later in Chávez's speeches as means for teaching his followers and potential followers and for identifying himself with Mexican-American listeners through both content and form.

Those migrant years brought Chávez into close contact with unionism. His father joined a series of unions attempting to organize farm workers; although none succeeded, César eagerly listened at the Chávez home when his father and uncle, Valeriano, talked about unions. Young César was fourteen when his father and uncle began to join other union members on strike and picket at night. The impression was lasting. "Because his father harbored a strong, if unstudied, conviction that unionism was a manly act of resistance to the employers' authority," wrote Daniel, "Chávez's attitude toward unions quickly progressed from vague approval to ardent endorsement."[19] At age nineteen Chávez joined the National Agricultural Workers' Union (NAWU), which—like its predecessors—would fail in its battle against growers.[20] Chávez would later identify this experience as the beginning of his career in organizing.

In 1944, at the age of seventeen, Chávez enlisted in the Navy, his preferred option to being drafted. He disliked his two years in the military, calling them "the worst of my life." He especially hated the regimentation and discrimination. Like many others, Chávez had hoped to learn skills in the military that would serve him as a civilian. But, he said, Navy discrimination forced Mexican Americans to be either deckhands or painters. If Filipinos and Blacks could not advance beyond kitchen work, Mexican Americans could not get even that. "Before the war," Chávez later told an audience, "the Navy had Blacks and Filipinos who were given kitchen jobs, but no Mexicans." During his two years, Chávez served on a destroyer escort doing weather patrol out of Saipan and was seasick much of the time. Subsequently he was transferred to Guam where he became a painter. In 1946, upon his discharge, he returned to migrant labor.[21]

One action Chávez took during his military years is frequently cited as an instance of his early inclination toward militancy. On leave in Delano, Chávez attended a movie in a theater that set aside one-fourth of the seats for Mexicans, Blacks, and Filipinos. Defying the rule, he sat in the larger section reserved for Anglos and Japanese. When he refused to move, he was taken to jail. His behavior followed easily from that he had witnessed as a child: "It was the first time I had challenged rules so brazenly, but in our own way my family had been challenging the growers for some time. That was part of life."[22]

After the war Chávez worked for a while in the forests of northern California and eventually settled in San Jose, California, in a barrio called *Sal Si Puedes* ("Get out if you can"), a section of the city "dirtier and uglier than the others."[23] (Later Chávez would challenge this dispiriting name in the rallying cry for his farm workers' movement: "*Sí, se puede*" ["Yes, we can"].) Most of the workers in Sal Si Puedes toiled in the vineyards and orchards near San Jose. Chávez described that period:

> I kept working in the fields because I've always been a farm worker. I worked there until 1952. At that time they would harvest the oranges by hand. . . . We worked on the fields, in 1952, I used to work at an apricot, nectarine, and pear ranch in San Jose. What happened next in San Jose, it's what changed my life . . . it's the beginning of what is happening now."[24]

During this time Chávez met two men who changed the course of his life: Father Donald McDonnell and Fred Ross. Father McDonnell, a Roman Catholic scholar stationed at a local mission, first encountered Chávez while visiting Catholics in Sal Si Puedes in 1952. Fluent in several languages, McDonnell taught Chávez about social justice and labor movements among farm workers and tutored him in the ideas of *Rerum Novarum,* Pope Leo XIII's encyclical pledging the church's support for workers and social justice. Chávez recalled sessions with the priest that often lasted past midnight: "I would do anything to get the Father to tell me more about labor history. I began going to the *bracero* [contract laborer] camps with him to help with Mass, to the city jail with him to talk to prisoners, anything to be with him so that he could tell me more about the farm labor movement."[25]

In June of 1952 the twenty-five-year-old Chávez encountered the man who would become his mentor in organizing, Fred Ross, a leader in the Community Services Organization (CSO), a self-help group for Mexican Americans that was sponsored by Chicago-based Saul Alinsky's Industrial Areas Foundation.[26] Ross later described the CSO as "a civil-rights, civic-action movement among the Chicanos with, at that time, the reputation of being the most militant and effective organization of its kind in the United States."[27] Ross first attempted to contact Chávez at his home, but a suspicious Chávez eluded him, having "never heard anything from whites unless it was the police, or some sociologist . . . coming to write about Sal Si Puedes. They'd ask all kinds of silly questions, like how did we eat our beans and tortillas. We felt it wasn't any of their business how we lived." When Ross persisted, Chávez decided to teach him a lesson, inviting him to a meeting of rough individuals Chávez had gathered to harass him. During the course of the meeting, however, Chávez became so impressed with Ross that he called off the planned harassment and joined with Ross. "As time went on," Chávez recalled, "Fred became sort of my hero. I saw him organize, and I wanted to learn. Right away I began to see that organizing was difficult. It wasn't a party. . . . I wanted to do it just as he did; so I began to learn. It was a beautiful part of my life. And eventually, like him, I became an organizer."[28] Ross was equally impressed with Chávez: "I kept a diary in those days. And the first night I met César, I wrote in it, 'I think I've found the guy I'm looking for.' It was obvious even then."[29]

Chávez soon volunteered in several CSO projects. One of his first efforts was a registration drive that signed up four thousand Mexican-American voters; another helped Mexican Americans gain their citizenship papers. After a period of volunteer work, Chávez joined the CSO as a full-time, paid organizer, first in Oakland and then in the San Joaquin Valley. He was "very frightened" at first, unsure if he could succeed.[30]

As a CSO organizer Chávez learned "what I used to call schemes or tricks— now I call them techniques—of making initial contacts." The individual being recruited, he said, must show interest in being active; then a successful organizer acts on that interest. "The main thing in convincing someone is to spend time" with the person. One technique he practiced was "to take a man with you in your car. And it works a lot better if you're doing the driving; that way you are in charge. You drive, he sits there, and you talk." Chávez spent considerable time figuring out what made people choose to become active, then figuring out how to keep them energized once they had made commitments. If an organizer is successful, he discovered, the individual recruited will find the personal qualities necessary to be able to work independently.[31] Chávez also learned that successful organizing demanded hard work and follow-through, for "if you go around preaching, telling people that things can be done, they begin to deposit their problems with you and expect you to do something for them."[32]

Chávez set out to improve his organizing skills by studying history's great leaders. He read voraciously, borrowing many books from local public libraries and particularly studying St. Thomas Aquinas, St. Paul, and works on Mexican-American history. "St. Paul," he commented, "must have been a terrific organizer, as he would go and talk with the people right in their homes, and sit with them and be with them." Chávez often employed one-on-one communication with prospective organizers. He claimed that "the only way I know is to spend an awful lot of time with each individual—hours and hours—until he understands and you've got him going."[33] "To have effective organizing you just have to talk," he believed; it was necessary to "talk to one at a time" to convince others also to become organizers. Through that process of talking, he would be "multiplying one's work."[34]

As an organizer, Chávez learned to admire Mohandas Gandhi, too—as an organizer who "wasn't afraid to move and make things happen. And he didn't ask people to do things he couldn't do himself."[35] Chávez would begin to study Gandhi's life and works. But his first exposure to the man was visceral:

> Since then I've been greatly influenced by Gandhi's philosophy and have read a great deal about what he said and did. But in those days I knew very little about him except what I read in the papers and saw in newsreels. There was one scene I never forgot. Gandhi was going to a meeting with a high British official in India. There were throngs of people as he walked all but naked out of his little hut. Then he was filmed in his loincloth, sandals, and shawl walking up the steps of the palace.[36]

The image of a poor individual such as Gandhi taking on the rich and powerful British must have been electrifying to a poor young Mexican American dreaming of taking on similarly powerful forces in the United States.

After studying leaders such as St. Paul and Gandhi, Chávez became convinced that an organizer could not get "anywhere unless you build an organization and work like hell to reach your goal." He tried a variety of tactics. He recruited members to the CSO through a "chain-letter effect" by arranging meetings and then convincing each person who attended to call a meeting to which a new group of people was invited. He believed that meetings had to be "short and to the point" because there was "nothing more disastrous than to have meetings which ramble on and on without any results." The gathering must have specific and "clearly defined goals. And, when you organize, you must do it bit by bit, very deliberately and carefully. It's like digging a ditch. You take one shovelful at a time." He learned that the group must be given concrete signs of success to keep it energized; that even a small accomplishment helps to build peoples' spirit and energy.[37]

Following each meeting, Chávez "would lie awake going over the whole thing, playing the tape back, trying to see why people laughed at one point or why they were for one thing and against another."[38] This habit of careful analysis contributed to his ability to convince and inspire potential recruits and thus develop the tools necessary to transform his audience. He also discovered that educating and helping people came naturally to him, partially as a result of the values and training he received from his mother. And once "you helped people," he found, "most became very loyal. The people who helped us back when we wanted volunteers were the people we had helped."[39]

Despite Chávez's study and practice of public address, he was so quiet that he often failed to make an impression. Dolores Huerta, who joined the CSO in 1959 and later became one of the UFW's leaders under Chávez, initially found Chávez "very shy" at CSO meetings and anything but memorable. Yet, she added, "It was strange. Everyone knew that wherever he was, things happened."[40] Chávez's puzzling impact on audiences—which baffled even those closest to him throughout his career—is one of the mysteries of his discourse that our book attempts to solve.

Chávez's quest to reach his goals, and to develop the rhetorical skills necessary to attain those goals, required an all-out commitment. The young organizer worked seven days a week, allowing himself time with his family only by involving all of them in CSO work. Once he made the decision to devote himself fully to organizing for his cause, other people would always come first in his life—and he would always feel happy and fulfilled in being in service to the poor.[41]

During his migrant years Chávez had learned the value of helping others from his mother. He recounted that "My mom and dad were . . . especially my mother was like . . . the CSO. . . . We were migrants but we were a service center. We did all kinds of work for people." That work included interpreting for those who spoke no English, helping people stranded on the highway because they were out of gas or their cars had broken down, and taking people to the hospital. "We were known as the people," he said, "but it was my mother, not us. Sometimes we got very mad at her, but she would commit us and we would do it. So I learned—seeing her doing that is what got me in the CSO."[42]

His CSO years taught Chávez many other principles of labor organizing. For example, Chávez's early confrontations with opponents showed him the importance of power: "I soon realized that you can't do anything by talking, that you can't do anything if you haven't got the power. I realized that the first time I went to a public office to do battle." The battle occurred during a CSO voter registration drive among Mexican Americans when Chávez quarreled with a registrar who denied him the necessary deputy registrars to sign up the large number of people he had convinced to register. After a campaign in which Chávez recruited many supporters to call the registrar, and after he personally pestered the official each day, the registrar agreed to provide extra staff. Chávez learned his lesson well: "Now I seldom like to go see my opponent unless I have some power over him. I'll wait if it takes all my life. And the only way you can generate power is by doing a lot of work."[43] Through this and other experiences, Chávez gained understanding of his foes and the means available to defeat them.

In the CSO Chávez determined how to provide services to the poor, a lesson he would later apply in building his own union. For example, he helped establish a CSO center to solve problems for individuals in need. His work in specific cases taught him when and where to apply pressure to assist the needy to reach particular goals. Later, when starting the union, Chávez would create a similar service center to help members solve their problems.[44]

Chávez discovered another useful tactic while attending a meeting in a small Pentecostal church in Madera. He noticed that the people at the meeting sang and clapped to express their deep commitment to their beliefs. From the people in Madera he took "the idea of singing at the meetings. That was one of the first things we did when I started the Union."[45]

One fundamental insight Chávez gained as an organizer was "never to go to the so-called leadership, but to go right down to the grass roots and develop leaders there." Avoiding established groups and the middle class because they were too concerned about protecting their own self-interest, he located rhetorical means that were particularly effective with farm workers. "When you're trying to recruit a farm worker," he discovered, "you have to paint a little picture, and then you have to color the picture in. We found out that the harder a guy is to convince, the better leader or member he becomes." Chávez would use this lesson, too, when starting his union, seeking leaders from among the workers.[46]

Chávez worked with the CSO from 1952 to 1962, eventually rising to the position of General Director. In those ten years, Fred Ross later wrote, Chávez participated in drives that "registered over 500,000 Chicanos to vote, brought U.S. citizenship and old-age pensions to approximately 50,000 Mexican immigrants, fought for installation of paved streets, sidewalks, traffic signals, recreational facilities and clinics, and forced a drastic curb on police brutality and 'urban removal' of Spanish-speaking residents from redevelopment projects in many of those same barrios."[47]

Even though the vast majority of CSO projects were in urban settings, Chávez's early background drew him toward work that would improve the lives of those he knew best, the farm workers. In 1958 the CSO, under Chávez's leadership, attempted to organize agrarian Oxnard in conjunction with the United Packinghouse Workers of America (UPWA). The idea behind the project was that the CSO would organize a Farm Workers Employment Committee, which would eventually sever its connection with the CSO and attach itself to the UPWA. Chávez successfully organized the workers, but when he left Oxnard the group lost energy and eventually disbanded.[48] The project was not a total failure, however; the lessons learned would prove useful when Chávez began to organize in Delano four years later.

Though Chávez enjoyed his full-time organizing with the CSO, his growing passion was to organize farm workers. Chávez had always believed that the CSO would eventually get around to the farm workers; "In fact," he said, "when I joined the CSO back in 1952, the first thing I asked Fred Ross was, 'what about the farm workers? I want to do something that will give the workers a union.'" If the CSO got big enough, he was assured, it would bring about a farm workers' union.[49]

By the early 1960s Chávez began to disagree with the direction the CSO was taking; he believed it was compromising its radical stance in order to attract middle-class members more interested in building the prestige of the organization than in organizing the poor.

In 1962 Chávez challenged the CSO to return to its activist roots by mounting a campaign to organize farm workers. When the leaders of the CSO refused, Chávez resigned. As Ross wrote, "He couldn't keep living with himself without trying again to organize the farm workers with whom he had shared his life."[50] Chávez outlined the reasons for his resignation: "More than anything else I wanted to help farm workers. I was a farm worker when I joined the CSO ten years before, and I thought the organization could help us. . . . I began to realize that a farm workers' union was needed to end the exploitation of the workers in the fields, if we were to strike at the roots of their suffering and poverty."[51] Once convinced of the need, Chávez quit the only secure job he had ever held to confront a task that would be extremely difficult economically and physically. "If you're outraged at conditions," he said, "then you can't possibly be free or happy until you devote all your time to changing them and do nothing but that. . . . But you can't change anything if you want to hold onto a good job, a good way of life, and avoid sacrifice."[52]

Soon after leaving the CSO Chávez was offered a position as an organizer for the Agricultural Workers Organizing Committee (AWOC), an AFL-CIO affiliate attempting to organize farm workers. He declined the offer in order to be independent. He also declined a job as a director for the Peace Corps in South America, turning down an annual salary of $21,000 to began organizing his own union at a salary of $50 a week.[53]

Daunting obstacles faced Chávez. The workers lacked money, spoke little or no English, and were often illiterate in both English and Spanish. As migrants, they often resided in one place only for a brief time, so could not be mobilized against the growers. In contrast, California agribusiness was a powerful industry that had systematically beaten back all attempts at unionization for nearly half a century, successfully enlisting the power of the police, the courts and laws, big corporations, and large financial institutions in support of their actions and interests.

Despite a unified, powerful, and often ruthless opponent, farm workers had attempted to organize on many occasions. As early as 1928, the Imperial Valley Workers' Union (*La Unión de Trabajadores del Valle Imperial*), an agricultural union mainly composed of Mexican Americans, attempted to improve conditions for workers. The union sought increased pay for picking melons, reform of the labor contractor system, drinking water in the fields, outhouses for employees, and accident insurance. That union was eventually defeated; others followed and initiated strikes such as those by five thousand berry workers in El Monte, and by cotton-pickers in the San Joaquin Valley, both in 1933. The cotton-pickers strike led to violence and the deaths of several workers.[54] The list of unions that had tried and failed to organize agricultural workers was extensive: the Industrial Workers of the World (IWW); the United Cannery, Agricultural, Packing, and Allied Workers of America; the UPWA; the Food, Tobacco and Agricultural Workers Union; and both the AFL and CIO before they unified as one organization. In many instances the growers used violent actions and terror to crush the incipient unions.[55]

Chávez's own family were no strangers to the farm workers' tradition of unionization. His father had been a member of several unions including the Tobacco Workers, the Cannery Workers, the Packing House Workers, and—most importantly—the National Farm Labor Union (NFLU), led by Ernesto Galarza. Chávez later would adopt some of the NFLU's creative tactics (e.g., the economic boycott) and would turn to Galarza for guidance in the 1960s.[56] Mentors like Galarza are useful to leaders of movements because they provide models to follow and can share their wisdom with those who attempt to change society.

Knowing the shortcomings of early unions, Chávez vowed not to repeat their mistakes, and he attempted to learn from the labor leaders who had preceded him. He devoured histories of unions and biographies of labor leaders such as John L. Lewis and Eugene V. Debs, and talked with farm workers who had participated in strikes in order to understand the tactics of union opponents and the failures of union organizers. "It was a sad history of defeat after defeat," he acknowledged; "strikes smashed with violence, the government in league with the growers, police helping to bring in scabs. But the more I studied the mistakes that were made in the past, the more I believed growers were not invincible." He also saw that many Mexican Americans—an ethnic group historically willing to join unions—did belong to unions, including large international groups like the United Auto Workers (UAW). If Mexican Americans would join the UAW, he reasoned, they should be ready for a farm workers' union.[57]

Notwithstanding his modesty and quiet nature, César Chávez was prepared to challenge the growers. He had experienced both the numbing poverty and indignities suffered by migrant workers and the contrastingly hopeful life of owning the land on which one worked for oneself. The family that raised him, the source of his deepest values, had demonstrated its commitment to protesting injustice in general and assuming leadership in the farm workers' struggle in particular. That family, which was itself resourceful and persistent in its battle against the oppressive conditions of migrant life, conspicuously endorsed the union as a vehicle in that struggle. And, as we discuss in chapter 2, Chávez's belief in God and religion buoyed him with the assurance that divine powers were aligned with the farm workers in their righteous cause.

His earliest years bequeathed Chávez a cause in which to believe and the values with which to challenge injustice in his first years as an adult. But Chávez himself discovered the means to battle for his cause, deepening his faith that he could and would succeed. The young organizer learned about the history of the labor movement and its relationship to his religion's conception of social justice; he also acquired both an unshakable belief in organizing and the necessary skills to be an organizer. Moreover, his studies of labor history and his experiences as an organizer and speaker in the CSO provided him with both an understanding of the private and public communication necessary to organize effectively and the ability to do it. When he settled in Delano to begin his lifelong campaign for farm workers, then, Chávez possessed the experiences, knowledge, attitudes, and talents to succeed in a cause theretofore deemed unwinnable.

Chapter 2

Chávez's Conception
of Rhetorical Communication

"Nothing Changes Until the Individual Changes"

The primary features of César Chávez's conception of public discourse grew directly out of the experiences and insights he gained from his life before starting the National Farm Workers Association (NFWA), later the United Farm Workers (UFW). Among his most powerful influences were the family and culture that had shaped him and formed his view of religion and unions, his experiences as a migrant worker, the discrimination he suffered, his training as an organizer and leader in the Community Services Organization (CSO), and his reading and the other experiences that created his belief in non-violence. Added to these influences were the multiple sources—continuing into the mid-to-late 1960s—of his vision of the union as a unique organization that was part of a larger social movement.

Chávez's conception of discourse lay at the heart of his lifetime of speaking and writing. It directed him to the rhetorical qualities that characterized his public address and motivated him to preach his message incessantly regardless of the immediate response of his audiences. In this chapter we outline his theory of rhetorical communication and identify major influences on that theory, focusing on his principles for communicating with the Mexican-American farm workers of his initial campaigns. In later chapters we show how he extended and expanded—but never fundamentally changed—his rhetorical theory and practice in order to appeal to audiences of all ethnic groups and occupations.

César Chávez became a national figure during the turbulent era of dissent and protest in the 1960s and early 1970s. During that period, as we have written elsewhere, "Mexican-American organizations and leaders implored their people to speak out for their share of the American Dream."[1] Chávez joined other prominent Mexican-American leaders in founding organizations that called for significant improvement in the lives of their people.[2] Those changes were necessary because Mexican Americans lived in substandard housing, suffered high unemployment rates, had a lower educational level than most groups in American society, were negatively stereotyped by the media, and were mistreated by police and the legal system. Mainstream American historians and social scientists often mistakenly stereotyped them as lazy, unintelligent, and passive—stereotypes that were, in the case of farm workers, perpetuated by the growers and their allies. In his discourse Chávez would undertake the task of drawing attention to the plight of farm workers and creating an organization to work to overcome those problems.

To redress the wrongs suffered by Mexican Americans, Chávez and other Mexican-American leaders would rely heavily on public discourse. Together they would create the themes, appeals, arguments, and symbols that, we have argued, "altered perceptions of events, people, and places and organized the scattered direct and indirect experiences of individual listeners into a broad and cohesive" group capable of creating change.[3] These leaders' discourse described the problems of the past and the present and then created an image of a better future. Chávez's own vision for an improved future centered on a strong union.

In order for Mexican-American leaders to succeed in their goals, they needed to create a rhetorical picture that would change the image of the past in the minds of audiences. This rhetorical enterprise required them to redefine the image of Mexican-American history as that of a passive people who had not protested, but endured. Mexican-American rhetors would therefore point to specific instances where Mexican Americans had actively challenged the establishment. For Chávez this rhetorical redefinition required that he present examples of how he and other farm workers had always openly opposed the corrupt system.

Mexican-American leaders also strove to convince audiences that they could overcome current social problems in the community by creating organizations to challenge the power structure. They strove to make listeners see themselves not as downtrodden, but as part of a vibrant culture with intrinsic dignity and laudable values. Thus rhetors would attempt to change perceptions by creating positive terms around which Mexican Americans could unite and by identifying common enemies as a way of building solidarity. Chávez chose the UFW as the vehicle by which farm workers could achieve power. He envisioned for his followers a better future once the people united, a future best achieved through the creation of a strong union.

To accomplish his goals with Mexican-American audiences, Chávez would need to appeal to their culture and the rhetorical traditions that reflected that culture. We have previously described how Chávez's cultural heritage had a powerful effect on his discourse.[4] With strong roots in Mexico, the Mexican-American heritage encompasses suffering, sacrifice, penance, the importance of family and church, suspicion of governments and politicians, fears of betrayal by leaders, and positive values such as pride and dignity. The Mexican past also contained a vital place for written documents and speeches. Chávez and other Mexican-American leaders would need to appeal to their rhetorical legacy and cultural heritage to be effective rhetorically. We discuss Chávez's ideas on and practices of rhetorically appealing to Mexican Americans in more detail toward the end of this chapter and in subsequent chapters.

One key element in the formula that accounts for Chávez's success as an orator/organizer was his capacity to embody his discourse. The Chicano activist José Angel Gutiérrez captured the essence of this capacity when he described Chávez as "the embodiment of a Chicano. Chicanos see themselves in César: clothes, personal style, demeanor and commitment. Chávez inspired himself. And, his inspiration moved Chicanos. . . . He was one of the migrants. He spoke plainly but articulated larger than life goals for migrants, especially that of building their own union."[5]

In his youth Chávez lived the life of a migrant farm worker, and later he made a conscious effort to identify himself with that style of life. During a Congressional hearing he was asked how long he had been in his present position. His response united him with the workers he led: "Well, I have been a farm worker all my life."[6] On another occasion he identified himself with farm workers by saying: "I started organizing when I was nineteen years old. I came out of the fields."[7] His years as an itinerant crop-picker, part of the Mexican-American community, he believed, allowed him to identify with migrant workers because he had "traveled their paths." This experience would not only give him an understanding of his farm-worker audience, it would be part of the rhetorical formula that made him effective with that audience. The persona he projected through his life and discourse illustrates what rhetorical critic Frederick J. Antczak called "the practice of rhetoricians who successfully identified themselves as like their audiences, only somehow more so."[8] The success of that identification is apparent in the following remembrance by Blanca Alvarado, vice-mayor of San Jose:

> . . . his identity as a Chicano, being Mexicano, being Indio, or being part of the ancestry of the people from here was clear, even though he didn't go around banging that drum. He didn't have to tell you that he was brown; he was brown. He didn't have to tell you that he thought in Indian ways because he acted in an Indian way.[9]

· · ·

Chávez himself keenly realized the need to identify with his audiences and counseled organizers to achieve identification with those being organized. One of his coworkers recalled:

> I remember César used to tell me, "You gotta dress like the people. You gotta talk with the people. Don't even drive a car. Don't take a lunch. Let the people feed you." I learned a lot because he taught me that you have to be where the people are and start organizing where they're at.[10]

Chávez would need all of his capacity for identification to reach his goals in organizing. As biographer Winthrop Yinger noted, Chávez faced the formidable task of the "molding of a transient, unskilled work force into a skilled and participative citizenry."[11] Believing that "people are the raw material"[12] that must be refined, and that organizers must talk with people, Chávez instructed: "If you talk to people, you're going to organize them. But people aren't going to come to you. You have to go to them. It takes a lot of work."[13] He argued that the movement must begin "where the people are, where they work is where you have to begin. The individual is the key to social change. Nothing changes until the individual changes."[14]

The changes would be dramatic once strikers began to put their bodies on the line through picketing and boycotts. Picketers had to physically commit to hours, days, and even months of walking a picket line—risking being fired from their jobs and enduring physical attacks from opponents. Those who organized the boycotts had to leave California to spend months and sometimes years in distant cities in the United States and Canada to create and maintain organizations that attempted to convince stores to stop selling boycotted products. In both cases strikers had to overcome their fear of violence, loneliness, and the prospect of failure. According to Chávez,

> We are dealing with fear. If we get rid of the fear, then it is easier. Once we confront the fear the struggle is not hard to fight. A man will think hard, very hard, before he joins a picket line. Once he does that, he won't think twice about staying out on the boycott for a year, two years. Once the farm workers get up on their feet and strike, they are not the same people. They begin to think differently about themselves.[15]

Chávez elaborated: "When you have people together who believe in something very strongly—whether it's religion or politics or unions—things happen."[16] And these things can be dramatic. "When the genius of a people is released, it is a powerful force," Chávez said; people "are developing before their own eyes. . . . It happens overnight. These things, when they get released, get transacted into ideas, into acts, into demands, into struggles. They are not corrupted. They are original."[17]

Chávez's coleader in the union, Dolores Huerta, reported that he inspired "the workers to organize, giving them the confidence they needed through inspiration and hard work and educating them through the months to realize that no one was going to win the battle for them, that their condition could only be changed by one group—themselves."[18] One of Chávez's followers added, "From Chávez, I learned to struggle for justice and to allow myself to evolve into someone who is committed to social change and who nonviolently pursues equality and fairness for the dispossessed of society."[19] This revised identity was also apparent in the way people described themselves. Joe Serna, a volunteer with Chávez in the 1960s who later became mayor of Sacramento, described how Chávez helped him change: "We used to call ourselves Spanish, not Mexican, because we were ashamed of our poverty. Ashamed because we were Mexican. César took that shame away."[20]

Chávez's speaking was a primary means by which he helped people redefine themselves and their prospects. Eliseo Medina, a successful organizer for the union, recalls that he was at first unimpressed when he saw Chávez give a speech: "So César gets up and he's this little guy . . . very soft spoken. I say, 'That's César?' You know, I wasn't very impressed. . . ." But Medina's view quickly changed: "The more he talked, the more I thought that not only could we fight, but we could win."[21]

Much of Chávez's belief that workers could win came from experiences within his own family, which provided many valuable insights into what it took to be an effective rhetor and union leader. The Chávez family had acquired a unity that gave its members strength to speak out against injustices in the fields. Without this solidarity, they might easily have fallen into the hopelessness that results from the isolation and powerlessness associated with the life of migrant workers. The Chávezes did more than speak out, however; Chávez saw himself as being part of "probably one of the strikingest families in California. . . . We were constantly fighting against things that most people would probably accept because they didn't have that kind of life we had in the beginning, that strong family life and family ties which we would not let anyone break."[22] This willingness to stand up against unfairness resulted in part from the fact that the Chávezes had not always been migrants. The displaced Chávez family, wrote labor historian Cletus E. Daniel, held "among its otherwise meager possessions a powerful legacy of the independent life it had earlier known, one that revealed itself in a stubborn disinclination to tolerate conspicuous injustices."[23]

Chávez applied his belief in family unity to his union. He attempted to transform the farm workers from a group of powerless and often fearful individuals into a strong family that could provide its members the identity, services, and influence necessary to alter their less-than-ideal lives. As he said, "We are a Union family."[24] Early in the development of the UFW Chávez outlined his view:

> The movement of the farm workers association is organized so that all the members of the family belong. Unity of life comes to our movement through the cooperation of the worker. The farm workers association is a collective undertaking, which, by collective means, works to provide the economic basis that the farm workers need to assure a better life, socially, morally, and economically. At the same time the association works to restore to man that independence and liberty which will assure him his dignity and solidarity with other men.[25]

Chávez fleshed out his conception of family by teaching that the structure of the union must fit the farm workers, not be "a neat business operation with no heart, [because] the workers will scoff; they will turn it down cold." In order to appeal to workers, the union would emulate a family by offering "cooperatives, credit unions, educational programs of a practical nature, money saving devices . . . these are necessary elements of any union planning on capturing the imagination of the farm worker. It must be grass roots with a vengeance."[26] Nor was this idea abstract; once during a protest march Chávez pointed to a worker in a field and said: "But whatever he needs to be, everything he's got inside him to be, we've got to help make that possible."[27] From his early years as a farm worker, Chávez also determined that the immense power of growers came largely through the weakness of farm workers; and that as farm workers gained strength, they would balance the power of their employers.[28]

Chávez was intimately aware of the barriers for success. "You see, the farm worker is an outsider," he lectured, "even though he may be a resident worker. . . . He is an outsider economically, and he is an outsider racially."[29] Chávez had experienced being an outsider, but he had also been taught that farm workers could improve their lives through direct action. Thus he proclaimed: "We don't let people sit around a room crying about their problems. . . . No philosophizing— do something about it." Once such actions brought dignity and worth, he reasoned, workers would be seen in a different light:

• • •

One of the most beautiful and satisfying results of our work in establishing a union in the fields is in witnessing the worker's bloom—the natural dignity coming out of a man when his dignity is recognized. Even some of the employers are seeing this point. Workers whom they previously had treated as dumb members of a forgotten minority suddenly are blooming as capable, intelligent persons using initiative and showing leadership.[30]

A witness to many such transformations, Chávez promised that he "could sit up all night and tell of the beautiful things that happen to people."[31]

Chávez's belief in the worth of individuals and in their ability to improve—and indeed his motivation for his lifetime campaign—grew out of his religious convictions. As a devout Catholic he described the church as "one form of the Presence of God on Earth" and a "powerful moral and spiritual force" in the world.[32] Relating his religious faith to his everyday life, he said: "Religion is a deep part of us. . . . Our religion and our life are inseparable."[33] Perhaps not surprisingly, he attracted many clergy as his top advisors and coworkers, such as Catholic priests Mark Day and LeRoy Chatfield and Protestant ministers James Drake and Chris Hartmire.

Acting out what biographer Jacques Levy called his "quiet, unpretentious piety," Chávez often went "unnoticed into churches to pray or to receive Communion, alone." His deep religious faith formed the foundation for his determination in the farm workers' movement. As he confided: "Today I don't think that I could base my will to struggle on cold economics or on some political doctrine. I don't think there would be enough to sustain me. For me the base must be faith."[34]

Chávez's faith justified his actions. His "deepest belief," wrote Winthrop Yinger, was that "sacrifice and selfless service to others lead to the authentic life." As Chávez stated, "We are men locked in a death struggle against man's inhumanity to man."[35] Chávez uncovered a spiritual basis for his militant crusade in the documents of the Second Vatican Council that emphasized justice and condemned the separation of the spiritual from the material. Father Mark Day saw Chávez as "both a mystic visionary and a pragmatist, with a heavy accent on the latter. As a student of social movements and forces, he knows that violence can only breed more violence. It leads to a tragic escalation that ends in the demoralization of one's forces. As a Christian, Chávez has a deep reverence for human life."[36] Chávez said that he saw himself as "literally commanded to do something" about people who were suffering; he was convinced that "even in the face of the biggest disappointment there's always that faith, that tomorrow's gonna be different."[37]

Although Chávez's deep faith gave him a means of identifying with members of his largely Catholic farm-worker movement as well as the motivation to preach his message, he charged that the Catholic Church itself had abandoned many of its ideals and teachings by siding with the growers rather than the workers. "Here in Delano," he would point out, "the church has been such a stranger to us, that our own people tend to put it together with all the powers and institutions that oppose them." He insisted that the church change its stance toward workers or suffer serious consequences: "But I think that a storm is brewing with the Mexican American and the church. Unless something is done very soon, the church leadership is going to have a hell of a time."[38] Eventually the leadership of his church supported the union, but only after several years spent ignoring his appeals for help.

The Catholic Church gave Chávez a moral grounding for his ideas, but he learned his practical skills in organizing and rhetorical communication during his ten years with the Community Service Organization. Like its parent organization, the Industrial Areas Foundation (IAF), Yinger wrote, the CSO advocated "coalition[s] of existing groups, confrontation to publicize issues, corporate structuring, strong emphasis on grass roots membership, and the local or neighborhood membership carrying the financial load (as opposed to outside monies being used)." In the CSO Chávez found techniques and strategies that would prove effective for the UFW. Throughout his career, according to Yinger, Chávez was never a "planner plopped behind a desk gazing idealistically at some organizational blueprint. His organizing style was . . . that of the quiet, grass roots activist-reformer out there, face-to-face with people. A migrant farm worker among farm workers."[39]

Fred Ross acknowledged that Chávez had "received a few ideas and concepts" from Saul Alinsky and himself. "But he developed his own philosophy and his organizing style," Ross insisted. "You know how well it has worked."[40] Chávez gave credit to Ross for his training, saying: "I paid attention to what he did, how he did things. I really wanted to learn how to organize. And I think I learned my lesson. I had . . . ten years under him. So when I came to organize farm workers, I had a lot of confidence."[41] Ross returned the compliment, claiming that after having worked with Chávez for several years, "there wasn't any question in my mind that certainly he was the best Mexican-American organizer in the United States."[42]

During his CSO years Chávez obtained a rich education in the pragmatic theories and everyday practices of organizing—a temporal means to give life to his spiritual faith. He came to realize, he said, that "you need a continuous program that meets the needs of the people in the organization." An organizer must work directly with those people being organized, however, rather than concentrating on activities like setting up meetings, having discussions, running surveys and studies, and originating programs. Chávez said that he learned that he had to organize people before he could write programs, and that the people being organized must be involved in writing those programs.[43] He also learned, he said, to "stay away from established groups and so-called leaders, and to guard against philosophizing," having watched professionals sit around and talk politics but engage in too little action and established groups become overly concerned with respectability and working through traditional channels "like taking a petition to the Mayor, or having tea parties with the PTA. . . . Once you become a respectable group you're not going to fight anymore."[44] Chávez's insights were transferred to his farm workers' union. For example, in both the CSO and UFW he observed that a leader must do all he could to help his supporters in all aspects of their lives. "If I thought someone had been cheated," he recalled, "I'd raise hell. . . . You always knew a friendly priest who would pay a call, a friendly lawyer who would write a letter threatening suit."[45]

While in the CSO Chávez was shocked when people labeled him a communist or rejected him because of his work for the poor. He developed the tactic of refuting attacks on his loyalty by, as Daniel noted, "cloaking himself in the respectability of the Catholic Church."[46] "I found out that when they [those who called him a communist or said he was disloyal] learned that I was close to the church," Chávez said, "they wouldn't question me so much. So I'd get the priests to come out and give me their blessing." In those days, individuals would listen "if a priest said something."[47] Although farm workers did not always accept the ideas of priests, the church remained a potent source of motivation for many of Chávez's audiences. Consequently Chávez had practical as well as moral reasons for incorporating the church into his movement as much as possible.

During one period Chávez organized for the CSO at night and worked in a lumberyard during the day. Initially his coworkers treated him in contradictory ways: Some warned him to be careful because he could be punished for his actions, others needled him about those actions. Eventually he detected a gradual change in their attitudes toward him—they had come to view him as a leader on the job as well as in the CSO. "It's a weird thing how the chemistry works. I think this is how the reaction to leadership begins to develop. Leadership many times is only a mental condition, more than anything else. They began to come to me with little problems that they had."[48] But although people would seek out organizers for help, Chávez knew, there would be precious little appreciation for their actions. Not expecting that appreciation was a theme of Chávez's discourse throughout his career. "I know good organizers who were destroyed," he noted, "washed out, because they expected people to appreciate what they'd done."[49]

Chávez offered a clear guide to the themes and means of the organizer/rhetor.

"In organizing people," he said, "you have to get across to them their human worth and the power they have in numbers." First, one must isolate a problem that needs to be solved; "then there has to be someone who is willing to do it, who is willing to take whatever risks are required. I don't think it can be done with money alone. The person has to be dedicated to the task. There has to be some other motivation."[50] Organizers must realize that they don't know everything, for "once you realize that, it makes you realize that other people have got to do things." And because the organizer does not know everything, organizing is a gamble: "I'll bet there are more failures in organizing than in any other endeavor you can think of. It's a very risky business . . . an awful lot of gambles you have to take almost daily."[51]

Chávez perceived organizing as "difficult only at the point where you begin to see other things that are easier. But if you are willing to give the time and make the sacrifice, it's not that difficult to organize." He decided that there were "some very simple things that have to be done in organizing, certain key things that nobody could get away without doing, like talking to people." "Just keep talking to people," he predicted, "and they will respond."[52] As Griswold del Castillo and Garcia concluded, Chávez's "almost instinctively knew that power lay in changing *people;* not by theorizing but by doing."[53] For Chávez, the primary tool for transforming people—for "doing"—was his rhetorical discourse.

In organizing farm workers Chávez always began with talk: "I just go to the first house in the labor camp or town and knock on doors." Rhetorical success was obtainable and even contagious: "I know that there will be at least a few farm workers in every town or camp who will be receptive to me. I also know that you can sell anything you want to sell if you really want to sell it." The organizer may have to knock on many doors, but "maybe at the fortieth or sixtieth house you find the one guy who is all you need." That one person would become part of a necessary core of dedicated individuals. "You are not really looking for members as much as for organizers," Chávez said. "But people don't know they are organizers when they actually are. Some of the best organizers don't look upon themselves as such."[54]

During his first strike, in 1965, Chávez established a lasting goal: to "involve our friends around the country. We've got to go to the public and tell them what is it that we need, and get them to help us."[55] Thus his public address campaign would focus both on the farm worker and on the public at large.

Chávez defined organizing as an educational process, and some of the best education came through actions that took place on the picket line and the boycott. "When you learn by doing," he came to realize, "you learn faster than by other methods. Once you have people who see what has happened, they become your best organizers." The picket line served as an excellent school to educate organizers and workers, for "if a man comes out of the field and goes on the picket line, even for one day, he'll never be the same." Confirming Chávez's analysis, one farm worker reported: "From him [on the picket line] we have learned . . . not only determination, dedication, and hard work, but unrelenting patience."[56]

Successful organizing required effective and determined leaders, a need Chávez frequently and thoroughly addressed in his public discourse. He outlined how early in life he became the leader in his own family: "At some point . . . I began to take over. . . . I began to take on other responsibilities and I liked it." Chávez's understanding of the need for skillful leadership deepened when he observed strikes called by earlier unions, particularly those he and his family had joined. As a youngster he had listened to workers talk about strike tactics, "overhearing late evening strategy talks and watching firsthand all the other confrontation tactics used by organized labor." Taking part in a strike called by the National Farm Labor Union (NFLU), he noticed that the strike suffered from a lack of leadership and faced other problems that worked against its success. On the other hand, as Daniel wrote, the experience "also produced a brief but equally keen feeling of exhilaration because it afforded an opportunity to vent the rebelliousness that an expanding consciousness of his own social and occupational captivity awakened within him."[57]

Chávez's youth taught him a kind of patience and adaptability that many leaders lack. His biographer Ronald Taylor wrote that because of their trials as migrants, Chávez and his followers "seemed to thrive on the conflict and the result was that the movement developed a unique character, a character consistent with the life and environment of the seasonal farm worker. César Chávez, as the son of a migrant farm worker, had learned to adapt to a life that had to be met day to day, a life that was chaotic and beyond the control of his parents."[58]

Once he became a leader, Chávez found that authority brought dangers as well as responsibilities: "It's very difficult because being a leader is only in peoples' minds," he related, "so you have to be careful because the moment they don't any longer perceive it, then you're not. . . . But the day they don't, if you continue to think they do, you're in trouble."[59] Early in the development of the union, Chávez summed up many of his ideas on leadership:

The missions of the leaders—which is the mission of any authority—is to sustain the movement, to keep the farm workers' association on its destined path, to do what always has to be done so that the goals of the association can be reached. If we want the movement to develop and the association to protect itself, it is necessary to maintain a unity of doctrine, a unity of methods, and a unity of structure which will assure the goals of that movement.

This unity means that we must make sacrifices but these are necessary to sustain the life of the whole organization; they are essential. When we decide on the goal of a particular work, it is necessary to hold on to it, not only with our lips, but always actively; it is necessary for this goal to become a rule of life. He who knows principles is not equal to he who loves them.[60]

While working toward the goals of the union, Chávez "learned a lot about planning and about strategies. . . . That is my first love . . . strategizing." As a strategist he first had to ensure that members were carefully organized and prepared, a task that required him to be like "a composer working night and day. . . . If there is no orchestra, there is no music. No one hears it." Convinced that people knew what they wanted and did not want, Chávez decided that "it's a case of staying with them and keeping your ears open and your eyes open."[61]

Chávez saw the ultimate goal of organizing as power. "Power is what the game's all about," he instructed, "but a lot depends on how the power is used." Convinced that power flowed from a large and committed membership, Chávez would dedicate much of his time and energy to recruiting and energizing UFW members.[62]

Though he willingly assumed the role of leader of his movement, Chávez did not want to be known as an administrator. He understood that administrators could easily become separated from the workers they led. "I'm not one," he admitted; "No one likes to be sitting behind a desk but that's the role I have to play now, I guess, whether I like it or not. I like to consider myself an organizer, not a real good one but a very persistent one." Chávez saw himself not as a bureaucrat but instead as an organizer/leader/rhetor; as Peter Matthiessen wrote, Chávez saw himself "as father of the Union family, praising, teasing, needling, cajoling, comforting, and gently chastising to maintain a balance in this huge and complex household. . . ."[63]

One of the most difficult tasks was to convince members that violence would not be an acceptable part of organizing. From the beginning Chávez realized that nonviolence posed difficult challenges but possessed great promise:

Nonviolence exacts a very high price from one who practices it. But once you are able to meet that demand then you can do most things, provided you have the time. Gandhi showed how a whole nation could be liberated without an army. This is the first time in the history of the world when a huge nation, occupied for over a century, achieved independence by nonviolence. It was a long struggle and it takes time.[64]

• • •

In Chávez's view, to practice nonviolence successfully demanded no less than a spiritual rebirth. Those in his movement must be at peace with themselves before working for "peace in the world." This sense of peace in turn required a ritual purification similar to that advocated by Gandhi. Chávez explained how Gandhi went through purification: "He prepared himself for it by his diet, starving his body so that his spirit could overtake it, controlling the palate, then controlling the sex urge, then using all of his energies to do nothing but service. He was very tough with himself."[65] And to achieve the needed purification, Chávez knew, individuals must endure suffering. Farm workers were well-prepared for this task: "Our people are ready to accept sacrifices. They have made many sacrifices in the decades of exploitation and humiliation they have faced as agricultural workers. They are ready to undergo more sacrifices in the course of their liberation."[66] Thus farm workers were the right people in the right place to initiate a major social change.

Chávez taught that action and leadership comprised essential elements of nonviolent protest, and that leaders who embodied their message were indispensable to the success of their agendas. He himself went through personal preparation as did Gandhi. "I am firmly convinced that nonviolence cannot exist only in books or on the seminar level on our university campuses," he lectured, "but it must exist in the flesh. I have always believed that people are the most important element we have. We must put flesh into our nonviolence rather than simply talk about it."[67] A successful nonviolent movement also demanded constant involvement by the leader. "You must do nothing more and nothing less than the movement," Chávez directed; "Nonviolence depends on the absolute loyalty of the leadership to their cause, and the ability of the leadership to attract and organize other people." "If we can just show people how they can organize nonviolently," he concluded, "we can't fail. It has never failed where it's been tried. If the effort gets out of hand, it's from a lack of discipline."[68]

Chávez learned from Gandhi many ideas about nonviolence, particularly that nonviolence required strategy and creativity, "a moral jujitsu" with which to keep opponents "off-balance." Studying Gandhi carefully, Chávez strove to understand the Indian activist's principles in their own historical setting. "I'd read a lot," the Mexican-American organizer admitted, "but all of it was in the abstract. It's difficult to carry the message to people who aren't involved. Nonviolence must be explained in context."[69] He could not practice nonviolence exactly as Gandhi had, Chávez said. Rather, "You've got to take the whole philosophy and try to adapt it to your needs. I want to experiment with some of the things he did but not imitate him, because I don't think that can be done."[70]

As a necessary agent for social change, the UFW would have to reach beyond the typical union goals of winning better contracts and job conditions. It would, Chávez taught, need to change the "economics of agriculture" in order to create a "social revolution" as the foundation upon which "a more human society can be built." Concerned that his union might lose its focus by concentrating exclusively on social issues such as voter registration, he warned that its immediate purpose was to improve the lives of workers on the job. He pledged "to find some cross between being a movement and being a union."[71]

Chávez instructed his followers that nonviolence could not be equated with "inaction—with not doing anything—and it's not that at all. It's exactly the opposite." Because nonviolence involved action, "it's got to be organized. There must be rules. There must be people following." He also had to persuade union members that "nonviolence is [not] cowardice, as some militant groups are saying. In some instances nonviolence requires more militancy than violence." The ideal places to teach and practice nonviolence were on picket lines and in boycotts, he said.[72] And by practicing nonviolence, his coworkers would have "unlimited, unrestricted . . . opportunities to be on the offensive. Constantly."[73]

Chávez argued that the boycott was an adaptation of Gandhi's ideas because it was a powerful nonviolent weapon that could be used as a teaching tool. The farm workers learned nonviolence by going to target cities to create organizations to picket markets that sold the produce (grapes or lettuce) that the union was boycotting. Meanwhile, union organizers recruited individuals from those cities to participate in the boycott, turning the boycott itself into a way of teaching people about the problems faced by farm workers as well as an economic vehicle to force the growers to agree to sign UFW contracts. Chávez spoke of the grass-roots value of a boycott:

> Gandhi said that the boycott was the most perfect nonviolent weapon available to people, especially poor people. Because the boycott is so simple, anybody can help. If a family stops buying grapes when they go to the store it is a tremendous help to the cause. They don't have to go on a picket line, they don't have to put money into it, they don't have to take time off their jobs, they don't have to take time off their busy schedules.[74]

As Chávez sought to seize the moral high ground by educating audiences about the nature of nonviolent tactics and their relationship to his union, he found himself redefining the term "union." In some respects his organization *was* a union as conventionally understood, but in other ways it appeared to be a social movement. He defined its aims as "broader than the traditional goals of unions. . . . It is more than a union as we know it today that we have to build. It is a movement. It is a movement of the poor."[75]

At times Chávez's commitment to nonviolent means superseded his commitment to his unionizing ends, just as his vision of a social revolution sometimes eclipsed his view of his union. "If to build our union required the deliberate taking of life," he declared, "either the life of a grower or his child, or the life of a farm worker or his child, then I choose not to see the union built. . . . We advocate militant nonviolence as our means for social revolution and to achieve justice for our people."[76]

As the 1960s ended, Chávez placed his union into the context of a broader moral movement, a millennial event heralded by activism and protest signaling "the biggest revolution this country has ever known." Convinced that his moral goals were part of a social revolution, he asserted with certainty: "We will win, we are winning, because ours is a revolution of mind and heart, not only of economics." Because the UFW consisted mostly of members of racial minorities, Chávez saw union issues as civil rights issues. To him the UFW was "a movement to change the conditions of human life" rather than "just another union."[77]

Victory would require changing attitudes, stimulating actions, and in some cases revising the public's own self-concept, a task Chávez believed to be possible and even likely. To Chávez the facts that God controlled events on earth and the union sought social change for just ends meant that the public would end injustices once it was informed of those injustices. In his master's thesis on Chávez, Ricardo Aecio Bomfin identified as one of Chávez's characteristic rhetorical appeals the attempt "to convince the masses that the love of justice is still in the hearts of Americans."[78] Chávez's unique conception of the nature and function of reform rhetoric caused him to view himself and other rhetors as vital parts of God's master plan to right the wrongs of the world and thereby essential in the UFW's quest to reach its specific goals.[79] Chávez's millennialism reflected a venerable tradition in Christian history. As had generations of believers before him, Chávez translated his religious convictions into secular actions. In his case, many of these actions were rhetorical in nature—a fitting application for a leader whose goals and means relied so heavily on influencing audiences.

An effective movement, Chávez decided, required rhetors who could fulfill the unarticulated hopes of many people and to instill the depth of caring that can motivate those people to make sacrifices. The final necessary ingredient was enlisting "enough people with one idea so that their actions are together like a wave of water which nothing can stop."[80]

Chávez knew that he had to be largely independent of external pressures in order to create his humane union. On numerous occasions he turned down out-side money because he felt that this support would carry obligations that would restrict his time and freedom to build a union based on his own ideas. "Even when there are no strings attached," he said in rejecting financial offers, "you feel you have to produce immediate results. This is bad, because it takes a long time to build a movement, and your organization suffers if you get too far ahead of the people it belongs to."[81]

As noted earlier, Chávez identified the "individual" as "the key to social change" and was convinced that "nothing changes until the individual changes." Unfortunately, he lamented, "the farm workers, especially those speaking only Spanish, are not a part of or participating in the society around them. We want to develop in them an awareness of citizenship, of civil rights and civil responsibilities."[82] Once farm workers acquired the proper attitudes toward citizen responsibilities, the movement could begin to effect broad social change.

The UFW was founded at a time when many people out of the mainstream in the United States were mounting active and well-publicized protests to change society. Chávez attempted to merge his movement with that struggle, to place the farm-worker movement in the broader social revolution. He saw his union's strikes as part of "a civil liberties issue, . . . a race issue, and . . . a desperate struggle just to keep the movement going against such tremendous odds." Thus his union became a symbol of the broader movement among Mexican Americans for civil rights. As Rodolfo Acuña pointed out, "Humane commitment and people's pride have been infused into the arena by Chávez so that La Causa [the cause] is also a movement, an insistence on a people's worth, a molding of a transient, unskilled work force into a skilled and participative citizenry."[83]

The authors of this book have argued elsewhere that the rhetoric of minority groups can best be understood when scholars consider "the rhetorical traditions of ethnic groups whose discourse they study."[84] In the case of Chávez, much of his discourse was grounded in his Mexican heritage. Because most farm workers were Mexican Americans, Chávez appealed to his and their common Mexican past. His office walls held posters of Emiliano Zapata, the UFW flag showed a black Aztec eagle on a red and white background (red and black were the colors of flags carried during strikes in Mexico), and UFW marchers carried symbols of the Virgin of Guadalupe. As historian Arturo Rosales noted, the farm workers' "theme song . . . was 'De Colores,' the theme song of the Catholic 'cursillo' [short course in Christianity] movement, a charismatic prayer and study association to which Chávez and many union members belonged."[85] Chávez frequently referred to the Mexican Revolution in his calls for action in strikes; and in his union activities he introduced numerous Mexican religious traditions such as pilgrimages, fasts, processionals, and masses. In his speeches he relied on the Mexican dichos, consejos, and cuentos he learned at his mother's knee—three rhetorical components effective in educating his audiences because the rhetorical means as well as the clear morals of the stories would be familiar to workers. "Hay más tiempo que vida," he would say, which means "'There is more time than life.' We don't worry about time, because time and history are on our side."[86] In his story of his attempt to organize workers in Oxnard in 1958, Chávez illustrated how he used a variety of such dichos during his organizing. When speaking to a worker about how workers needed a union because they were badly treated, he said: "The farm worker's the low man, too, you know. Maybe we'd better get together. 'Hombre, sin hombre, no vale nada,' I tell him in Spanish. 'We either hang together or separately.'"[87]

The still-present Mexican past also surfaced in Chávez's use of pilgrimages and marches. A common event in Mexican history, the pilgrimage still exists in the twentieth century. During Chávez's life numerous pilgrimages took place daily in Mexico, particularly to the Basilica of the Lady of Guadalupe. Chávez yoked his own pilgrimages to that past and present:

> . . . there is a meeting of cultures and traditions; the centuries-old religious tradition of Spanish culture conjoins with the very contemporary cultural syndrome of "demonstration" springing from the spontaneity of the poor, the downtrodden, the rejected, the discriminated against bearing visibly their need and demand for equality and freedom. . . . a trip made with sacrifice and hardship as an expression of penance and of commitment—and often involving a petition to the patron of the pilgrimage for some sincerely sought benefit of body or soul.[88]

These periodic marches dramatized the problems facing farm workers and also built the solidarity crucial to the success to the union.

Other links with Mexican history and culture were Chávez's appeals and actions based on suffering and self-sacrifice. As Dolores Huerta explained: "I know it's hard for people who are not Mexican to understand, but this is part of the Mexican culture—the penance, the whole idea of suffering for something, of self-inflicted punishment. It's a tradition of very long standing."[89] Jim Drake, a Chávez advisor for many years, underscored the "unique understanding of suffering" possessed by Mexicans, who lived in a world where suffering has been "ritualized, institutionalized, especially in the work of the Franciscans." "Mexicans believe that from suffering you get strength rather than death," Drake stated; thus the strike gave purpose to the long-time suffering of many UFW members.[90]

Chávez's most publicized acts of sacrifice and suffering were his fasts. The most famous, which lasted from February 14, 1968, to March 10, 1968, grew out of his concern about mounting violence between union members and the growers. The fast attracted widespread attention among workers, the media, and growers; and it had an educational effect on workers that Matthiessen described well: "It taught the farm workers that Chávez was serious about nonviolence, that it wasn't just a tactic to win public support; and it taught them what nonviolence meant."[91]

This chapter has discussed sources that shaped César Chávez's theory and consequently his practice of rhetorical communication. It has positioned Chávez's views of discourse within a broader context that includes his interrelated conceptions of union leadership and organizing, the UFW, nonviolence, reform, social movements, and God's plan for the world. From his Christian perspective of God as all-powerful and in control of events on earth, Chávez saw his farm workers' movement as more than a mere union of workers: It was a collection of exploited people who together were part of God's millennial plan to better the world—in this case to attain justice for the farm workers' union as a representative of moral force. To accomplish this task would require that farm workers act boldly rather than merely philosophize or lament their plight. Leaders must speak out against injustice and talk with workers, addressing and organizing audiences on a grassroots level to convince some of those farm workers to become organizers who would in turn spread the union's rhetorical appeals and build support for the union. Those new organizers and many other farm workers—who would support the union but not serve as organizers—would need to find in themselves a means to overcome the fear that had kept them silent, an intense willingness to sacrifice and struggle for the just cause of farm workers, and a dignity as humans that would insulate them from the attacks and discouragement that would surely come. They would become intelligent, informed, and committed agents in his movement. Those who would become active organizers would undergo the greatest self-redefinition, taking on new selves that would feature extraordinary patience, commitment to nonviolence, willingness to labor long and suffer deeply for their cause, and dedication strong enough to overcome a to-be-expected lack of appreciation for their efforts.

The organizers' discourse would need to inform listeners and readers of the clear moral cause of the farm workers. To enlist rhetor/organizers from audiences, those addressing them would need not only to be skilled at crafting and delivering their messages; they would need to be able to identify with audiences and be adaptable in their tactics. To his rhetorical formula for Mexican-American audiences, Chávez added the need to adapt rhetorical tactics to Mexican-American rhetorical traditions and practices including symbolic events such as fasts and marches. And although neither rhetor/leaders nor organizers could expect appreciation for their sacrifice and hard work, only they could unify audiences into a moral union.

On a broader scale, farm-worker rhetor/leaders would need to convince the American public of the truth and justice of their cause. If they made their case carefully and clearly, public opinion would inevitably respond to their just cause and assure their ultimate victory. Chávez was certain that his moral leaders would succeed rhetorically—and the movement would succeed materially—if they presented their message skillfully. He was certain that these leaders could infuse individuals and groups—both farm workers and the general public—with the power to change the world. The entire enterprise would rely on nonviolence, a tactic suitable to farm workers because their history of oppression and sacrifice allowed them to be purified morally and thereby attain the necessary spiritual health for successful nonviolence. But at the center of the moral enterprise was rhetorical discourse, the sine qua non of Chávez's plan to change the world.

Chávez's unusual view of discourse would direct him to his rhetorical means and message and thus would be the primary source of what we will call his *rhetorical profile*. By this term we mean the rhetorical behavior that characterized Chávez's communication with his audience. This behavior included the extensiveness of his rhetorical campaigns; his substantive message as seen primarily in his themes, arguments, and explanations; and his various other rhetorical tactics, qualities, and characteristics—from use of language and patterns of organization to creation of personae and their respective importance to and place in his discourse.

Chávez's rhetorical profile was indispensable to his successes with audiences and consequently to his major accomplishments as a reform leader who made rhetorical discourse the center of his career. Before we begin to consider closely his rhetorical career, therefore, we present in the following chapter our approach to his discourse and our model for analyzing it, evaluating it, and illuminating the deeper rhetorical dynamics that accounted for its effects on audiences and hence Chávez's accomplishments in his career. Because Chávez's idiosyncratic worldview and goals channeled him to somewhat unusual rhetorical ends and means, our approach and model will itself be unconventional in many respects. Accordingly, it will challenge and expand conventional precepts from rhetorical theory and, to a lesser degree, social movement theory.

After we have laid out our theoretical starting points and principles in chapter 3, subsequent chapters examine each period of Chávez's career. Throughout these chapters we focus on his discourse, both that which he used to recruit union members and teach American society of the plight of farm workers, and that with which he sought to enlist many kinds of audiences to support his movement. Our story of Chávez's rhetoric attempts to provide a detailed and textured contour of his techniques and strategies within the historical context of issues he faced, a clear explanation of the dynamics of his rhetorical interaction with audiences, a close examination of changes that occurred in his discourse, a fuller sense of the prominence and power of his discourse in his career, and an elaborated version of his conception of discourse as he developed that conception more thoroughly later in his life.

Chapter 3

The Rhetorical Criticism of Reconstitutive Discourse

A Model for Analyzing Chávez's Public Address

César Chávez's conception of discourse was situated within his worldview of God's grand plan for him and society. Seeing himself as an agent of God's will, Chávez sought to change his audiences in fundamental ways. In his initial attempts to organize in Delano, California, he would use public address to redefine farm workers so that they would lose their fear and lack of confidence and become organizers and coworkers in his organization. Later he would expand his audiences by appealing to volunteers for his movement, consumers committed to his boycott, and others supporting various political, legal, and social issues. Thus "persuasion," in its sense of shifting an attitude on an issue, was not Chávez's main goal: He aimed for nothing less than the rhetorical reconstitution of listeners and readers who would then act out their new definitions by working with him to reach his goals. Seeing his movement as part of God's plan, and drawing from his own study and practice of discourse, Chávez believed that rhetorical transformation was both vital and achievable. His rhetorical profile would allow him to effect just such a transformation.

Crucial to an understanding of Chávez's discourse, then, is an understanding of reconstitutive discourse. Although scholars we discuss in this chapter have recently introduced such a critical approach, no one has moved past general considerations to provide a model for application. In this chapter we construct a model of reconstitutive discourse suitable for analyzing and evaluating Chávez's public address.

Speakers such as César Chávez who employ messages designed to fundamentally change the lives of their listeners—whether those changes are temporary or permanent—provide some of the most intriguing studies for critics and teachers of communication. In such cases rhetors appear to redefine or *reconstitute* rather than merely persuade their audiences. Reconstitution requires auditors to adopt an altered identity and often to act out a new way of life. In this way the born-again Christian, the cult member, the newly converted political zealot, and many others see themselves as different in fundamental ways from their former selves. They have experienced something more profound than a mere change in belief or attitude.

Textbooks on public speaking customarily treat informing, persuading, and entertaining as the ends or functions of discourse. These books, like the field's most popular textbooks in rhetorical and communication criticism, contain little or no discussion of discourse that constitutes or reconstitutes audiences.[1] If reconstitutive discourse depends on a particular rhetorical dynamic that is not necessary for persuading (or informing or entertaining), however, students and other critics may possess what critic and philosopher Kenneth Burke has called a "trained incapacity" to appreciate and understand the discourse that has the greatest impact on them and others.[2] This incapacity may help to account for why scholars and other writers have attributed little of the successes of this quiet and seemingly uncharismatic man to his discourse.

We are not proposing that all discourse that persuades lacks capacity to reconstitute or change an audience's view of its character, or that discourse that defines or redefines an audience cannot also persuade on an issue or idea. Rather we are claiming that discourse that reconstitutes the character of an audience contains rhetorical qualities and invites rhetorical processes particularly appropriate and in some cases indispensable for the task of changing character. Whether reconstitutive discourse is defined as possessing a means, dynamic, and end that classifies it as a kind of persuasion, or whether it is different enough to be isolated as a kind of discourse in itself, is an interesting question but not one vital to our study. What is more important to this study is that the direct end of reconstitutive discourse—to change the character of the auditor—differs significantly from that of most persuasion and calls forth a particular set of rhetorical means.

To explore the qualities and workings of reconstitutive discourse, a necessary step before presenting our model, we begin by reviewing rhetorical critic Frederick J. Antczak's approach to discourse and examining subsequent scholarship that applies and extends his approach. In his 1985 book, *Thought and Character: The Rhetoric of Democratic Education,* Antczak proposed a non-Aristotelian starting point for the conception of rhetoric. Aristotle, long the starting point for discussions of rhetoric, defined it as the ability, in each case, to "see the available means of persuasion."[3] In contrast, Antczak viewed *identification* rather than persuasion as rhetoric's end, and the merger of a rhetor's thought and character its means. Antczak explored "the limits and capacities for intellectual reconstitution inherent in the specifically democratic audience" and proposed an important place for the "powers, functions, and obligations" of rhetoric as a major instrument of that task.[4]

Antczak drew primarily upon the works of three theorists—Plato, Kenneth Burke, and particularly Wayne Booth—to explain how a rhetor's merger of character and ideas allows members of an audience to discover, expand, and activate latent moral qualities in themselves. "A rhetoric is successful," Antczak reasoned, "insofar as it reconstitutes and frees audiences to participate in the constitutive conversation for themselves—participate as themselves, as women and men thinking, or rebels or reconcilers or whatever new character with which . . . the listener can identify." This reconstitution releases individuals from "the yoke of custom and convention" and in doing so can "open intellectual and moral possibilities that constitute a truer freedom."[5] Only through this merging of persona and ideas in discourse, by identifying and educating audiences through the agency of one's self as well as one's arguments, themes, and explanations can this reformulation of listeners take place. As noted earlier in conjunction with descriptions of Chávez, the audience must perceive the leader as like them, only "more so." The leader/rhetor represents "the achievable bests in his audience . . . what his audiences could become if they were educated to the deepest meanings and richest possibilities of their identity."[6]

Antczak took from Plato the concept that a rhetoric that can intellectually and morally reconstitute audiences (rather than merely indulge them by telling them what they want to hear) must make use of the characters of both audiences and speaker.[7] Burke provided the concept of identification as the center of the rhetorical enterprise, what he called a "consubstantiality" achieved between rhetor and auditor through the symbolic sharing of "substance"—or what Burke calls "whatness"—a person's attitudes, experiences, values, friends, occupation, activities, and whatever else unconsciously and consciously makes up that person's identity.[8] Booth, over the past forty years one of America's most influential voices in literary studies, supplied the perspective that "the primary mental act of man is to assent . . . 'to take in' and 'even to be taken in'" through rhetorical exchanges: "By understanding and being understood, by taking in other selves, we expand our moral and intellectual capacities, we expand our identities themselves."[9] Arguing that the author emerges through the narrative text to shape a reader's response while that reader is engaged in the text, Booth established the *implied author* as a central factor in the rhetorical workings of literary texts.[10] Thus Plato, Burke, and Booth all view a rhetor's character or *persona* as an essential component in rhetorical transactions wherein that rhetor reconstitutes audiences.

Antczak applied his critical approach—which he later described as relying on "Boothian concepts" that generated "at least an approach, if not a full-blown methodology"[11]—to the public discourse of Ralph Waldo Emerson, Mark Twain, and Henry Adams. Each figure was a lyceum rhetor who used reconstitutive rhetoric to reformulate audiences, liberating listeners to think and act more creatively, intelligently, and humanely.[12] All three orators delivered extraordinarily well-received speeches despite committing a long list of oratorical offenses in organization, style, delivery, or substance that would make their addresses appear unworthy of success even in a beginning public speaking class. Antczak's approach produced a provocative explanation for the dazzling effects of these three speakers: Each rhetor rhetorically combined his person and ideas to reconstitute rather than merely persuade audiences. Emerson, for example—this shy and often coldly impersonal transcendentalist—delivered speeches that were oddly organized, strangely argued, frequently bereft of transitions, and were sometimes concluded so abruptly that they startled audiences. Yet the man and his rhetorical manner communicated a personal if ethereal image that unified him with his substantive ideal and the idea of "man thinking," clearly illustrated by him in his speeches as a man "thinking aloud." This merging of thought and character allowed listeners to see themselves as thinking, self-reliant beings who must trust and enact their thoughts much as this man Emerson before them was trusting and acting out his own.[13] By melding persona and ideas in discourse, by simultaneously identifying with and educating audiences through the agency of one's self as well as one's arguments, themes, and explanations, a rhetor can reformulate an audience.

Antczak illustrated and expanded the uses of his thought/character approach in several subsequent studies. In a chapter in *Rhetoric and Pluralism: Legacies of Wayne Booth,* he critiqued Martin Luther King Jr.'s influential and constitutive narrative on civil rights, "Pilgrimage to Nonviolence." Through King's combination of persona and ideas, Antczak argued, the audience was "taken in" by King even as King himself was changed by being "taken in" by the audience. Those readers of King who participated in his text's language were moved to emulate King's example by reformulating themselves into a synthesis of Christianity's opposing wings of fundamentalism and liberalism.[14]

King narrated his own conversion to nonviolent protest by describing how he synthesized his fundamentalist upbringing, which had the potential to impel action against sinful practices but which focused too little on the material suffering of the world, with his liberal theological education, whose idealistic "love your enemies" philosophy distorted the analysis of real problems of sin in a dangerous and strife-torn world, diffused the energy to fight them, and diluted the tactics needed to resolve those problems.[15] This combining of theological and practical selves required King to become a Christian activist using nonviolent means to bring justice on public issues. By revealing how he himself had justified his actions through a synthesis of real-world, everyday concerns and moral principles, King incarnated his argument and called forth from committed followers "resources of strength and courage and empathy" that they may not have known they possessed.[16] Careful and serious readers of King's narrative, wrote Antczak, "at least for the time of their engagement with the text," identified with King's person and ideas and thus entered "a way of life" as a spiritually motivated activist that prepared them for pilgrimages to nonviolent activism "in their own lives" similar to that undertaken by King. The effect on King and the entire civil-rights movement, Antczak contended, irreversibly melded "pragmatic effectiveness" with "moral character" and fused "expediential concerns with philosophical ones."[17]

Following Booth, Antczak's essay on King focused not on "after effects" of the discourse but on "the quality of life lived in the company we keep with a work's implied author." This focus is infused with ethical concerns because, in the words of Booth, "insofar as the fiction has *worked* for us, we have lived its lives for the duration; we have been *that kind of person* for at least as long as we remained in the presence of the work." To Antczak, such "ethical criticism" focuses "not primarily on the measuring of effects, but on describing with intersubjective precision the way of life constituted and enacted, the quality of life lived while we are the kind of people, communicators, and moral agents whom the text invites and teaches us to be. . . ." Enacting Booth's "non-consequentialist focus," Antczak concentrated on ethical judgments rather than pragmatic effects.[18]

In several other essays Antczak demonstrated the applicability of his critical approach. A study of King's speech announcing his deep commitment to opposing U.S. involvement in the Vietnam War revealed the discursive community constituted in the text between the author and audience implied by the text. In King's attempt to unite the two major protest issues of the times, he merged his ideas and personae in order to reformulate both sets of likely auditors, who could each then extend the "American values of revolution, freedom, and democracy."[19] Antczak found a similar intertwining of ideas and personae in John F. Kennedy's speech before the Houston Ministerial Association in 1960. Although Kennedy—who would become the first Catholic president of the United States—had not made religion a part of his campaign, many American Protestants had deep concerns about his independence in matters of church and state. Citing a personal history that implicitly documents his claims, Kennedy's speech "functionally defines the ideal audience" as magnanimous enough to support a Catholic candidate for President at the same time as it defines Kennedy as possessing the fairness, respect for all religious beliefs, and ironclad commitment to the Constitution necessary to qualify a presidential candidate of any religious faith. Auditors who participated in the discourse community constituted by the text would no longer be inclined to dismiss Kennedy's candidacy on religious grounds—at least while they participated in the text.[20]

Antczak, Booth, and others have applied the thought/character critical approach both to illuminate grounds for ethical judgments of public address and to explain the audience's engagement with the rhetor during its participation in the text. That participation can, of course, have a different and darker side, one with less-than-liberating effects, as with fascism in Spain in the 1930s.[21] Here the fascist party became the mere extension of its leader, José Antonio Primo de Rivera, who rhetorically interacted with audiences along dimensions emanating from the intricate, dynamic, and reciprocal interplay of his ideology, his substantive themes and arguments, the picture of himself he communicated to his audience (his first persona), as well as his *second persona*,[22] the rhetor's explicit and implicit depictions of the audience. Antonio's rhetorical identification resulted not only from his substantive themes and arguments, but from the ways in which he presented his message as well as the person he appeared to be through descriptions of his heritage, life, appearance, and self in speeches and writings.

As one of the authors of this book has written, the ideology Antonio communicated emphasized "eternal values, timeless truths, the need for faith, spiritual essences embedded in a nation, the hierarchical ordering of humans, and an emphasis on voluntary actions by an elite minority of activists who possessed knowledge of truth and would boldly follow their leader to overthrow the present political regime in favor of a fascist state." The second persona developed in his rhetoric depicted an audience of heroic followers who had the "personal qualities necessary to seize the government and enforce their idealistic vision upon the majority, i.e., the qualities of bravery, boldness, action, discipline, sincerity, unwillingness to compromise truths, and willingness to sacrifice all for the spiritual cause." These ardent believers should, Antonio taught, expect "a very special person" to lead them, one who possessed the qualities expected of all fascists as well as additional qualities required of leadership of a fascist movement: "superb linguistic skills, broad general knowledge and deep understanding of history, and an aesthetic sensibility necessary to grasp and communicate spiritual essences, universal truths, and eternal values."[23] Through his first persona, Antonio embodied the qualities of both the ideal fascist and the ideal fascist leader. His resulting identification with audiences was essential to reformulating and thereby animating auditors who would enact the fascist agenda through their slavish obedience to a mythical leader and mystical ideology, their eager willingness to use violence to achieve its ends, and their smug superiority that translated into scorn for those who opposed them and hence did not understand "eternal truths."

One specific example of how Antonio created his own persona was through his use of poetic language. His own eloquence and preference for poetic expression were rhetorically appropriate for a rhetor who spoke of the need for a single leader whose essential qualities included eloquence and poetic sensibility—how else could the leader grasp and communicate to the masses the eternal truths of the romantic themes of fascism? By frequently referring in his discourse to poets and renowned literary works, by sometimes reading poems to begin or end speeches, and through his well-publicized fraternization with Madrid's literary elite, he reinforced his image as a man of letters with an aesthetic bent. In his case, then, one source of his identification with his substantive message lay in the ways he depicted his poetic nature.

This analysis of José Antonio's rhetoric emphasizes the importance of the second persona's workings in reconstitutive discourse by identifying a special and vital rhetorical characteristic in fascist discourse (and perhaps in other reconstitutive discourse). Antonio subtly—and at times explicitly—defined audiences so that they would expect a leader with the particular qualities he would reveal through his own first persona. This cyclical rhetorical process continually expanded and deepened his identification with those audiences as it "happened" that his own personal qualities were precisely those they expected in their sought-after leader.

These and other writings on reconstitutive rhetoric form the foundation from which to build a model for the analysis of reconstitutive discourse. Such a model draws its explanatory power primarily from the Burkean concept of identification, which rests on the human need to overcome separation and estrangement from other humans. Burkean theory posits that the need for identification may be conscious or unconscious; that separation and its accompanying feelings of estrangement are universal and motivate all humans; and that estrangement is both inherent to humans (because our different nervous systems prevent us from duplicating the perceptions and understandings of other humans), and human-made through the hierarchies of class, achievement, appearance, etc., that further divide us. Language and communication compensate for that division and allow humans to bridge their differences symbolically and thus to satisfy longings for oneness with others. Hence to Burke, human language is never neutral, but is always colored by choice that reflects the human drive to identify, and communication offers a means of achieving cooperation between and among beings who are fundamentally separate.[24]

The three parts of our model of reconstitutive discourse are the *first persona,* the person whom the rhetor appears to be in the eyes of the audience; the *substantive message,* which consists primarily of the themes, arguments, and explanations in the text of the rhetor's message; and the *second persona,* the auditor depicted implicitly and explicitly by the rhetor. These parts are reciprocal and synergistic in the dynamics of the reconstituting rhetorical act.

THE FIRST PERSONA

The first persona has long been viewed as an influential component in communication. In this book "first persona" is defined as the audience's view of the rhetor's personal qualities as communicated to and perceived by the audience. This definition expands Booth's idea that the implied author is constructed entirely within the text; it acknowledges that first persona is also constructed from non-textual sources that may or may not be controllable by the rhetor—the rhetor's own life history, for example, or the rhetor's family heritage. These non-textual sources can powerfully shape the rhetor's first persona for a particular audience and thus can partly account for the resulting rhetorical effects on an audience's character and actions—as, we are attempting to show, they did for Chávez. *Personal qualities* are defined broadly to include heritage and other sources that make up what the audience sees in the rhetor. The elevation of *ethos*—a speaker's character, intelligence, and good will—as one of the three engines of persuasion in classical rhetoric, particularly in the rhetoric of Aristotle and his followers, virtually ensured centuries of consideration of the speaker as a major source of persuasion. Burkean theory, which takes something of a different perspective on the rhetorical act, features identification of speaker or author with audiences as vital to forming attitude and inducing action.[25] A straightforward instance of identification takes place whenever humans overtly share their substance—as when a politician speaking to an audience of farmers says "I grew up on a farm myself."

Just as neo-Aristotelian critics expanded Aristotle's conception of ethos by making a speaker's heritage, life, appearance, and other sources available for analysis along with the speech text once considered its sole source, so Burke expanded the source of a rhetor's identification with audiences by considering subconscious motives in the audience. Burke proposed that such forms as argument, style, and arrangement could secure an auditor's unconscious identification with a rhetor. By reasoning in the ways an audience typically reasons or wishes to reason, by organizing ideas and evidence in ways expected by an audience, and by creating and fulfilling expectations through familiar stylistic devices, a rhetor can achieve a degree of identification with audiences.[26]

It makes intuitive sense that an audience's identification with a speaker plays an important part in the impact of that speaker's message on that audience. Perhaps the rhetorical potency of persona comes from a fundamental human need to identify with others, to share in common humanity whether failed, noble, or undistinguished. Perhaps humans simply find other people and their stories irresistible because part of each of us is made from the stories of others. Walter R. Fisher claims that "one's life is . . . a story that participates in the stories of those who have lived, who live now, and who will live in the future." In Fisher's view, "Humans are essentially storytellers."[27] Stories about other humans continue to be the most appealing to audiences. From the oral accounts of ancient seers to the celluloid or print-created characters that attract contemporary movie-goers and novel readers, audiences have long identified themselves with those they watched, heard (and heard about), and read (and read about), participating in the dramas of life created via their imaginations. Out of this propensity toward identification is created the continued power of face-to-face communication, the visible reach of rhetoric to affect audiences unmoved by dialectic, and the appeal of human motives that prodded Burke to transfer psychiatric insights from Freud to the symbolic world of rhetoric.[28]

THE SUBSTANTIVE MESSAGE

The themes, arguments, explanations, and evidence that comprise the substantive message in the texts of reconstitutive discourse often allow rhetors to embody—and thereby in some cases to become indistinguishable from—their ideas, ideology, or movement. Such embodiment can occur explicitly and obviously, as when rhetors claim that they have lived out the principles advocated in their message, or are demonstrably living out those principles. It can also occur implicitly, as when rhetors use such means as language, delivery, appearance, or organization to prove their enactment of their arguments, appeals, and agendas.

As a general rule, when a rhetor identifies with a message, auditors who identify with that rhetor will be inclined to identify with the message too. The power of identification may thus be transferred from the rhetor to the message. This rhetorical dynamic is not one of persuasion alone, where facts and arguments are combined with other appeals to convince or persuade audiences and shift their attitudes or beliefs; it is fueled by identification. An audience's identification with a rhetor simultaneously identifies that audience with the substantive message in that rhetor's speech or essay or film or other form of communication. The rhetorical potency of identification is therefore magnified, with both the rhetor and message connecting closely and personally with the audience.

Studies of public address have found that a rhetor's communicated self-portrait can merge with a substantive message to exert considerable influence on audiences. Rhetorical critics Karlyn Kohrs Campbell and Kathleen Hall Jamieson have discussed how a rhetor's personal "enactment" of a message, wherein the speaker "incarnates the argument, [and] "is the proof of the truth of what is said," can be vital to that speaker's rhetorical impact—for example, in Barbara Jordan's Keynote Address at the 1976 Democratic convention, or in John F. Kennedy's speech, "Ich bin ein Berliner."[29]

Martha (Solomon) Watson proposed that a study of a rhetors and their rhetoric can reveal much "about the relationship between specific ideologies and their inherent rhetoric. Clearly, one's ideology constrains the arguments one uses and colors the presentation of those arguments." She argued that embodiment was a powerful rhetorical tool because it "bridges ethos and logical arguments" and because the rhetor "enacts the principle of argument she/he is discussing. . . . This strategy is particularly useful to leaders of social movements who can embody the principles they advocate"—leaders, she noted, such as Martin Luther King Jr. and Gandhi. She might have added César Chávez to the list.[30]

Documenting the dangers of a negative enactment that can project an unattractive persona, Solomon demonstrated that anarchist Emma Goldman's unconventional personification of her message was consistent with her ideology but drastically reduced her appeal to most listeners. While "Red Emma's . . . flamboyance, flouting of social mores, and outspokenness were virtually prerequisites for proponents" of her anarchist ideology, her enactment of these prerequisites forfeited her capacity to identify with the larger and far-more conventional public that held the power to bring about the broader social changes she sought.[31]

THE SECOND PERSONA

The ability to redefine audiences and to induce them to take on and act out aspects of a new way of life requires effective use of the second persona. Paralleling Booth's view of the first persona in literature as an "implied author," rhetorical critic Edwin Black defined second persona as a text's "implied auditor."[32] We expand this definition by viewing the second persona as being explicitly as well as implicitly communicated by the rhetor. For example, rhetors sometimes baldly point out the qualities audiences possess or should possess, as when José Antonio told auditors that they should become bold, courageous, and active fascists—obedient to party ideology, responsive to spiritual appeals, and willing to risk their lives to enact his agenda. More often the qualities of the second persona are implied, however, as when a rhetor calls for actions that require particular personal qualities to be enacted, or addresses an audience in a way that implies their level of understanding, intelligence, sensitivity, or other qualities.

The second persona adds reconstitutive force when a rhetor projects a first persona and articulates a message that calls for auditors who possess the characteristics that comprise that second persona. In fascist discourse, for example, the substantive message called for brave, bold, active, and unquestioning followers who would elevate spiritual concerns over purely material ones, and who would honor nation and leader over world and self. When Antonio, through his first persona, identified himself with both his ideology and audience, and then fashioned a second persona consisting of personal qualities that he held and that his substantive themes and agenda requested of listeners and readers, he achieved a powerful multilayered identification with audiences and was able to reconstitute an aimless conglomeration comprised primarily of street toughs, students, and other disaffected elements into a dedicated cadre of believers who would serve as shock troops for his rebellion.[33] Not all of Antonio's prominent personal qualities were meant to be adopted by his audiences. For example, his obvious depth of learning, education in poetry, and elevated heritage (he was the son of an army general who for several years was dictator of Spain) were necessary ingredients of the leader he told audiences to expect, but not the followers themselves.

By identifying with the rhetor and message, audiences can be adjusted to a second persona that tells them who to be and how to act. The personal qualities embodied by the rhetor and called for by the message thus are reified in the portrait of the audience. The second persona presents audiences with an altered identity so that they can more easily bring to the surface their own qualities necessary to accept, adopt, and act out the rhetor's substantive ideas, personal qualities, and agenda for action.

The three parts of the model of reconstitutive discourse interact in a variety of ways. In some cases, for example, the substantive message may be much more important than the first persona in working reciprocally with the second persona. Here rhetorical critic Maurice Charland's examination of *Québéçois* discourse is instructive. Drawing broadly from the scholarship of Burke, Black, and rhetorical critic Michael McGee, as well as from contemporary writers on narrative, structuralism, hermeneutics, and related topics, Charland argued that Québécois rhetors created rather than persuaded audiences. Constitutive public address thus preceded these audiences' existence as audiences, before persuasion of them as audiences was possible. To create audiences, Charland contended, speeches and writings must rely heavily on the second persona—on the narratives that define and depict audiences and auditors—within the context of the text, the framework of ideology, and the material world inhabited and influenced by human agents. To Charland, because such discourse constitutes rather than persuades, Burkean identification rather than neo-Aristotelian persuasion forms the cornerstone of the rhetorical act.[34]

Regardless of whether a rhetor's particular goal is persuasion or reconstitution, the rhetorical power created by the merging of personae and message can be undermined when the speaker acts inconsistently with the identification established with the audience. In his fantasy theme analysis of presidential candidate George McGovern's handling of the "Eagleton affair," rhetorical critic Ernest G. Bormann found that the widespread public perception that McGovern had dismissed his vice-presidential running mate for base reasons of political expediency conflicted with McGovern's persona of being "not really a politician . . . [but] an honest, sincere, decent man who just happened to be in politics." McGovern had based his 1972 presidential campaign on the idealistic vision of a "New Politics" that, Bormann wrote, "encompassed all of life from aesthetics to social style." In a period of protest and idealism, McGovern's followers—a representation of what we would call his second persona—were idealistic, a "dedicated and mighty army of hard-working volunteers who finally were to get their chance within the system."[35]

In the terms of our model of reconstitutive discourse, it was the rhetorical combination of McGovern's message, his first and second personae, and the prevailing cynicism toward political leaders and longing for purity in leadership that coalesced into a message and audience that had brought McGovern success in the primaries and won him the Democratic nomination. When the "Eagleton affair" sullied his sanctified persona during the general election campaign, the damage was considerable; as Bormann noted, "the New Politics rhetorical vision lost its power to generate commitment and action and to attract new voters."[36] When discourse seeks to create audiences by merging rhetor and ideas, any major fissure between the persona and thought will break the rhetorical identification necessary for reconstituting an audience.

Our reconstitutive discourse model differs from Antczak's thought/character approach by featuring three parts in the model and by diffusing considerations of the rhetor's thought and character through these three parts. First and second personae receive separate and equal scrutiny, as do the rhetor's substantive message or themes, arguments, appeals, and evidence. We replace the term "character" with the phrase "personal qualities" in order to broaden attention to sources outside the rhetor's immediate text, for example, the rhetor's heritage. And in contrast to Black's definition of second persona and similar definitions offered by Booth and Antczak, we emphasize the explicit as well as the implicit construction of the audience by the rhetor. Particularly in public speeches, orators sometimes directly tell listeners who they are or should be.

A second major innovation in our model is that while both Booth and Antczak focus on the audience's engagement in the text at the time of its reception, the reconstitutive discourse model applies to effects long past those experienced in the moment. For example, rhetors who wish their audiences to be "born again," to act out the unconventional agenda demanded by some cults, or to follow the demanding dictates of Spanish fascism, usually intend to prepare audiences to live the message long after their direct engagement with the text and rhetor. Committed religious followers are expected to carry out their convictions in the days after hearing the sermon; cult members may themselves be directed to be proselytizers, whereby their new personae can be used to recruit further cult members; and fascists in Spain were urged to take to the streets to fight zealously and courageously for their cause, acting out their new identity long past any direct contact with rhetor and message.

A final major difference between the two perspectives is that the model of reconstitutive discourse allows but does not direct the critic to make the ethical judgments desired and demonstrated by Booth, Antczak, and others. Booth makes clear that he is not focusing on the consequences or effects of rhetorical acts, that he is concerned primarily with ethical judgments about rhetors who engage audiences during their participation in the text. As he put it, critics should focus not on a narrative's "future effects" on readers but instead, as we have noted, on "the kind and quality of company it offers while the reader is engaged in it."[37] Such concerns for ethical considerations are obviously crucial and of great value to students, critics, teachers, and society alike. And indeed, when one considers a rhetorical act that fuses the rhetor's thought and personae, ethical analysis is invited. However the reconstitutive discourse model need not focus exclusively or primarily on ethical judgments of the goodness or badness of a rhetorical act, but may seek only to explain and judge if the rhetor accomplished his or her intended effect. While transformations of audiences can depend on qualities the critic sees as moral, qualities similar to those that Antczak examined in his book and articles cited above, they can also arise from qualities amoral or even immoral as in the case of José Antonio. Whatever the morality, critics and teachers of rhetoric strive to explain rhetorical influence. Because such pragmatic rhetorical consequences are important to understand, our model is designed to give insights into causes and effects of these consequences. To help to remove exclusive or dominant emphasis on ethical concerns, the reconstitutive discourse model substitutes the topics of personal qualities or personae for that of character.

In contrast to traditional canons and models of public address, the reconstitutive discourse model provides a somewhat different orientation and set of critical questions for critics who seek to understand the rhetorical dynamics of messages that reconstitute audiences. Analysis of a given case of reconstitutive discourse need not feature all three elements of the model, of course. And in any case, reconstitutive discourse can fail to reconstitute but still succeed in persuading rather than redefining how auditors views themselves.

There have always been rhetors whose impact on audiences is explosive but whose discourse resists explanation by conventional theories and principles in rhetorical and communication theory. Some of these rhetors may have combined personae and ideas to achieve the potent identification necessary to reformulate their audiences. Thus charismatic rhetors need not necessarily be supercharged performers or communication-textbook exemplars but instead may communicate personae and a set of rhetorical characteristics that meld with their substantive ideas. To account for the rhetorical effects of such rhetors—in which group Chávez clearly belongs—we have revised, extended, and particularized the thought/character approach to ethical criticism and proposed the reconstitutive discourse model.

Although the rhetorical dynamics featured in the reconstitutive discourse model are also often present when persuasion succeeds through subtle-to-obvious rhetorically induced shifts in the beliefs and attitudes of audiences, the dynamics addressed in our model seem ideally suited to induce reconstitution. They therefore may be often or always present when audiences take on new selves. The multiple layers of identification, the rhetorical depiction of personal qualities required for a new identity, the identification with rhetor and message in a way to coax or push the auditor into the mold depicted in the second persona—all are rhetorical components that invite reconstitution. In addition to being designed to reveal the rhetorical elements in such reconstitution, the reconstitutive discourse model directs attention to the reciprocal and synergistic nature of the identification fueling the rhetorical process. For example, the model focuses analysis on how a rhetor's first persona and substantive message can contribute to the definition and picture of a second persona. To facilitate the examination of links between the first persona and substantive message, the model directs attention to sources of identification embedded in the easily overlooked syntactic corridors and linguistic corners of texts—places, we will attempt to demonstrate, where Chávez added to his identification with message and audience.

Not only does our model of reconstitutive discourse serve to revise and extend traditional rhetorical approaches to analyzing and evaluating discourse, it has the potential to help scholars revise conventional thinking about social movements.

Most rhetorical studies of social movements focus on external events that affect individuals in a movement or on the stages through which a movement evolves. They ask questions such as: What caused an individual to participate in the movement? What tactics did the leader employ to lead the movement? How did the leader adapt to events that affected the movement? Left largely unaddressed are questions of how leaders rhetorically change the character, and hence the behavior, of their followers, and of how leaders reconstitute audiences who then form the nuclei and bodies of social movements and carry out their agendas.[38] Prior studies generally do not concentrate on how individuals look inside themselves or how leaders work to change the self-concepts of followers.

Rhetorical critic James Andrews displays this emphasis on external events in his discussion of rhetorical imperatives or "situations or events which compel certain people to take some kind of concrete action. The isolation and examination of these imperatives," Andrews reasoned, "can provide significant information regarding the ultimate goals of the movement and the nature of those who create and sustain it."[39] The critic who employs Andrews's definition of rhetorical imperatives looks for external events or situations that shape the movement and force its leader to adapt or change tactics. The reconstitutive discourse model can add to Andrews's approach by explaining how a leader helps individuals to change their perceptions of their own characters, enabling critics of social movements to explain the animating dynamics of movements by looking to individuals as well as events.

In addition to describing the stages of movements, critics have also dissected the nature of rhetorical leadership in movements. In 1970 rhetorical critic Herbert W. Simons explained the complicated rhetorical choices that leaders face, concluding that in order to be successful, a leader's rhetoric must fulfill a series of requirements, the leader must understand the means available to accomplish those requirements, and the leader must be able to overcome problems that threaten achievement of those goals.[40]

For a movement to be successful, Simons argued, leaders must meet three broad requirements:

1. "They must attract, maintain, and mold" group members "into an efficiently organized unit." The group must be willing to follow a program, be loyal to the leader, and be willing to work. The leader must help form a hierarchy and convince others to adhere to it.

2. "They must secure adoption" of their goals and ideas by the establishment.

3. "They must react to resistance generated by the larger structure." Leaders must constantly react to changes in tactics and discourse produced by the establishment.[41]

A leader must be able to reduce the rhetorical problems facing the movement by adjusting to problems such as maintaining a sense of cohesion in the group, gaining respectability outside the group, balancing the incompatibility of organizational efficiency and needs of the members, and negotiating the differences between group expectations and role definitions. Leaders must seem to be what they are not, adapt to several audiences at once, and satisfy a movement requirement for "diversity of leadership types" that include the "theoreticians, agitators, and propagandists [who] must launch the movement; [and] political and bureaucratic types [who] must carry it forward."[42]

Rhetorical critics Charles J. Stewart, Craig Allen Smith, and Robert E. Denton built on Simons's thinking by contending that leaders of movements need two or more of the following three attributes to be successful: prophecy, pragmatism, and charisma. To be charismatic, they claim, a leader must possess a powerful personality and tend "to be a showperson with a sense of timing and the rhetorical skills necessary to articulate what 'others can as yet only feel, strove towards, and imagine but cannot put into words or translate into action.'"[43]

The studies of leadership cited above thoroughly describe a leader's powerful effects on a movement. Although their introduction of the concept of charisma moves close to the appeal of Chávez and others who reconstitute, they do not probe the rhetorical processes that generate the charisma of a quiet rhetor such as Chávez, who appeared to be anything but a "showperson." While these and other scholars have defined charisma in various ways, perhaps the most-quoted definition comes from social theorist Max Weber:

> The term "charisma" will be applied to a certain quality of an individual personality by virtue of which he is set apart from ordinary men and treated as endowed with supernatural, superhuman, or at least specifically exceptional power or qualities. These are such as are not accessible to the ordinary person, but are regarded as of divine origin or as exemplary, and on the basis of them the individual is treated as a leader.[44]

"What is alone important," Weber claims, "is how the individual is actually regarded by those subject to charismatic authority, by his 'followers' or 'disciples.'"[45]

To Weber, charismatic authority occurs in individuals who are working outside the system to create change. Other scholars support Weber's view. "Historically," wrote professor of Management Jay Conger, "we find that charismatic leaders have always personified the forces of change, unconventionality, vision, and an entrepreneurial spirit."[46] Because charismatic leaders function most effectively outside the system, Weber argues, it is difficult if not impossible to transfer that charisma to work from within:

In its pure form charismatic authority has a character specifically foreign to everyday routine structures. The social relationships directly involved are strictly personal, based on the validity and practice of charismatic personal qualities. If this is not to remain a purely transitory phenomenon . . . it is necessary for the character of charismatic authority to become radically changed. Indeed, in its pure form charismatic authority may be said to exist only in the process of originating.[47]

In an attempt to show the interrelationship between charisma and rhetoric, rhetorical critic George P. Boss outlined nine attributes that may be useful in analyzing charisma and charismatic individuals:

1. Charismatic individuals may be seen as having a "gift of grace" or "divine gift" that sets them off from ordinary people. This gift may be supernatural or may exist as a belief on the part of the individuals that they have been chosen for "a special mission."

2. Charismatic "leader-communicators" are those who have strong followers who recognize their leadership qualities. Leaders must have demonstrated "heroic spirit" and great deeds. Leader-communicators are recognized by their use of nonverbal and verbal behaviors, but most of all they communicate orally in a superior manner.

3. Charismatic leaders have an "inspiring message." Leaders must spread the message through nonverbal and verbal means, but the "most vital presentation . . . will consist in the moving oral performance of the leader-communicator."

4. Charismatic leaders attract to themselves groups of "idolatrous followers" who are "faithful listeners, responders, and doers."

5. Charismatic leaders and their followers have a "shared history," which provides a sense of family or community. Audiences and leaders "participate as well in a common national culture—in its linguistic, social, political, and economic heritage," which allows leaders to use the myths of the culture.

6. Charismatic leaders have "high status." Once leaders achieve that status, however, they are forced to take on new roles and tasks, even to achieve "miracles" for followers.

7. Charismatic leaders have a sense of mission or "idealistic crusade." The leader and the mission become inseparable. In order to achieve this goal, leaders will take on images of selflessness and renounce economic benefits.

8. Charismatic leadership "is a uniquely personal response to a crisis in human experience." Such a crisis induces a leader to enact a series of appropriate actions and messages to overcome the crisis.

9. Charismatic leaders must achieve "successful results": unless the crusade appears to be accomplishing its avowed purpose, "there is little likelihood" that the leader will retain a charismatic aura.[48]

The descriptions of charisma provided by Weber and especially by Boss fit Chávez in many ways, but miss him in others. The in-so-many-ways seemingly ordinary Chávez violates Weber's definition of the charismatic persona possessing exceptional if not seemingly supernatural powers and personal attributes beyond those of ordinary people. And while we can recognize Chávez in Boss's descriptions of charismatic leadership, where is the consideration of the dynamics of the discourse that produced or contributed to creating his nine attributes? An application of Boss's checklist would report but not explain Chávez's superb ability to communicate, his inspiring message, his worshipful followers, his high status, his personal response to a crisis, and his successful results. Nor does Boss provide an avenue for understanding how Chávez became inseparable from his mission—an inseparability our model can depict as the result of a rhetor embodying his or her substantive message and mission.

This chapter has proposed that a model of reconstitutive discourse can make a significant contribution to the understanding of communication, in this study the discourse of César Chávez. The model seeks to extend traditional understanding of rhetoric and of social movements. In subsequent chapters we apply the model frequently as we tell the story of Chávez's rhetorical career.

Chapter 4

Finding His Message and Forming His Union, 1963–1970

From 1963 to 1970, the beginning period of his career as a union leader, César Chávez sought to transform an audience of disorganized, individual farm workers into a cohesive union, and an audience of potential—if, for the moment, uninterested—supporters into a vibrant movement capable of defeating entrenched agricultural interests in and beyond California. This transformation would require that he convince both farm workers and his broader audience that they were not powerless but possessed collective power that would lead to inevitable victory, and that they must use their power to advance their just cause. Such reconstitution of audiences is predicated on powerful rhetorical identification between speaker and listeners, between leader and followers. To create his union, Chávez would need to establish a rhetorical identification based not only upon his substantive message of themes, arguments, explanations, and appeals, but also upon personae that reflected who he was and what he stood for as well as what his audiences were or could become.

This chapter delineates Chávez's substantive message as he developed and presented it from 1963 to 1970 and examines his personae and the other rhetorical elements that contributed to or complemented that message. First we develop the historical context of this opening period of Chávez's career as a union leader of farm workers and a civil-rights speaker. We then study the discourse he created in response to the historical context. The chapter closes with an extended analysis of a representative speech from this period.

Chávez settled in Delano with his wife, Helen, and eight children because of family concerns as well as the unique characteristics of the labor force in the area. It was in Delano that he had met Helen Fabela, and it was there that they had married.[1] When asked why he selected Delano as his base, he stated: "The answer is simple. I had no money. My wife's family lived there, and I have a brother [there]. And I thought if things go very bad we can always go and have a meal. . . . Any place in the [San Joaquin] Valley would have made no difference." Coworkers believed that the major reason was the presence of his brother Richard, for Chávez had often said that he and Richard were inseparable.[2]

Perhaps the best tactical reason for choosing Delano was its relatively stable work force. Grapes require year-round tending, including pruning, tying, girdling, cultivating, and spraying; and Delano's many semi-skilled jobs attracted a contingent of farm workers who lived permanently in the area. In 1968, for example, 32 percent of the seven thousand harvest workers in the Delano area resided there throughout the year. Because their work was more permanent, grape workers earned more money than did most farm workers. According to John Gregory Dunne this financial stability allowed them to be "less apathetic than migrants whose overriding considerations are the next job, the next meal, and hence more susceptible to an organizing effort." Chávez understood well that Delano and the San Joaquin Valley contained many resident workers who were already members of small union-like organizations or were sympathetic to unions.[3]

Certain that his righteous cause would achieve success if explained clearly and with force, Chávez embarked upon an exhaustive rhetorical campaign that featured speeches, writings, conversations, and non-discursive symbolic events such as fasts and marches. His initial goal was to educate audiences on the value of a union of farm workers and on the place of that union in history, and then to convince them to join or otherwise contribute to the union.

To finance his rhetorical campaign, Chávez would work a few days in the fields and then use the money earned to buy gas and materials. Helen often worked in the fields with him; when his expanded organizing responsibilities prevented him from field work, she supported the entire family. Several groups offered money to help fund his organization, but he turned them down because he wanted to implement his own ideas on organizing rather than being directed by outside groups.[4]

In his Delano campaign Chávez began to apply the knowledge he had gained from being a farm worker, Community Service Organization (CSO) organizer, and labor historian. He described his plan: "I drew a map of all the towns between Arvin and Stockton—eighty-six of them, including farming camps—and decided to hit them all to get a small nucleus of people working in each. For six months I traveled around, planting an idea." During his first trip through the valley Chávez drove throughout the area, getting the lay of the land, studying the crops, and seeking reactions to the idea of forming a union. When he saw workers in the fields, he would attempt to talk with them. He described his opening tactic: "The first thing I would ask for was the boss and if the boss was close by I would ask him for a job." If the boss was not around, "I would then ask the first person I saw what he thought about unions, just like that, first good morning and then to the question." He recalled "two reactions": Some workers would look at him, "lower their heads," and work even harder; "but from every one hundred men, from every one hundred men that I spoke with one . . . [perhaps] said it was time. And they would say it with assurance, and you already know what they said, 'We're tired.'" When he met those prospective union members, he would take their names and addresses "and then they would have me that night talking to them, only those." Sometimes he would go for weeks without finding such a person; often, when he did, the person was a woman. "Let me tell you that it is not the men who are the more courageous ones," he later told an audience, "there were more women than men that said, 'It is time to start fighting.'"[5]

When Chávez asked workers about their feelings toward creating a union, many reacted with disbelief or fear but a few applauded his inquiries. Those few were essential to his cause, he found, for "when they overcame their fear, almost all of them would agree a union was a good thing. But almost all of them thought that it couldn't be done, that the growers were too powerful."[6] To reconstitute his audience, he would need to instill in once-fearful migrant workers the belief that a union would allow them to stand up successfully to growers.

Before he engaged in face-to-face organizing, Chávez often passed out a questionnaire, "a little card with space, for name, address, and how much the worker thought he ought to be paid." He and his family distributed eighty thousand such cards door to door, in camps, and in grocery stores.[7] The information he received helped him understand the needs of the workers, formulate specific goals for the union, discover rhetorical appeals that promised to be effective in his public discourse, and gather facts and ideas upon which to base his identification with workers.

The heart of Chávez's organizing consisted of tedious, time-consuming face-to-face discussions and house meetings. "We had hundreds of house meetings," he remembered; "Sometimes two or three would come, sometimes none. Sometimes even the family that called the house meeting would not be there." Chávez adapted his community-organizing techniques to the process of recruiting: "I ran these house meetings different than we did in CSO, because it was important for me to learn what the workers wanted. They had to teach me what they needed. I spoke very little in those first meetings, and I listened to what they had to say." He noticed that people behaved differently in their homes: "It was unbelievable how their attitude changed, how different it was from when I talked to them in the fields." This changing attitude was a first step in the process of re-constitution. At the meetings he demonstrated his sensitivity to rhetorical communication by talking not of a union but of a vaguely defined organization composed of like-minded individuals. Realizing that unions and strikes had failed in the past, he did not want his organization linked to those defeats.[8]

Chávez's immediate goal was to build trust and "plant an idea." He frequently established the necessary trust by helping individuals in need. As his reputation spread, more people approached him for help. His CSO experiences had taught him how to work with governmental authorities and thus prepared him to assist some individuals with their immediate problems. Through his assistance to others he brought leaders as well as supporters into the organization.[9]

Fortuitous incidents led Chávez to several of his most effective recruiting techniques. During the early years of the union, he later recalled, "We didn't have any money at all . . . none for gas and hardly any for food. So I went to people and started asking for something to eat. It turned out to be about the best thing I could have done, although at first it's hard on your pride. Some of our best members came in that way." "If people give you their food," Chávez began to understand, "they'll give you their hearts."[10]

Setting himself a timetable, Chávez decided that if he could not organize a union "in three years, then we couldn't do it. But we made a firm promise among ourselves that if we couldn't do it, we'd never blame the people, we'd blame ourselves." Within one year he had recruited enough members to hold an organizing convention in Fresno. In September, 1962, 230 people from sixty-five communities met to form the National Farm Workers Association (NFWA). Delegates wrote a constitution, created a dues structure, and elected Chávez as president and Dolores Huerta and Gilbert Padilla, organizers Chávez had recruited from the CSO, as vice-presidents.[11] Thirty days after that convention, about 350 people had signed up to join the union. Six months later, it had 12 dues-paying members.[12] The organization would change its name several times in the 1960s, eventually settling on the United Farm Workers (UFW).

Chávez realized that an emblem could serve as a powerful symbol for the new union, "something that the people could make themselves, and something that had some impact." Eventually his brother Richard "suggested drawing an eagle with square lines, an eagle anyone could make, with five steps in the wings." Chávez selected the colors, a red background featuring a black eagle on a white circle. Red and black flags had historically been used in strikes in Mexico, so the design had strong roots in the Mexican-American community that comprised the major source of union membership. Chávez's cousin Manuel, who was not an artist, created a design that could be easily reproduced. The flag became a powerful symbol that provided a means of identification among workers in later strikes and linked many members to their Mexican past.[13]

The new union offered a wide variety of support. It instituted services needed by the workers, eventually creating a credit union, cooperative food store, drugstore and service station, burial insurance, and a newspaper. It also provided legal counsel and grievance committees to assist union members with problems at work.[14]

An indispensable additional element in Chávez's plan was to build support from outside the union. During the first years of his Delano campaign, much of his outside audience consisted of religious groups. In his travels as an organizer, he had met dedicated farm-worker–union supporters among the members of the California Migrant Ministry, a mainly Protestant group. He wondered why the Catholic Church did not have a similar program to help migrant workers. Why do "Protestants come out here and help the people, demand nothing, and give all their time serving farm workers," he asked, "while our own parish priests stay in their churches, where only a few people come, and usually feel uncomfortable?" He was shocked to see priests siding with the growers rather than following what he believed was church doctrine that called upon priests to help the poor and the workers. Although many growers were Catholics of Italian and Yugoslavic descent who exerted pressure on church officials and gave generously to the parishes, the church would eventually contribute significantly to the union movement. As Chávez reminded the clergy: "The churches *had* to get involved. . . . Everything they had taught for two thousand years was at stake in this struggle."[15]

To maintain his fragile union in its early years, Chávez tried to avoid premature strikes. He believed that the union would lose any confrontation until the time was right for the challenge and unless the union had the strength to defeat the growers. This was a period in which the United States was open to social reform. As Chicano labor leader Bert Corona said, "It took the combination of the civil-rights movement that was sweeping across the land involving Black people as well as new groups of people which later became the reservoir of support for the farm workers. César Chávez recognized this." Corona related how Chávez called a meeting of Chicano organizers in Delano in the spring of 1965: "He made a very strong point . . . that the reason the farm workers organizing drive could win in the days ahead was because they could ally themselves with a new feature in American social and political activity—the movement for civil rights, the movement of the youth, and the movement of the poor—to become involved in doing something about the farm workers' needs."[16] In order to appeal to those groups, according to historian Francisco Rosales, Chávez cultivated a "Gandhi-King image that fascinated Americans, many who viewed with mis-giving the rough-and-tough mainstream unions like the Teamsters."[17]

By 1964 several developments were already hastening the day when the union would have the necessary power and proper climate in which to act. U.S. Secretary of Labor Willard Wirtz had in the past tried unsuccessfully to convince growers to recruit domestic workers, but ultimately had permitted some *braceros* (contract workers) to enter the country under an agreement that guaranteed them $1.40 per hour for their labor and specified that they could not be hired unless local workers received the same wage. The bracero program, which began during World War II, ended on January 1, 1965, because of pressure from all sides: Churches and Democrats opposed the program on humanitarian grounds, Republicans believed the program led to moral decay in society, and unions were concerned that braceros lowered wages for domestic workers and made unionization of workers more difficult.

By failing to renew the bracero program, according to Rosales, Congress "took a lethal weapon from the growers."[18] Meanwhile, as the civil-rights movement was inspiring Mexican Americans in the Southwest to take bold action, the daily life of the migrant remained far from satisfactory. Itinerant farm workers earned the lowest wages of all workers and worked in miserable conditions.[19] Sanitation facilities were absent, dangerous, or exploitative. Stan Steiner reported, for example, that at one ranch "the field boss charged his hands 25¢ for a cup of water, and at a farm in the Delano area, sixty-seven workers were forced to drink from one cup, which was an empty beer can." And according to John Gregory Dunne, ranches routinely lacked portable field toilets, forcing women workers "to squat down several rows over from where they were picking," where, the women charged, "their foreman used to sneak after them and watch them."[20]

Although Chávez would have preferred to delay until the union was more prepared, he led his initial strike in May, 1965, among rose workers in McFarland, California.[21] After a brief strike the rose workers won a pay increase, but returned to work without signing a union contract. Chávez said that the union "wanted to hold out for a contract and more benefits, but the majority of the rose workers wanted to accept the offer and go back to work." Even though the victory "was a small one," he said, "it prepared us for the big one."[22] Chávez next led his union in a series of small strikes to perfect its tactics[23] and prepare workers for the larger strikes he believed they would face several years in the future. Subsequent events, however, drastically foreshortened that future.

The strike that catapulted Chávez and his union into public notice began in Delano on September 8, 1965, when two thousand Filipino workers of the Agricultural Workers Organizing Committee (AWOC) left their jobs because they were being paid less than braceros. The union demanded $1.40 an hour or 25¢ a box for picked grapes. AWOC had earlier won such demands in the Coachella Valley of Southern California and expected similar success in Delano; but as the strike dragged on, AWOC realized that it needed help. AWOC's leader, Larry Itliong, approached Chávez and invited his NFWA to join the strike. Although Chávez still questioned the readiness of his group for a major strike, he moved decisively to join the cause because he did not want to see the Filipino strike broken. The NFWA's leadership agreed to support the strike, and scheduled a mass meeting for September 16, Mexican Independence Day, to ask the active membership to ratify that decision. The turnout surprised Chávez: "We were astounded, we had like six thousand workers. We were ready to strike and we took a vote and we struck. And we said, 'God will provide.' and we struck." Later when asked why he relied on God, Chávez stated: "There was absolutely no way that I could [do it without divine help].... I had no money. I had no idea. All I knew was ... they wanted to strike. ... We couldn't work while others were striking."[24]

The choice of Mexican Independence Day was symbolically charged for a union whose membership was mainly Mexican Americans. Speaking at the meeting, Chávez compared the labor battle to the Mexican Revolution fought by his and his audience's ancestors: "One hundred and fifty-five years ago in the state of Guanajuato in Mexico," he said, "a padre proclaimed the struggle for liberty. He was killed, but ten years later Mexico won its independence." Steiner argued that by invoking "the spirit of Father Hidalgo—the George Washington of Mexico—" Chávez cast himself in the powerful image of a revolutionary leader. This image identified him with the revered leaders of the Mexican battle for independence, connected Mexican-American workers to their rich Mexican tradition of dissent, and brought their Mexican past into their American present. After some discussion, union members voted to strike. Reaching its moment of destiny, the union initiated a strike that would last from 1965 until 1970, a strike frequently marked by violence against workers and their supporters.[25]

Once the strike began Chávez sought to inform and convert the broader public. He traveled throughout California to speak on college campuses to "galvanize support for the striking workers." Television news crews helped publicize the event by filming the picket lines, especially when there were confrontations. Newspapers and national magazines sent reporters to interview Chávez, opening larger audiences to his messages; and Chávez linked his cause to the expanding national concern over civil rights by explaining that farm workers sought fundamental human rights."[26]

A few weeks after the strike began, Chávez marveled at the attention it had attracted:

• • •

The name Delano is now known throughout the state. It is becoming known throughout the nation. Not because of its rich land and fine location, not because of its friendly and industrious people, not because of its beautiful mountains in the east or sunsets in the west. . . . Delano is on the map because of a bitter strike—a strike which will be 100 days old before we reach Christmas.[27]

In August, 1966, a year into the strike, the two cooperating unions joined to form the United Farm Workers Organizing Committee (UFWOC), affiliated the new union with the AFL-CIO, and named Chávez its first director.

The war between Chávez and his opponents quickly polarized the San Joaquin Valley. The growers had long controlled the region and were unwilling to relinquish their immense power. In his book on the strike, Dunne noted that the isolated area took its rhythm from the cycle of crops and possessed a prevailing ethic similar to that of "the nineteenth-century frontier. . . . It is precisely this rhythm, this tone, this insulation, this ethic which made the Valley unable to understand an intense, unschooled Mexican American named César Chávez."[28]

The owners initially reacted in a manner typical of establishments under attack: They made light of the threat and belittled the union and its leader.[29] Arguing that the strike did not even exist, grower Martin Zaninovich stated: "There is no strike among Delano farm workers. . . . The so-called strike is pure myth, manufactured out of nothing by outside agitators who are more interested in creating trouble in the United States than in the welfare of the farm workers."[30] Others attributed unacceptable motives to Chávez's actions by dismissing him as a "social revolutionary and not a labor organizer," and calling him a "power-hungry opportunist, who is amassing a small fortune from the dues of the workers and the contributions of do-gooders. All he is able to offer in return are empty promises."[31] Further attempting to reduce Chávez's credibility and persuasiveness, the growers maintained that the workers had always been happy before Chávez arrived. Grower Bruno Dispoto claimed that "the workers have always gotten along well with us. They make good money. . . . They are our neighbors here and we were getting along well until the troublemakers started." Another grower, Jack Pandol, said, "Our workers have never shown any dissatisfaction. They are proud to work for us." Pandol even proposed that Mexican Americans were made for a migrant life: "It's the nature of these people to move from place to place."[32]

Chávez refuted growers' claims by relating that "just like the Southern plantation owner used to say about his negroes . . . , ranchers in Delano say that the farm workers are happy the way they are."[33] He also disputed the characterization that everyone in Delano was happy until he and other outsiders had stirred up the contented workers: "The chamber of commerce would like people to believe that Delano is a sweet, simple American town where everybody loved his neighbor until us troublemakers came," when in reality, he said, it was a violent place where different groups of people had long been bitterly divided.[34]

As the strike gained momentum, growers and police who took their side began harassing Chávez and his supporters. At each picket line workers and their sympathizers were photographed and files established to track them. Police followed strikers and leaders wherever they went. All visitors to union headquarters had their license-plate numbers recorded. Acts of violence were common—cars were shot up, motorists tried to run down picketers, and some picketers were assaulted.[35] At times the harassment aided Chávez's cause. For example, in 1968 a group of ranch workers walked off their jobs after union representatives had talked with them. Chávez, the Reverend Chris Hartmire of the California Migrant Ministry, and a Catholic priest, Father Victor Salandini, accompanied workers who went to retrieve their belongings at the ranch. All were arrested for trespassing, stripped naked, and chained together, including Chávez, Hartmire, and Salandini. The resulting publicity elicited sympathy for the strikers and hostility toward growers.[36]

Four groups that consistently fought Chávez were the California Farm Bureau, the California Grape and Tree Fruit League, the South Central Farmers Committee, and Whitaker and Baxter, a San Francisco public-relations firm hired by the growers. Some residents of Delano also formed organizations to challenge Chávez, adopting names such as "Citizens for Facts," "Men Against Chávez," and "Mothers Against Chávez." The citizen groups distributed letters, leaflets, and pamphlets that associated Chávez with a communist conspiracy. The Citizens for Facts even charged that Chávez and his followers were not farm workers: "FACTS ARE: Chávez and his cohorts have imported the long-haired kooks, professional loafers, winos and dregs of society to carry their Huelga [strike] banners. The true farm workers are in the fields working."[37]

Alternative union-like organizations were created to oppose the UFW. With names such as the Kern-Tulare Independent Farm Workers or the Agricultural Workers Freedom to Work Association (AWFWA), the organizations described themselves as the true representatives of workers. Later both alternative "unions" were proven to be front organizations for growers' groups and quickly faded from sight.[38] This failed attempt to divide the farm workers actually helped Chávez by alienating many workers from the growers and associating the growers with dishonest tactics.

The growers eventually recognized that Chávez was a serious threat. One grower perceived the situation in the darkest terms. After asking Chávez to detail his plans, he stated: "Give us a program and we'll try to find some meeting ground. We're not inhuman. But all Chávez wants to do is replace my power structure with his."[39]

To be flexible and avoid repeating past failures, Chávez adjusted the union's strategies to specific situations and invented new tactics when necessary. He consistently taught his followers that tactics must evolve and change. For example, he created mobile picket lines to seek out workers in the fields and employ them there as picketers rather than to picket only the entrances to farms as previous unions had done. Again demonstrating his emphasis on communication to change behavior, Chávez defined the purpose of "roving picket lines" as "to try to communicate to workers wherever they were closest to the road where we could communicate with them."[40] As part of Chávez's pragmatic approach, the union did not strike all growers. Workers, including Chávez's supporters, needed to earn money or they would be forced to move out of the area and thus weaken the strike.[41]

One of Chávez's biographers, Eugene Nelson, noted that the strike employed "a dozen innovations: balloons with "Huelga [Strike]" painted on them flying gaily over the vines; new and more provocative signs: 'A crime against God and man,' 'Think,' 'United we stand, divided we fall'; red-and-black Mexican strike flags whose mere appearance suffices to discourage prospective scabs in Mexico . . . and dazzling and highly effective new songs and chants. . . ."[42] And there were other weapons: For example, one young striker planted a false rumor that two thousand college students would show up to picket on a particular weekend. Fearing such a large number of picketers, the growers pulled nearly all of the workers out of the fields. The rumor accomplished as much as any picketing could have done.[43]

Another new tactic focused on artistic communication. The union established El Teatro Campesino, a theater group, to teach farm workers to carry their message to new audiences. Luis Valdez, head of El Teatro, related how the group toured "farm-worker towns across the Valley," creating rallies where they told farm workers about the strike and related matters.[44] Chávez described El Teatro Campesino's role in the union:

Well, it helped with the workers. . . . It was street theater. . . . It was able to deal with three important things. One was just [to] deal with . . . like we're here to stay. . . . The other thing he was able to [do was] ridicule . . . growers . . . which was great. Not attack them. But ridicule. . . . Then deal with the internal problems we had about the strikebreakers or being afraid . . . . Oh, the Friday night meetings would be jammed with people . . . because even though we were losing the strike . . . they're still coming because the teatro was there.[45]

Occasionally the farm workers' methods went beyond those that Chávez had approved. Spies and "inside agitators" sent to work in non-picketed ranches would engage in slowdowns or sloppy work to reduce the harvest. When picketers appeared, the secret unionists would lead workers out of the fields to join the strikes. Although Chávez was uncomfortable with such actions, they proved effective.[46]

Chávez infused his strike with traditional symbols of Mexican-American culture and the Catholic religion. At the suggestion of women among the strikers, Chávez introduced religious services near the picket lines. At one ranch he and his brother built a small chapel in the back of a station wagon, started an around-the-clock vigil, and announced on radio that mass would be held. Many worshipers appeared for the services, including some who left the fields to join in the mass; these strikers met with nonstriking workers whom they frequently proselytized.[47]

The most publicized example of advancing the strike by enacting Catholic traditions from Mexico occurred in the farm workers' twenty-one-day, 250-mile march from Delano to Sacramento in 1966, one of the many UFW-sponsored masses and marches that raised public awareness of the plight of farm workers while simultaneously creating internal solidarity among workers.[48] This march took the form of a pilgrimage, a powerful tradition in the Spanish-speaking world where, as we have argued elsewhere, such marches are "an expression of penance and commitment."[49] Uncovering the origins of this particular pilgrimage, Luis Valdez recalled that the organizers' belief that "something had to be done, we'd gotten to a stalemate, and so, César came up with the idea of a pilgrimage." On the way to Sacramento, the feeling of solidarity grew while "little bands of farm workers kept joining," culminating in ten thousand people gathered at the capitol to celebrate.[50] The march was a vivid refutation of the charge that the union lacked the support of workers; the rhetorically sensitive Chávez understood "that a large turnout for the march would counter the accusations leveled by the growers."[51]

Simply by participating in the march, workers would be bonded to the union. As Chávez shrewdly observed, once people could be convinced to participate in an activity they would be different or would be reconstituted: "So we have the teatro, the Virgin, we had the flags, but see people marching and . . . [they're] participating. They're committing themselves because their compadre . . . [or the boss] in the car sees them in the march, they can't deny it. Now they're committed, now they have to support it."[52] Chávez also saw the march as a way to link him and his cause to Martin Luther King Jr. and the entire civil-rights movement: "Dr. King had been very successful with that [marches]. So anyway, it was a great experience for us. Oh, it was very difficult to march for twenty-one days, but it was like God-sent, it was fantastic, it helped us a lot."[53]

Chávez emphasized the close association of the march with the Mexican tradition's value of sacrifice. "This was an excellent way of training ourselves to endure the long, long struggle," he explained. "This was a penance more than anything else—and it was quite a penance, because there was an awful lot of suffering involved in this pilgrimage, a great deal of pain."[54] In a speech given in Spanish he elaborated on the important place of sacrifice for Mexican Americans:

> Ever since our ancestors we've seen primarily in Mexico that people are willing to make sacrifices. That is why our union is strong. Because the root of the union is sacrifice. Once we understand this, we can look years back and see that for many years we've had the idea of sacrificing ourselves to obtain something good for us and for our people. That is why my fellow people that I ask you for one last sacrifice, a big sacrifice that will take you to victory, a work sacrifice, a sacrifice to do it without violence, a sacrifice to work hard, and ordinarily to arrive at the final victory that is about to come.[55]

Chávez's strong Catholic beliefs further manifested in religious pictures, statues, and pictures hung on the walls of his office as well as in such traditional practices of the church as pilgrimages and fasting. Of particular importance was the Virgin of Guadalupe, a symbol present at nearly every meeting, procession, or march. In the early days of the union many of Chávez's advisors were priests and ministers who helped him in a variety of ways, from planning finances to arranging his itinerary to editing the union's newspaper, *El Malcriado*.[56]

Chávez's 25-day fast in 1968 was the single event that probably attracted the most widespread attention to his cause. Robert F. Kennedy, long a friend and supporter of Chávez and the farm workers, attended a mass and broke bread with the weakened Chávez as he ended his fast. The former U.S. attorney general lauded Chávez for sacrificing "against violence, and against lawlessness . . . on behalf of people who suffer so tremendously in this country, namely so many of our farm workers, and particularly the Mexican Americans and other of minority groups who have not had the protection of the laws. . . ."[57] "I think that César Chávez has been a good example," he told the nation; "I think César Chávez has been very influential. . . ." Kennedy himself could also be rhetorically effective for the cause, as illustrated by the well-publicized suggestion he made to Kern County law enforcement officials at a Senate subcommittee hearing after a sheriff had proposed stopping the peaceful assembly of protesting farm workers: "Could I suggest in the luncheon period of time, that the sheriff and the district attorney read the Constitution of the United States?"[58]

Kennedy ranked among the most visible UFW supporters. Winthrop Yinger noted that the Senator's "political power could open some closed doors," that he "may have been the Union's most important ally. He was an acknowledged champion and advocate for the poor—American Indians, people of Appalachia, farm workers."[59] As journalist Sam Kushner observed, "No other American politician could have drawn the response that the grape-pickers gave Kennedy—chiefly because no other had done so much to deserve it."[60] Kennedy's endorsement certainly gave the union and its leader increased legitimacy in the minds of many members of the public. Chávez acknowledged the debt:

> Robert Kennedy came to Delano when no one else came. Whenever we needed him, whenever we asked him to come, we knew he would be there. He approached us with love; as people, not as subjects for study—as Anglos usually had done—as equals not as objects of curiosity. He helped the oppressed. His were HECHOS DE AMOR. Deeds of Love.[61]

Chávez reciprocated the assistance by actively working for Kennedy's 1968 presidential bid. Kennedy had asked Chávez to be one of his delegates to the Democratic national convention, in part because he needed Chávez's support to gain Mexican-American votes in California. Kennedy's victory in that primary showed the power of Mexican Americans at the polls. His assassination on election night was a terrible blow to Chávez and the union; the UFW and its leader had lost a powerful friend.[62] Steiner described Chávez's sadness: "'I have no taste for politics in my heart,' Chávez told me after Kennedy's death. In his grief, he would say no more."[63]

Chávez's best-known tactic was the boycott. Early in the strike he realized that he could improve his chances for victory by putting economic pressure on growers. Asking consumers to refuse to buy products produced by firms that did not recognize the union, Chávez initiated the first boycott in December of 1965 against the grapes produced by Schenley Industries. When Schenley signed with the union in 1966, Chávez announced a second boycott, against the DiGiorgio Corporation. Other growers began to help DiGiorgio in the fight, so Chávez broadened the boycott to include all grape producers. The grape boycott continued until 1970, when the growers agreed to union contracts.

In order to build a functioning boycott, Chávez dispatched volunteers to cities throughout the United States. Receiving little or no salary, the volunteers had to raise their own money, find places to lives, and recruit local volunteers to build boycott organizations. As the years went by they discovered many tactics that made the boycott effective. Among the wide variety of techniques the union employed were a sit-in at the Jewel Tea Company near Chicago, a campaign to convince people to write postcards and phone the headquarters of A&P stores in Philadelphia, and a "balloon-in" at supermarkets in Toronto where balloons inscribed with the legend "Boycott Grapes" floated through stores. By sending organizers throughout the country, Chávez began to reach for new audiences.[64]

Appearing at televised press conferences in the late 1960s, California Governor Ronald Reagan presented the case against Chávez and his boycott. Reagan began by attempting to gain credibility by referring to his own union credentials: He had been an officer in a labor union (the Screen Actors Guild) for twenty-five years, and six times its president. Reagan accused Chávez of going "over the heads of the workers to management" and relying on an ill-advised grape boycott as well as on "coercion and threat and demonstration and so forth." Although he acknowledged the contracts Chávez had won, he labeled Chávez's organizing and boycott efforts a failure. But Reagan belied his own easy dismissal of Chávez when he warned that "what we all have to keep in mind is that the grape boycott's just the first domino in a whole series" that could "move through the agricultural community of California."[65] Later, after Chávez had won contracts from many grape growers and was now boycotting lettuce, Reagan's warnings appeared prophetic. The Bud Antle Company's Robert Antle, a powerful rancher in the valley and probably the most visible representative for the lettuce growers, admitted that the boycott had disrupted business and been effective.[66]

In 1970, after a dramatic and draining five-year fight, the union won most of its demands and many grape growers signed contracts with the United Farm Workers. Chávez had become a national figure and the UFW had confounded history and expectations with its successes. We now turn to a close examination of the rhetor and the discourse that was indispensable to achieving these successes.

Although they had a long tradition of joining labor unions, many Mexican-American workers held themselves aloof from Anglo organizers/rhetors in established unions, whom they suspected of seeking to lure them into the organizations that had traditionally discriminated against them for the sole purpose of collecting their dues. "What the farm workers clearly lacked," wrote Dunne, "was indigenous, Mexican-American leadership." Organizing Mexican Americans into a successful union required a leader/rhetor with Chávez's qualities. As Luis Valdez observed:

> Chávez was not a traditional bombastic Mexican revolutionary; nor was he a
> gavacho—a gringo, a white social worker type. Both types had tried to orga-

nize the raza [Mexican-American people] in America and failed. Here was César, burning with a patient fire, poor like us, dark like us, talking quietly, moving people to talk about their problems, attacking the little problems first, and suggesting, always suggesting—never more than that—the solutions that seemed attainable. We didn't know it until we met him, but he was the leader we had been waiting for.[67]

Valdez's description of Chávez recalls Antczak's view that an orator succeeds with an audience by speaking "that which they recognize as part of them but which they were not yet ready to say."[68]

The leader the farm workers had been awaiting turned out to be an unpretentious man who often went unnoticed in groups. "Outwardly," recorded one observer, "César Chávez does not appear to be very different from the average Mexican farm worker. His quiet, almost shy manner and his unpretentiously dull clothing make it very difficult for all but those who know him to spot him in a crowd."[69] Yinger described his first meeting with the man who embodied the image of a farm worker: "Half a dozen farm workers stood in the middle of the office gesturing and talking rapidly in Spanish. I did not recognize César Chávez. This is an important circumstance to underscore. He is not a celebrity you can easily spot in a crowd. He is an archetype; he is a farm worker." Peter Matthiessen provided this often-repeated description:

> The man who has threatened California has an Indian's bow nose and lank black hair, with sad eyes and an open smile that is shy and friendly; at moments he is beautiful, like a dark seraph. He is five feet six inches tall, and since his twenty-five-day fast the previous winter, has weighed no more than one hundred and fifty pounds. Yet the word "slight" does not properly describe him. There is an effect of being centered in himself so that no energy is wasted, an effect of density; at the same time, he walks as lightly as a fox. One feels immediately that this man does not stumble, and that to get where he is going he will walk all day.[70]

Clearly Chávez differed in manner from most celebrated speakers of his time. Rosales captured the quietly charismatic advocate in these words: Chávez "did not possess an imposing figure; he did not swagger or project a tough persona, as did many militant activists of the era. Chávez's short stature and soft-spoken, quiet demeanor was often mistaken for the stereotypical look of passivity rather than forceful leadership."[71]

This unique labor leader found promising rhetorical possibilities in Delano. To seize the moment, he would need first to educate farm workers of the need for a union and then convince them to reconstitute themselves into activists who could defeat an industry that had never been effectively unionized. At the onset of this educational campaign he presented a pragmatic justification of his union: "The United Farm Workers Organizing Committee is a labor union. The farm workers are one of the largest work forces in America that are not organized. Those of us who are in the union feel that the best way of bringing those benefits that other Americans are enjoying now because of unions is through their own union." As he canvassed the country, Chávez encountered "a large and increasing demand for organization from many places. . . . Almost everywhere I go to speak, somewhere in the vicinity there are farm workers. So a network is being built." "It will take many years," he continued confidently, "but . . . we know that a union of farm workers is going to be built somehow because the workers are on the move, and they want a union."[72]

Convincing audiences of the need for a union required that they learn of past injustices that the union would correct. Chávez's instruction began with the story of the less-than-honorable history of agriculture in California. "You must have some of the background of agriculture in California to understand what we have been doing," he said as he informed his audiences about the ways in which large corporations had often amassed their land holdings through questionable means and followed equally dubious practices to obtain the water needed to irrigate their crops.[73] With so much land and water, he said, growers needed cheap labor to work their property profitably; accordingly, they recruited and then exploited ethnic groups throughout the world. Chávez detailed how the growers had begun using Chinese workers after the railroads had been completed in the 1860s. The initially docile Chinese quickly determined that farm work would bring them the money necessary to buy their own land. When they began to do so, legislation was passed barring Chinese men from ownership of land and from marrying Caucasian women. As the Chinese abandoned agricultural work to settle in the cities, growers turned to poor white workers. By the turn of the century they began to bring in Japanese workers, who proved to be equally independent and began to rent land for their own farms, which prompted growers to import workers from India and the Philippines. In the 1920s, Chávez said, growers turned to Mexico for laborers who could move quickly and inexpensively to the United States, where they, too, would be discriminated against. "One grower," Chávez related, "explained that Mexicans were good for California land work because they were short and close to the ground."[74] On many occasions Chávez claimed that farm workers had not been covered by protective legislation simply because most were Mexican Americans.[75] Sometimes he compared the farm workers' problem to that which plagued "Negroes . . . for many years": token legislation.[76]

When Chávez addressed the issue of growers importing legal and illegal Mexican nationals to break strikes, he broke from the views of many Chicano groups by condemning such immigration. In 1970 he assailed the illegal use of "green carders" and "wetbacks"—the latter a pejorative term he used more than once in public—and he charged that growers colluded with the Immigration and Naturalization Service to import more workers from Mexico.[77]

Chávez's history lesson covered the long struggle to organize workers into unions. During the "last sixty or seventy years," he instructed, "unions tried to organize, beginning with the Wobblies way back in the beginning of the century. . . ." The battle was particularly difficult because "farm workers are excluded from the National Labor Relations Act, therefore, there are no rules, no regulations to organize by in agriculture." At a tremendous disadvantage in their battle with growers, the workers had never been organized into an effective union.[78] Even in 1970, at the end of his first period of organizing, Chávez continued amassing facts to educate listeners. He told a television audience that despite some victories, his union was in a similar position to "industrial workers . . . of the turn of the century," the 1920s, and the early 1930s. "One of every three jobs in California is in . . . a four, or five billion dollar [farm] industry," he reported.[79]

Chávez portrayed crop-pickers as mistreated by growers and unable to secure a decent wage, living a harsh life in which they were controlled by external forces. He compared farm workers' poverty in the 1960s to conditions during the Great Depression of the 1930s. Conceding to his audiences that many listeners would not fully understand the harshness of life during the Depression, he quickly added that many people "had been living it and experiencing it for many years. And farm workers are living it still, though most other people today don't even realize it."[80] The invisibility of farm workers to many segments of society contributed to the lack of attention to their plight; and their anonymity in turn invited mistreatment on and off the farms. One striking symbol of on-the-job abuse was the mandatory use of short-handled hoes in thinning certain crops. "You have to caress a plant tenderly to make it grow," Chávez related from direct experience, "and the short hoe makes you bend over and work closer to the plant. But a good man can work just as well with a long hoe, without the exhaustion."[81] Matthiessen wrote that Chávez's criticism of the short hoe in speeches to workers always elicited a "wild cheer of anger and approval. . . ."[82]

To quantify the callous treatment of workers, Chávez cited the number killed in accidents while being transported to the fields in rickety buses and trucks. After one accident, he spoke angrily:

> There have been too many accidents in the fields, on trucks, under machines, in buses. So many accidents involving farm workers. People ask if they are deliberate. They are deliberate in the sense that they are the result of a farm labor system that treats workers like agricultural implements and not human beings. These accidents happen because employers and labor contractors treat us as if we were not important human beings. . . . The trucks and buses are old, and unsafe.[83]

"How long will it take," he pleaded, "before we take seriously the importance of the workers who harvest the food we eat?"[84] Those who died were "important human beings," he said, "because they are from us. They are important because of the love they gave their husbands, their children, their wives, their parents—all of those who were close to them and needed them. . . . They were important because of the work they do. . . ."[85]

The public's lack of concern underscored Chávez's opinion that many members of society did not grant farm workers the respect given to other individuals, and that even well-meaning people patronized them. Despite his acknowledgment that farm workers lacked money and power, Chávez did not ask for or want pity. He belittled patronizing actions by the union's earlier volunteers as evidence of "idolizing the poor. . . . Like farm workers are saints, you know." Such behavior was harmful, he reasoned, because it did not improve the lives of either workers or volunteers. As he told readers, "You can't help people if you feel sorry for them. You have to be practical. This type of feeling doesn't carry you for more than what it carried those people who were helping us. After a while it becomes old, and there is no real basis for doing things that you're doing."[86]

Rather than being seen as objects of pity, workers should be treated as human beings with intrinsic dignity, he insisted. In his "Letter From Delano"(1969) Chávez set forth his views to E. L. Barr Jr., President of the California Grape and Tree Fruit League:

> You must understand—I must make you understand— . . . our membership and the hopes and aspirations of the hundreds of thousands of the poor and dispossessed. . . . [We] are, above all, human beings, no better and no worse than any other cross-section of human society; we are not saints because we are poor, but by the same measure neither are we immoral. We are men and

women who have suffered and endured much, and not only because of our abject poverty but because we have been kept poor.[87]

On other occasions Chávez argued that growers denied dignity to workers out of sheer ignorance of the lives of their employees. Thus employers saw workers as comfortable in their lives, ". . . like a big happy family here—men singing down by the camp at night. Women praying to their plaster saints. Kids playing after work." Chávez compared the growers' idyllic view to the one that formerly justified slavery: "They think people live by the hour and not by the year. . . . They say the farm workers are happy living the way they are—just like the Southern plantation owner used to say about his Negroes."[88] Unlike the farm owners, Chávez said, the union had concern for all people, including "the least of our brothers. . . . We're concerned for everyone and particularly concerned for the poor." He and his coworkers were dedicated "to change things so we can get justice and dignity for our people." Such justice and dignity could best be attained by first creating meaningful employment for everyone.[89]

In "The Plan of Delano" (1966) Chávez and his coauthors had made clear that the union was much more than an ordinary workers' association that sought economic advances:

This is the beginning of a social movement in fact and not in pronouncements. We seek our basic, God-given rights as human beings. Because we have suffered, and are not afraid to suffer in order to survive, we are ready to give up everything—even our lives—in our struggle for social justice. We shall do it without violence because it is our destiny. To the growers and to all those who oppose us, we say the words of Benito Juárez, "Respect for another's rights is the meaning of peace."[90]

In this letter he pictured the conflict of growers as "a death struggle against man's inhumanity to man. . . . This struggle itself gives meaning to our life and ennobles our dying."[91]

Adherents who joined and participated in Chávez's righteous cause and union were promised personal power. Chávez credited his union for providing poor farm workers with the power necessary to improve their lives, adamantly telling audiences that the union must be built by farm workers and owned by farm workers if those workers were ever to attain power.[92] Arguing that only through such power could the poor remedy the wrongs committed against them, he constructed the following simple comparison: "To try to change conditions without power is like trying to move a car without gasoline. If the workers are going to do anything, they need their own power." The necessary power, he taught, was political as well as economic, for unions could influence legislation and attitudes.[93]

Even a strong union would face enormous challenges from formidable foes. Chávez warned that the established power structure would seek to divide its challengers so that individual union members would be defending themselves rather than their people or movement. In Delano harassment by the growers often elicited such self-defense. A few months after the Delano strike began, Chávez talked of just this kind of harassment: "On September 16th when the Delano workers voted to strike the grape growers, they took a pledge to conduct a nonviolent strike. Many months have passed since that day. Many of us have been cursed, our women have been insulted by the growers, our wives, mothers, sisters, and many of us on the [picket line] have been arrested." Picketers were attacked and sprayed with pesticides, growers drove their cars into the picket lines, and cohorts of growers shot at strikers. Often the police seemed sympathetic to the growers' illegal attacks on strikers. The harassment of workers shaped Chávez's rhetorical responses. "The first two years of the strike," he declared, "I spent most of my speaking engagements and my time getting support to get the growers and cops off our back." The public responded to his call: "We once had over a hundred telegrams and maybe three hundred phone calls to the Delano chief of police in a three-day period. They came from all over the country. Churchmen called him, lawyers, union leaders, government officials, U.S. senators, congressmen."[94]

Chávez attributed his success in outmaneuvering growers to the moral rightness of his cause: "We outsmart them many times. We have a just cause and I guess this is 90 percent of the case." Acknowledging the practical as well as the metaphysical, he also credited his experience in recognizing that his antagonists tended to respond predictably and in stages. Chávez became a theorist of social movements by delineating the stages that the establishment goes through in reacting to agitators and their movements: "At the first stage, they ignore us. . . . Then they ridicule us. . . . Next comes the repression. Eventually—after a long time—comes the respect." Chávez realized that once organizers understood that establishments tend to function in predictable ways, the organizers could make necessary adaptations; a savvy organizer could "push a button here or do something there, and we know what the reactions will be, sometimes three or four or five steps ahead. It's natural. They're reacting like human beings with money and with land. They're afraid. They feel threatened."[95]

Chávez identified labor contractors as representing one of the most hated practices he would seek to end. His own family had been exploited by those contractors during his days as a migrant worker, and the corrupt system continued to exploit workers well into the 1960s. Chávez began his educational campaign on the issue by introducing his audience to contractors. The labor contractor, he instructed, was generally a former farm worker who knew the work force and was a recruiter, supervisor, provider of transportation, and bookkeeper. Although a former worker and often a Mexican American, the contractor viciously oppressed workers and represented "a remnant of the system of peonage." To eliminate the system, Chávez's union sponsored hiring halls governed by workers themselves.[96]

Chávez found that the Teamsters Union was an equally dangerous foe. On several occasions in the 1960s Chávez believed that he would reach an understanding with his union rivals. For example, in 1967 after an agreement over jurisdiction with the Teamsters, he said that he had received a "no raid agreement that's very, very good. We'll organize the fields, they'll assist us whenever they can in the organization of the field workers for our union." The agreement would succeed, he announced, because "we're experiencing very good cooperation from them." As the decade passed, however, the Teamsters reneged on their agreements and then broke completely with the UFW. Chávez blamed the breakup on the Teamsters' inability to understand the UFW's ideological differences with traditional unions. "The Teamsters never could understand how our farm workers would go out on strike or work for the Union without pay," he said in an interview; "They don't understand what we're trying to do, because it isn't part of their history. They just haven't done what we have done. Most unions haven't." What made his task especially daunting, he charged, was that the Teamsters and growers worked "hand in glove," which was "a hard combination to beat."[97]

Notwithstanding the collective strength of his adversaries, Chávez remained unshakable in his conviction that the righteousness of the UFW's cause would allow farm workers to triumph. At the base of his pyramid of reasoning lay his belief in God. He told an interviewer in 1969 that he tried to apply "the teachings of Christ" as expressed in the Roman Catholic encyclicals. "I think," he confided, "you need very little else to make things work." To these Christian principles he added the influence of Gandhi, whose accomplishments showed that a leader must "get people involved and keep them involved in what would be a "long, long struggle. . . ." From Gandhi he learned that "by setting the example, you get others to do it. That is the real essence but that is difficult. That's what separates ordinary men from great men." In Chávez's union, poor people would "take a very direct part in shaping society" and making decisions.[98]

Chávez painted his picture of the union's struggle on a vast canvass by proclaiming: "People are not going to turn back now. The poor are on the march: black, brown, red, everyone, whites included. We are now in the midst of the biggest revolution this country has ever known." To reach their goals, workers had an array of potent tactics: "We shall strike; we shall organize boycotts; we shall demonstrate, and we shall have political campaigns. We shall pursue the revolution we have proposed. We are sons and daughters of the farm workers' revolution, a revolution of the poor seeking bread and justice." His ultimate goal was nothing less than a new social order for the farm workers in the fields. Positioning his movement in a millennial perspective, he assured readers that farm workers neither feared nor cringed "from the confrontation. We welcome it! We have planned for it. We know that our cause is just, that history is a story of social revolution, and that the poor shall inherit the land."[99]

The oncoming social revolution could only succeed, in Chávez's view, through a unique movement that would combine elements of traditional unions with aspects of the civil-rights movement. His new union would focus on ideals and education, thereby transcending the typical interests and activities of unions:

> I have often been asked what kind of a union I am trying to build and what type of society I want to see in the future. It seems to me that, once the union members are taken care of in terms of better wages and working conditions, the union must involve itself in the major issues of the times. The problem often arises that a group gets too involved in its own successes and doesn't have time for anything else. It is my hope that we keep ourselves focused on our ideals. It is much easier to profess something by words and not by deeds. Our job, then, is to educate our members so that they will be conscious of the needs of others less fortunate than themselves. The scope of the worker's interest must motivate him to reach out and help others. If we can get across the idea of participating in other causes, then we have real education.[100]

In September of 1965, when the strike began, union leaders told followers that three primary tactics would fuel their movement: the strike to build a union; a boycott and public address campaign to "go to the public and tell them what it is that we need, and get them to help us"; and the practice of nonviolence. Chávez later talked of how he pursued these three goals in the ensuing "fifty-eight and a half months," until for "the first time the farm workers had a union, and 158 contracts had been signed."[101]

Chávez had to educate workers on each of his union's goals. For example he had to show workers that the strike was a legitimate tactic. "Look," he said in Spanish to an audience of crop-pickers, "for years and years they've tried to make our people think that strikes are wrong. . . . The strike is not wrong because it is the weapon that all workers have used, all the farm workers. The strike is used everywhere with all the workers, all around the world to obtain benefits that the worker needs to benefit himself only." Chávez then informed his listeners about the importance of strikes, teaching that "a strike with the support of the worker, is a strike to be fought because the great necessity to win exists, and because it leads to better benefits. Our freedom as workers depends on winning this strike, if we lose this strike we'll lose our benefits, and even more important and dangerous, we would lose our freedom and democracy as farm workers."[102]

Chávez was convinced that his education of the workers and the general public would lead to the creation of an uncommon organization able to bring together people who had historically failed to unionize. "We have been beaten every time," he admitted, "beaten into the ground. Now it's like a dam where the water has been backed up, backed up for all those years, all of a sudden there is a small breakthrough. Now we don't want just a small change. We have waited too long."[103] The job of a leader/rhetor was to let loose this reservoir of physical and moral energy to attain the union's just goals.

Chávez attached his union to the moral issue of civil rights. "So what I'm saying," he summed up, "is that the work of civil rights and the work of unifying can also be done by unions." But first workers must be taught about their civil rights; and the Spanish-speaking in particular must attain "an awareness of citizenship, of civil rights, and civil responsibilities."[104]

Chávez the teacher sought to transform individuals. As he said, he strove to enable his audiences to "rise above mere material interests," a change that would require "a cultural revolution among ourselves—not only in art but also in the realm of the spirit." This transformation would require a powerful rhetorical identification with audiences to liberate a set of their latent qualities, especially among those whom Chávez identified as "poor people and immigrants . . . [who] have brought to this country some very important things of the spirit. But too often they are choked, they are not allowed to flourish in our society."[105] Farm workers especially, he explained to an audience at a rally in 1966, must lose "that great fear that they've had in the past, the fear that kept them many times in ignorance and also unable to organize."[106]

When young activists in the Chicano Movement dismissed Chávez's divinely endorsed blueprint for the future and spurned his reliance on nonviolence and racial cooperation, he separated himself from their means but held hope for unity. "When La Raza means or implies racism, we don't support it," he explained, "but if it means our struggle, our dignity, or our cultural roots, then we're for it." "Every man who comes to the picket line is our brother, immediately, regardless of color," he lectured in 1970; and he promised not to provide ammunition for growers who during the prior eighty years had successfully pitted races against each other.[107] Chávez made very clear that no manifestation of racism would appear in the UFW.[108] Taking this theme outside California, he told an audience at a national convention of AFL-CIO union members gathered in Texas in 1967 that he was not "building a Mexican-American union" or a "Negro union" but instead was "building an AFL-CIO union" that would fight for the rights of all workers.[109]

Farm workers and Mexican Americans did not make up Chávez's only audiences. Through his words and acts he affirmed the importance of outside volunteers who would form one part of a phalanx of supporters needed for success. The first volunteers he recruited were college students, often those who had been active in the civil-rights struggles in the South in the early 1960s or in campus dissent movements. He identified his initial reason for recruiting them: "In the beginning, the staff people didn't understand the whole idea of nonviolence, so I sent out the word to get young people who had been in the South and knew how to struggle nonviolently. . . . They were very good at teaching nonviolent tactics." Busloads of students assisted the union in its strike against grape growers, earning Chávez's admiration for being "the first people who have ever come to us without a hidden agenda. They just want to help us—to be servants—and that's a really beautiful thing."[110] He considered a person "willing to give us his time" as more important than one "willing to give us his money"—and thus "the students and young people are so valuable. . . . They are not involved in a lot of things yet. . . ."[111]

Chávez had learned the value of cooperation among diverse groups during his first boycott. He confirmed that "our philosophy of cooperation with all groups has helped us a great deal" and applauded his coworkers and followers for developing their skills in respecting the "beliefs and ideals" of all people. He enunciated his practical principle: "We try to get them to help us on their own terms."[112]

Chávez singled out the Catholic Church as a vital institutional member of his team. His strong Catholic beliefs as well as the church's influence on union members motivated him to seek help from that powerful wing of Christianity. When he had first moved to Delano, he had discovered that his parish church was not close to its worshipers and that its priests would not assist him in organizing. The church even denied him use of its auditoriums for union meetings. It appeared that the many growers who were Catholics controlled the parishes.[113] As the union grew and pressure mounted for Catholic involvement, however, church leaders responded by assigning Father Mark Day to be the union's chaplain. On hearing that news, Chávez penned this partial compliment: "Finally, our own Catholic Church has decided to recognize that we have our own peculiar needs, just as the growers have theirs."[114]

In Chávez's view, poor people traditionally had appealed to the Catholic Church for material aid in the form of food and clothing but had not requested church involvement in activities like grass-roots organizing. It was now time, he said, to ask the church to do much more: "I am calling for Mexican-American groups to stop ignoring this source of power. It is not just our right to appeal to the church to use its power effectively for the poor, it is our duty to do so. It should be as natural as appealing to government . . . and we do that often enough." He taught that religious institutions had much to offer his cause, for "the church we are talking about is a tremendously powerful institution in our society, and in the world. That church is one form of the Presence of God on Earth, and so naturally it is powerful. . . . It is a powerful moral and spiritual force which cannot be ignored by any movement."[115] That moral force, combined with the union's clear and compelling message, could hasten the day of the union's victory.

Churches, whatever their denomination, could minister to individuals with spiritual needs as well as to movements with moral goals. Chávez elaborated: "When poor people get involved in a long conflict, such as a strike, or a civil-rights drive, and the pressure increases each day, there is a deep need for spiritual advice." Without that advice, movement leaders would see "families crumble, leadership weaken, and hard workers grow tired. And in such a situation the spiritual advice must be given by a friend not by the opposition."[116] In Salinas during the lettuce strike in 1970, one priest captured the spirit of Chávez's appeal to the church when he called the UFW "more than a union. . . . Here, also, in this movement is a spirit . . . of a people who want to be free, . . . who no longer want to be captive, . . . who want to determine for themselves how they are going to live."[117] Armed with the spirit of God in this righteous cause, promised another priest in Salinas, "you will overcome. Viva la causa. Viva César Chávez." A third priest prayed that supporters of the farm workers' movement would "find the meaning and purpose You have given us when You called us sons and made us heirs to life."[118]

The political system was another potential ally. In the "Plan of Delano" Chávez stated: "We seek the support of all political groups and the protection by the government which is also our government, in our struggle." After being "treated like the lowest of the low" because others had determined their fate throughout history, workers had become "tired of words, of betrayals, of indifference." Times had changed and farm workers would no longer be ignored by politicians: "Through our strong will," he declared, "our movement is changing these conditions. Due to our movement, farm-worker leaders are developing who are faithful to the ideals and the propositions of the farm workers. They shall represent us. WE SHALL BE HEARD."[119]

Carrying his rhetorical campaign directly to the center of political power, Chávez testified before the U.S. Congress to educate legislators on the special needs of farm workers. He linked his union to broader issues of civil rights, arguing that farm workers were "essentially" ethnic minorities who if they had been Anglos would not have been excluded from protective legislation for workers.[120] When asked, "Where do you stop being an organizer and start being a civil rights advocate?" he replied: "It's one and the same."[121] Yet in Chávez's message, economics was even more important than race; and poor people of all colors formed his movement in this "beautiful period of history."[122]

Concerned that farm workers had been left out of most major labor legislation and in particular were not covered by the 1935 National Labor Relations Act (NLRA), Chávez asked for modifications in laws like the original NLRA and opposed restrictions imposed by subsequent labor laws. More generally, he called for "the American people and the Congress to help us build our union with some special help in the face of some especially stubborn opposition of long standing."[123]

Speaking in 1966 at a rally in Sacramento, Chávez acknowledged the invaluable participation by many groups in the union struggle that began in Delano. He cited Protestant, Catholic, and Jewish "church leaders and churches"; Mexican-American political groups such as the Mexican-American Political Association (MAPA); the CSO; the civil rights movement; students; the AFL-CIO; and the International Longshoremen's and Warehousemen's Union.[124] In interviews in 1970, Chávez scanned the variety of his supporters. He credited his union's strength to his "very formidable . . . army of men and women who are dedicated to seeing that social justice be brought to these workers," including people from universities, some of whom quit their jobs to work in his movement. He then acknowledged "a very, very strong following" with a "spirit of solidarity and a real desire to battle for justice," a following consisting of "friends throughout the country," not only of farm workers but of people in the cities who included religious groups, labor, students, and ethnic groups. "Without the support from the cities," he proclaimed, employers would "destroy us in no time flat."[125]

Although outside helpers were vital, the UFW's organizers and leaders themselves bore primary responsibility for moving the organization forward. Chávez argued that "the mission of the leaders—which is the mission of any authority—is to sustain the movement, to keep the farm workers' association on its destined path, to do what always has to be done so that the goals of the association can be reached." In this enterprise, he insisted, unity of doctrine, methods, and structure was essential.[126]

Infusing his campaign with sources of rhetorical power often discussed by scholars of communication, Chávez taught union organizers to embody the goals and ideology of their organization. In this way organizers could acquire the potential to duplicate Chávez's own reconstitution of audiences. In 1970 he reported the fruits of his rhetorical labor, noting that his most gratifying moments came when individuals grew into their dignity; "you can see individuals, workers, grow-ing by leaps and bounds, leaps and bounds."[127]

The first step in embodiment, he directed, was "to work more than anyone else" in the groups being proselytized. Many followers withheld a deep commit-ment to the union because they feared their organizers would resign and the movement would die. To convert those reluctant cohorts, an organizer must "be able to say, I'm not going to be here a year, or six months, but an awful long time—until when they get rid of me they'll have leaders to do it themselves."[128] In front of a college audience in 1970 Chávez laid out a work-hour calculus: "The only way I know to organize is to work; if the troops work eight hours, or ten or twelve, you work at least one and a half times more."[129] Thus the organizer must be seen as the model for the group.

Notwithstanding the arduous labor, the organizer should not expect any thanks for the effort. "If an organizer comes looking for appreciation," Chávez warned, "he might just as well stay home. He's not going to get any, especially out of a group that's never been organized or had any power before." Chávez readily sup-plied examples of organizers who were destroyed and rejected because they ex-pected people to appreciate what they'd done.[130] Moreover, he urged listeners to take no credit for victories; and he himself had this characteristically modest exchange with a reporter in 1966: "Did you have any idea that you would be-come so influential when you first started out your union organizing efforts?"; Chávez: "No, . . . I'm not that influential. It's a passing thing . . . that has caused a lot of attention, because it's a very just struggle. But it'll pass and . . . we'll be alone pretty soon."[131]

Other qualities important to facilitate embodiment included willingness to sacrifice and to favor spiritual over material rewards. Chávez recounted his own example of leaving the security, income, and comfort of his position with the CSO in order to launch his crusade in Delano. It was a difficult decision, he confided, yet "we can't change anything if we want to hold on to a good job, a good way of life, and avoid sacrifice."[132] In 1970 he told television viewers that 95 percent of the strikers who began in 1965 "lost their homes and their cars," but "in losing those worldly possessions, they found themselves."[133] Carrying far beyond California his belief in the power of suffering and sacrifice as penance, Chávez included in his fragment-sentence outline for short addresses to AFL-CIO audiences in Denver and Miami the headings "We accept our suffering as a down payment to have our own union," and "We will suffer for the purpose of ending the poverty, misery, and injustice. . . ."[134] Addressing an audience of union members in Texas, he said quietly but firmly that he and his fellow workers would accept the "sufferings we have gone through," and that "we draw strength from our despair."[135] Speaking first in Spanish and then in English at a rally in 1970 in Salinas on his way to a courthouse to offer himself to be arrested in protest over an "unconstitutional act," Chávez proclaimed: "We have no other course but to give our whole bodies and our spirits to the cause. . . ." He asked everyone present not to fast but to accompany him to jail as their penance.[136]

A model of the sacrifices he requested, Chávez and his family lived in Delano in what Steiner called "conspicuous poverty. . . . In an era of affluent unionism, such a way of life is an anomaly for a union leader."[137] Steiner described Chávez's motivation not as martyrdom but as a steadfast belief "that the leader of the poor has to live as the poor do, not for their sake, but for his own; the sanctity of his soul and peace of mind demand it of him."[138] The motivational appeal of sacrifice and penance particularly appealed to Mexican-American audiences, for suffering and sacrifice are prominent values and grow directly from Mexican-American heritage, history, and religion.[139] Not neglecting rhetorical considerations, Chávez also insisted that such sacrifice as that which he displayed on his fast proved the depth of commitment of an organizer's advocacy of nonviolence.[140]

Reflecting his conviction that a righteous cause would succeed if it were understood by enough people, and if it were communicated through an extensive rhetorical campaign, Chávez labeled organizing an "educational process."[141] To be successful in this process demanded calculated planning as well as faith and courage. Referring to his own experiences, Chávez described how he initially contacted workers in their homes: "We went around to the towns, played the percentages, and came off with a group." He also disclosed some of the frustrations of those early years: "There were times, of course, when we didn't know whether we'd survive. We'd get members and then they would drop out. . . . They would come and use us, and after they had gotten what they wanted, they had second thoughts. At times it took a lot of faith and courage not to turn against the people." But in the end, he added, he had successfully organized his union.[142]

Chávez shared many lessons from his experience. "From the strikes of others," he observed, "I've learned some very basic things, that have to be taken care of if you're going to exist. I learned that all strikes were decided in the first few weeks" and therefore the organizer must pour all of his or her energy into that initial period. Recognizing that earlier organizers had called strikes too early in the development of their unions, the UFW union leaders did not strike until they were well organized.[143]

Chávez's followers also learned from him that they and their union must function like a family, a principle consistent with Chávez's theme that his union was part of a broad and cohesive millennial movement for justice for all oppressed people. His own family's positive influences on him during his migrant years no doubt contributed to this vision. As Chávez proudly announced: "We are a family bound together in a common struggle for justice. We are a Union family celebrating our unity and the nonviolent nature of our movement."[144] The "Plan of Delano" emphasized essential elements of the union family:

> We shall unite. We have learned the meaning of unity. We know, from other unions, the reasons why workers organize. The strength of the poor is also in unity. We know that the poverty of the farm worker in California is the same as that of all farm workers across the country—the Mexicans, Filipinos, Blacks and poor whites; the Puerto Ricans, the Japanese, the Indians, the Portuguese and the Arabs—in short, all the races that comprise the oppressed minorities of the United States.[145]

Once more fusing practical and moral considerations, Chávez portrayed unity and inclusiveness as bulwarks against the growers' historical practice of dividing workers along racial lines, a tactic that kept "wages down and . . . unions out." Racial division would fail in Chávez's union, however, for he was determined that all races work together.[146] "We have many ethnic groups in our union," he said in his matter-of-fact delivery to AFL-CIO listeners, "Mexican Americans, Negroes, Filipinos, Portuguese, Puerto Ricans, Arabs, and believe it or not, a few Jews. And we work side by side and there is no real difference."[147] As he wrote on his speech notes for an AFL-CIO audience in Miami, "Mexican American—Negroes—Filipinos—Portuguese—Arabs—Jews—We all work together—but not . . .[to be a] minority union [but an] AFL-CIO union."[148]

Chávez's union family departed from the typical concerns of other labor organizations by emphasizing the moral—as well as the practical—imperative of nonviolent means to achieve its goals. Again Chávez called on followers to act out a principle appropriate to a moral movement, and again he himself embodied the principles of nonviolence in his personal life. As Yinger said, "Examples of it [nonviolence] may be found in all the rhetoric of Chávez and in most of his life style."[149]

Chávez enacted nonviolence as he preached it, and endured the hardships of sacrifice as he advocated it. Using rhetorical means to communicate his own nonviolent struggle and its hardships, he told listeners that he had gone to jail three times, and his wife twice. Once when traveling home together from being jailed they worried about how to tell their children of their ordeal—a worry that ended immediately when the Chávez children cheerfully welcomed home their parents by saying, "Hi jailbirds."[150]

Appropriate for one who defined his role as that of a teacher, Chávez explained in detail to others what nonviolence entailed. A widely misunderstood weapon against injustice, he taught, nonviolent means were not easy or "cowardly" but an "effective" and "very powerful" practical method. To succeed with that method, however, "people have to understand that with nonviolence goes a hell of a lot of organization. We couldn't be nonviolent . . . and win unless we had a lot of people organized around nonviolence up and down the United States and Canada."[151] As Roberts notes, effective nonviolence required creative strategies: "Nonviolence calls for hardnosed organizing, for a minimum of dramatics and a great deal of understanding of what the situation is—to be able to assess the opposition, being able to win by winning small victories constantly, and by not letting yourself be locked into a position where you can't move because you are cornered."[152] If his followers employed nonviolent means, Chávez instructed, they could expect to capitalize on the "great compassion for them from the American public in general."[153]

Chávez presented his protests as "militant nonviolence . . . our means for social revolution and to achieve justice for our people. . . ." His "Letter from Delano" promulgated the principle that involving "masses of people in their own struggle" would prepare the farm-worker movement to convert the "frustration, impatience, and rage that blow among us" into a nonviolent force that would capitalize on the truth that "free men instinctively prefer democratic change and even protect the rights guaranteed to seek it."[154] Thus although admitting to "hate the agribusiness system that seeks to keep us enslaved," Chávez advocated that "we shall overcome and change it not by retaliation or bloodshed but by a determined nonviolent struggle carried on by those masses of farm workers who intend to be free and human."[155]

Chávez enacted such nonviolent protest even as he preached it. In 1968, concerned that UFW members were ready to give up on nonviolence, he began a fast to convince his followers of its continuing need. Although he had previously fasted for brief periods, his twenty-five day fast in 1968 attracted far more attention. In a speech at the end of the fast he explained his reasons: "I undertook this fast because my heart was filled with grief and pain for the sufferings of farm workers. The fast was first for me and then for all of us in this union. It was a fast for nonviolence and a call to sacrifice."[156] And it was effective. Chávez chronicled that some twenty thousand people, mostly farm workers, had visited the union headquarters, Forty Acres, during the fast, many or most participating in religious services there. To Chávez, "the most important thing was [that] people were there and they were participating."[157] The *Los Angeles Times* reported that for the first time "a nationally prominent union leader had resorted to fasting as a method of calling on followers to refrain from violence of any kind." The *New Republic* reported that the hunger strike was "generally thought to have united California's farm workers behind Chávez's leadership and established him as a hero, a man indistinguishable from his cause."[158] The man and his message were now inextricable.

Chávez understood well that the fast, along with pilgrimages and marches, drew appeal from the Mexican cultural orientation that features penance and suffering. He compared the tradition of fasting in India to that in Catholic Mexico where "'penitencia' is part of our history." He provided vivid examples to show that such pilgrimages remained prominent in Mexican culture: "Daily at any of the major shrines of the country, and in particular at the Basilica of the Lady of Guadalupe there arrive pilgrims from all points—some of whom have long since walked out the pieces of rubber tire that once served them as soles, and many of whom will walk on their knees the last mile or so of the pilgrimage." Chávez also cited "penitential processions, where the *penitentes* would march through the streets, often in sack cloth and ashes, some even carrying crosses, as a sign of penance for their sins, and as a plea for the mercy of God." Such marches, he asserted, were "in the blood of the Mexican American." He then turned his attention to his immediate protest where "many of the 'pilgrims' of Delano will have walked in such pilgrimages themselves in their lives—perhaps as very small children even; and cling to the memory of the day-long marches, the camps at night, streams forded, hills climbed, the sacred aura of the sanctuary, and the 'fiesta' that followed."[159]

Marches comprised another important component in the union's campaign. The most famous UFW march was in 1966, traversing the 250 miles from Delano to Sacramento in twenty-one days. Contending that the procession reflected both his venerable Mexican and present-day American heritages, Chávez wrote that it was "a meeting of cultures and traditions; the centuries-old religious tradition of Spanish culture cojoins with the very contemporary cultural syndromes of 'demonstration' springing from the spontaneity of the poor, the downtrodden, the rejected, the discriminated-against baring visibly their need and demand for equality and freedom." The march educated many people about the plight of the workers. Elizabeth Sutherland Martínez and Enriqueta Longeaux y Vasquez chronicled its effect: "Almost every night, the marchers would stop in a small town or village along the way and hold a meeting with the Raza who lived there. People talked, sang, and grew closer. Many of them had not heard about the Huelga and the union before; now they signed up with the union."[160]

In the "Plan of Delano," issued on the eve of the march to Sacramento, Chávez underscored the importance of such marches in his movement. It began:

• • •

We the undersigned, gathered in Pilgrimage to every agricultural area of the United States, make penance for all the needs of Farm Workers. As free and sovereign men and women, we do solemnly declare before the civilized world which judges our actions, and before the nation where we work, the proposition we have formulated to end the injustice that oppresses us.

The Plan professed consciousness of the march's "historical significance" derived from the sacrifices and suffering of generations of farm workers whose "sweat and our blood have fallen on this land to make other men rich."[161]

California Governor Edmund G. "Pat" Brown was absent when Chávez and his marchers reached Sacramento after their 350-mile walk; in his comments in response to that absence, Chávez merged Mexican Americans and his movement. "Farm workers particularly, and the Mexican-American community throughout the state in general," he complained, were hurt at the governor's snub. The governor had missed an historic opportunity, he added, because it was "perhaps the first time in the history of the state, that the Mexican-American citizen of the state has made it a special point to come and see the governor. . . ."[162]

In the founding decade of his union César Chávez produced in his discourse a cohesive set of themes, arguments, explanations, appeals, and evidence. To understand that discourse more thoroughly, we now closely examine a lengthy speech he delivered to AFL-CIO chief Walter Reuther and other labor leaders on April 1, 1967. This speech is representative of much of Chávez's rhetorical manner and technique during the period covered in this chapter and therefore allows us to identify elements of his rhetorical profile during his initial years as a unionist.[163]

Chávez began the speech with a gracious acknowledgment of "Brother Reuther and friends," and then immediately laid out his topic: "I'd like to take what time I have to bring to you, at least in part, the story of the strikers in the Delano area." He included in his short introduction a light sprinkling of humor, noting "one difficulty in getting up to speak before groups": He had been in jail three times recently because of the strike, he said, each time for "using microphones to talk to scabs in the fields. So every time I get to speak before people and I see these things in front of me, I get somewhat uneasy."

After expressing the appreciation of Delano workers to "members of the UAW [United Auto Workers], Brother Reuther, all of the leadership," he clearly forecast a part of his rhetorical plan for his audience; he was there to "tell you some of the specific things" the UAW and its leadership had done for farm workers. Although he could not cover all the helpful actions, he said, "there are some important things, in my opinion, that should be shared with you."

His ensuring history lesson began with two rhetorical questions: "Have you ever considered land—a lot of land—a lot of free water and a lot of cheap labor? Have you ever considered what this combination can do and is doing in the West?" His answer was that growers, for the past seventy or eighty years, had grown rich and powerful and used their money and influence to control legislation affecting farm workers. In simple and clear language he traced the lesson we have already examined: growers developed a labor-contractor system that first used Chinese workers, then Japanese, Indians (from India), Filipinos, and "lastly they got the Mexican." "The Negro," he added, "they didn't have to import." The growers had adjusted skillfully to historical conditions such as the exodus from Mexico during the Mexican Revolution or the shortage of workers during World War II, inventing such methods as the bracero program to maintain their wealth and power.

Chávez's transition sentence to the next section of his speech was characteristically clear and simple: "But while all of these things were taking place there were attempts to organize workers." In his brief review of the history of farm workers' efforts to organize, Chávez cited the example of a strike in 1905 by cotton pickers in Whitland, California, emphasizing that such organizing attempts were always defeated. Yet the past had value to his own movement, for, as he told labor leaders, "we in the union, even before we started to organize, wanted to know really everything that had been written and talk to everyone available . . . involved in past strikes and to find out why they had failed so often."

Chávez said that he had learned that one major problem was that unions were both organizing and striking at the same time. In five consecutive sentences that showed his use of personal and simple language, he noted the present state of farm workers: "We are excluded from the protection of the National Labor Relations Act. We can't go to the employer and say we got 30 percent, or 50 percent or 100 percent of the workers signed up and we want you to recognize our union. Or we couldn't go to the Board and ask for an election. We can't do either one. We may have 1,000 percent signed up and they won't give us that protection."

"Then, the other problem," he pointed out in another clear transition and forecast, was that the great cost of organizing farm workers had historically discouraged international unions from entering the fields—including attempts of the AFL as early as the mid-1930s. Too, he said, outside unions had come in only after local workers had struck in unwinnable cases, a pattern of failure that yielded an important lesson to Chávez and his unionizing cohorts. Applying what they had learned, he and fellow organizers had started a small independent association. When they found willing workers, they required them to pay dues and participate as organizers, thereby keeping alive the association. These workers had little money to give, he said; but once they gave, they made a commitment and would attend meetings. "And while they were there," Chávez said, "we were taking advantage of educating them."

Chávez said that he had also learned that organizing had failed because of the patronizing habit of romanticizing the poor people and ethnic minorities who had been victims of discrimination. Chávez and his union redefined farm workers as humans who could participate effectively as organizers. And once a worker was treated "as a human being," he said, that person could be helped as a human being.

Chávez's rendition of the strike in September of 1965 relied on precise information: statistics of hourly wages; number of days between meetings; the precise time of the first strike ("five-thirty in the morning"); the number of hours (within twenty-four) it took for the Delano city council to pass a resolution condemning the union for its ties to communism; the number of Delano Catholic priests (three) who quickly met and condemned the strike; the amount of money given to strikers by the California Migrant Ministry ($500); and a detailed review of the union's preparatory efforts to focus on broader issues facing workers in the community in which they lived. When the 1965 strike was finally called, Chávez related, he and his cohorts had been preparing with little outside notice for four and a half years.

Because he had learned that violence by workers had doomed earlier strikes and also made it difficult for them to rest their appeals on justice, Chávez said, he had convinced workers to be nonviolent and thereby aligned his movement with a contemporary movement for justice that was unknown to most farm workers: the civil-rights movement. On several occasions the strikers' nonviolence was met by growers who shot at them with guns. "They were very poor shots and didn't hit us," he told listeners. "In a period of seven days we had fourteen incidents where they actually fired a gun at the strikers. And not even in one case were we able to get the district attorney to take that case. They wouldn't take it."

For the first three or four months of the strike, Chávez confessed to his audience, "Things looked very bad for us." Every institution in the community was against them, they had no money, and they were only a "scab" group—not even an official union. Then, he said, on December 17, three months after the strike had begun, Walter Reuther himself had come to Delano, had come from the airport on a "cold" day to the picket line in "the local railroad yard," and said: "'Does this picket line ever march?' And the people said, 'No.' 'Yes.' And he said, 'Well, let's march.' And before I could say that we had a regulation against it, he started marching and we followed. And everybody started marching." That evening, he said, Reuther had spoken at one of the workers' largest meetings ever in Delano, and pledged vital money to the strike effort. For the first time the strikers had felt that they had outside support. After working with the AFL-CIO on the strike, the crop-pickers had found much in common with the larger union and within a year had merged with it.

Chávez began the last part of his address with another clear transition: "I would like to point out some of the other things because we don't have too much time. You haven't eaten and I haven't eaten. There are some things that I would like to leave with you to give you an idea of what we are going through." In narrative style, mixing quotations of police officers with descriptions of his own activities, Chávez recounted early discussions with one Sergeant Dodd who told him that the cry of "Huelga" communicated links to a Communist Party. Chávez had tried to convince Dodd that "although I wasn't blond I was still an American, and about my rights and the Constitution, the Supreme Court decisions and so forth." Despite Dodd's warnings to the contrary, Chávez bowed to workers' decisions—after a long meeting full of debate—and allowed "forty-four workers including my wife and six or seven ministers" to return to the picket line where they "spaced themselves fifty feet apart and shouted HUELGA at the top of their lungs." All were arrested by police and jailed in Bakersfield. Chávez then related how he immediately changed his plans and drove to Berkeley the next morning where he addressed an audience of students and asked them to give their lunch money to bail out the workers. He received $6,600, returning that afternoon to Bakersfield to bail the strikers out of jail.

Chávez began the end of the body of his address with a narrative of the pilgrimage from Delano to Sacramento, a rhetorical tactic designed "to keep the movement moving" during a period of little activity. The precedent-setting agreement with Schenley soon had come, and the financially strapped union had moved against DiGiorgio. With organizers scattered across the county, no money for support, and another long battle looming, Chávez had again met with Reuther, who donated seven cars to return the organizers to Delano.

Chávez concluded his speech by sharing his "one grave concern about the American labor movement," a movement he modestly admitted he did not "quite understand yet" because he was "very new in it yet." He saw the unions as badly divided, he said, and asked how the "capitalists" had forged "at least twenty-five years ahead of most of the unions"? More specifically, he asked, why were there "so many laws to control the activities of unions"? "We're in a bit of trouble, you know," he confided, "for not believing things are as they are." It would be one of Chávez's rhetorical goals in his career to make clear how things were and to move past the trouble in which labor found itself.

This example of Chávez's early speeches represents his rhetorical profile, although it differs in one significant way by not relying on the lengthy stories he often told.[164] It does show his commitment to a clearly presented and well-supported case for his just cause; his heavy reliance on facts to support arguments organized in an unusually clear pattern featuring many helpful transitions; a lucid, simple, repetitive and personal style of language designed to inform rather than to draw attention to himself; and a modest persona that stood aside in favor of his substantive message. He was gracious toward supporters and showed little rancor toward his enemies. This rhetorical profile, so appropriate for a man who taught the inevitability of divinely ordained success if the public could be informed, allowed him through obvious and subtle ways to merge himself with his message. Chávez combined his thought and character as he embodied his message, forging a powerful multileveled identification with audiences as he sought to transform them into supporters and animate them into activism.

By 1969 César Chávez's movement had, he believed, "educated an awful lot of farm workers, in the respect that it's not impossible to have a union, that it's possible, and we've broken the barriers."[165] What he had earlier believed would take ten to fifteen years had been accomplished in seven.[166] His public address deserves considerable credit for this success, for he featured his own public communication at the very heart of his effort to found and build his union and social movement during its first years. From 1963 to 1970 he developed his rhetorical profile as he doggedly and indefatigably spread his message through his speaking, writing, and nondiscursive symbolic events such as marches and fasts. That message drew from his experiences as a child of migrants, as a migrant worker, as an organizer, and from his resulting worldview that contained his interrelated notions of God's millennial plan for the world, the direction of contemporary history, and the divinely ordained power of reform rhetoric. It reflected both a practical understanding of what made for effective discourse and an idealistic commitment to moral goals and means.

Chávez's substantive themes, arguments, and explanations fit very well with both his own character as revealed in his first persona and his depiction of his audience in his second persona. After the successful grape strike, he became, in the words of *Time* magazine, "a man indistinguishable from his cause."[167] As such, he communicated a fusion of thought and character that allowed him to identify powerfully with those who heard, read, and saw him. He was thus able to reconstitute audiences into committed unionists and members of a social movement dedicated to a higher cause than mere material gains for members of organized labor. These newly constituted followers found within themselves the qualities necessary to overcome their fears, sacrifice for the cause, forego material rewards and others' appreciation for spiritual accomplishments and self-satisfaction, advocate the union's case despite long odds against success, remain committed to eventual success regardless of setbacks, restrict themselves to non-violent means in the struggle, and offer moral and financial backing for an idealistic movement.

To exert such impact on audiences, Chávez first fashioned a substantive message that emphasized the lessons learned from history, the need for human dignity, and the necessity of obtaining the power only a union could give workers to battle an array of enemies that included agribusiness, Teamsters, and legislators. He depicted his union as part of a righteous social movement to change the world, a movement that required that its rhetor/organizers reconstitute audiences. In his rendition of this reconstitution, rhetors—and those in his audience whom he had converted to activist rhetor/organizers—must embody their message by demonstrating faith in their war of words, a modest manner, a capacity to sacrifice for and fearlessly pursue their cause, a preference for spiritual rather than material goals, and a commitment to unity, nonviolence, and inclusion. These qualities were consistent with a substantive message that pictured the unionists' righteous case as part of a social movement of the oppressed, a movement guaranteed of ultimate success if facts and arguments were presented widely. Such a message would accordingly be presented clearly, factually, and modestly with attention placed on the ideas and facts necessary to educate audiences. Chávez also taught his followers to employ various other tactics and strategies he had learned and to conform to communication conventions of the Mexican-American culture when addressing Mexican-American audiences.

Chávez embodied his own message through his manner and means of communication, through his heritage, and through the way he lived his life. He amply demonstrated his faith in his rhetoric of moral and practical education; and education was an appropriate goal for one who taught that God would ensure success if rhetors for a righteous cause informed audiences of the facts and arguments of their case. Accordingly, Chávez presented his message incessantly and with confident assurance of its success, organizing and clearly wording his discourse so that it rested on arguments and explanations backed by ample evidence.

Through his own life of sacrifice, dedication, simplicity, and lack of pretense, Chávez further mirrored his substantive message. At times he explicitly told audiences of his identification with his cause and with farm workers, as when he described how farm workers throughout the nation were "suffering the same things you and I are suffering in Delano."[168] At other times, he implied the connection of his ideas to the way he lived his life and communicated his message, as when he cautioned listeners to remember that "in defeat there must be courage. But also, that in victory there must be humility."[169] Thus he could identify with his farm-worker audiences in order to reformulate a disorganized and fearful group of crop-pickers into confident, bold, and dedicated followers who would become organizers and form the nucleus of the first successful farm workers' union. Meanwhile, he identified with broader audiences to persuade them to change their actions or to reconstitute them into ardent and necessary backers who enacted their new identities by volunteering in the movement, donating money, changing eating habits to honor the boycott, and providing whatever other support they could.

The final element in Chávez's rhetorical equation was his second persona. He defined Mexican-American farm workers as having lost their fear and possessing inherent dignity as well as trust and confidence in his divinely ordained movement. They were thus depicted as working hard and sacrificing to the point of suffering in his nonviolent crusade to right the injustices he had illuminated, injustices that he proposed should elicit cheerful support rather than paternalistic pity. He asked potential organizers and other non–farm-worker audiences to recognize the same sense of injustice, privilege similar personal qualities, and enact some of the same agenda. Through his own first persona as a moral, courageous, hardworking, self-sacrificing, dedicated man who trusted his clearly presented case of facts and arguments to carry out God's will, audiences not only identified with him but through identification with his second persona received added rhetorical inducement to move into the mold he had created for them. Thus both personae and his substantive message worked together reciprocally and synergistically to afford the rhetorical identification necessary to reconstitute his audiences.

Griswold del Castillo and Garcia underscored Chávez's reliance on discourse and spectacular effects on audiences, noting that his "main activity during the early months of the strike was to travel around the state to the college campuses to give speeches and galvanize support for striking members"; that he conducted a "grueling speaking tour of California to promote the boycott"; that his speeches induced Gil Padilla and other top unionists to join him in his early quest to build a union; and that such powerful impact had an effect on groups of listeners, as when an audience in Delano cheered him for "a good ten minutes, as pandemonium breaks out: 'Viva México! Viva Puerto Rico! Viva César Chávez! Viva la unión!"[170] Identifying "a new national consciousness . . . inspired by the examples of César Chávez," the two biographers delineated key elements in the labor leader's audience: "Hundreds of volunteers [who] lived on poverty wages in the large cities" while organizing the grape boycott, "scores" of religious leaders and followers who "donated time, money, facilities, and energies to the farm workers' cause," organized labor which gave needed money and volunteers, and the "millions of Americans [who] gave up eating grapes."[171] We would add that Chávez's "example" was skillfully communicated in the discourse upon which he relied so heavily, forming a rhetorical combination of thought and character that was instrumental in his "inspiration" that transformed fearful farm workers into bold organizers, uncommitted college students into unpaid volunteers, friendly liberals into generous benefactors, and the general public into supporters of the boycott.

As Chávez reformulated disorganized farm workers into a vibrant union, and as he created an audience of active supporters from a broad range of the American public, he also supplied inspiration for the Chicano Movement among young Mexican Americans in the 1960s and 1970s. By speaking out to a broad audience, by emphasizing issues of race as well as union issues, and by drawing upon Mexican-American rhetorical conventions and history, he extended his influence deep into Chicano groups. Rodolfo Acuña expressed a common view: "César Chávez gave the Chicano Movement a national leader. In all probability Chávez was the only Mexican American so recognized by mainstream civil rights and antiwar movements."[172] In 1969 a young Chicana made the point in more personal terms: "I think that he's the first Mexican American in this nation that has kept our power, that has shown that the Mexican Americans want liberty, . . . justice, and that we are all working to fight for justice until we get it. And I think every one of his followers would give their life for César Chávez."[173]

The potency of Chávez's discourse, and the centrality of it to his successes, was difficult to understand for most outside observers. In 1966 Charles Kuralt, for example, depicted Chávez's movement as "awfully amateurish by uh, professional union standards," and asked: "How can they really hope to accomplish anything?"[174] Indeed, if judged by criteria of modern management, Chávez had little hope of defeating the Teamsters or winning any contracts. Yet his discourse allowed him to achieve uncommon effects on audiences of various kinds of people; those supporters in turn found the motivation, directions, generosity, and, in some cases, the new self-concept and abilities not only to support and win the strike and to acquire contracts but—in the years to follow—to record a dazzling series of equally-unlikely triumphs.

Chapter 5

Rhetorically "Working towards Creating the New Man"

Chávez Maintains the Movement from 1970 to 1975

During the first half of the 1970s, César Chávez gained public stature as he continued to teach his version of truth. In December of 1970 growers achieved a major, if temporary, victory when Judge Gordon Campbell ordered Chávez to the Monterey County jail for defying an injunction against boycotting products of Bud Antle, Inc., a prominent target of the farm workers' union. Chávez's imprisonment—his first time in jail for union activities—was marked by prayer vigils, masses, and protests numbering as many as three thousand supporters outside the courthouse; several celebrities visited him inside the jail. "Boycott the hell out of them," Chávez had cried to his supporters as he was taken into custody; the resulting publicity advanced that agenda.[1] After twenty days in confinement Chávez was ordered free on appeal by the state supreme court; the following April, in a unanimous decision, the supreme court found Campbell's injunction unconstitutional. No longer a little-known labor leader, Chávez was now a national figure who commanded widespread respect because of what he and his union had accomplished. He was a "liberal hero" (*Time* magazine) and "a social visionary" (*Nation*).[2]

By 1971 Chávez had acquired the celebrity status to be invited to attend fundraising events with members of Congress and other major public figures. At one such occasion, Congressman Abner J. Mikva (D-Illinois) referred to the large range of support for Chávez "that spanned Gloria Steinem to Mayor Daley."[3] In 1973, on the occasion of establishing the Martin Luther King Farm Worker Fund to teach people to work nonviolently for social change, Coretta Scott King introduced Chávez as a man who "exemplifies the true spirit of love, of truth, of justice and who comes to us at this time in our history to challenge us and to remind us that this spirit and this spirit alone will be the force that will bring us to the community of justice with peace and brotherhood."[4] Chávez's new status was additionally evident in the introduction he received before delivering a speech in 1974: "Our friend this afternoon, our guest this afternoon . . . [is] a humble man. He is small in stature, but historians will surely write him as a giant among men."[5] To a large extent, Chávez's rhetorical campaign had achieved the broad appeal he had intended: As *Newsweek* later wrote, he had been "embraced with equal fervor by *campesinos* [farm workers] sweating in the California vineyards and chic liberals summering in East Coast resorts."[6]

In this chapter we examine the interrelated complex of issues, events, and discourse that comprise the story of Chávez's career during his years of triumph from 1970 to 1975. We begin with a historical narrative of this period, then probe deeply into his public address, paying particular attention to whether and how his rhetorical profile and message changed in response to changing challenges as well as his changed image. We then look closely at how he adapted his message and means to Spanish-speaking audiences, and introduce a problem in leadership born ironically of the rhetorical crusade that had accounted for his prominence, power, and accomplishments.

In 1970, even as Chávez's stature grew to heroic proportions with many audiences, he encountered a powerful new foe. The Teamsters Union—in violation of its own agreement to organize drivers and warehouse workers but leave those working in the fields to the United Farm Workers (UFW)—entered the campaign to organize the lettuce fields. Some growers turned to the Teamsters rather than sign with Chávez, and a bitter power struggle ensued. In 1971 Chávez and the Teamsters forged an agreement that again gave the UFW jurisdiction over farm workers and the Teamsters jurisdiction over drivers and workers in the packing sheds.[7]

Freed temporarily from resource-draining rivalry with the Teamsters, Chávez's union reached its peak of power and influence in 1972 with 147 contracts covering fifty thousand jobs. It now staffed thirty-three boycott centers throughout the nation, each directing union activity in its region, and it employed some six hundred volunteers to assist with various activities.[8] By this time, as *U.S. News and World Report* commented, Chávez had clearly become one of the best-known and "probably the most controversial" American labor leader.[9] But peace between the two unions and for Chávez was to be short-lived.

In 1973, upon the expiration of the three-year contracts the UFW had negotiated with growers, the Teamsters again violated agreements with Chávez, signing more favorable pacts with growers for wages of $2.30 per hour, 10¢ less per hour than the UFW contracts. In addition, the Teamster pacts abolished Chávez's innovation of hiring halls, restoring the former method of using labor contractors.[10] Speaking in 1974 to an United Auto Workers (UAW) audience, Chávez presented a statistical overview of what had happened in the Coachella Valley: "On April 15 at midnight, we had thirty-four contracts. The next morning we had two contracts and the Teamsters had thirty-two contracts." Chávez accused the Teamsters of being "a company union . . . doing the dirty work of the employers to destroy unions. . . ." No Teamster contract had ever resulted from an election where farm workers could freely choose between the two unions, Chávez claimed, calling for free and fair elections. In such an election, he asserted, "farm workers would vote 90 to 95 percent" for the UFW. Perhaps aware of these facts, Teamsters consistently refused to participate in elections.[11] And because the Teamsters already had the contracts with the growers, they didn't need to worry much about what the farm workers thought.

Chávez later looked back on April of 1973 as "the worst of our times."[12] During these bleak days, UFW membership dropped significantly from around fifty thousand to perhaps ten or fifteen thousand. Jack Pandol, a strawberry-farm owner who had become a chief representative for growers, suggested that Chávez and his association of workers had been permanently defeated. Chávez and his cohorts had replaced worthwhile negotiating with "a bunch of speeches," he said, and during the prior three years, Chávez's "mismanagement" had reduced his organization's effectiveness.[13] When a reporter subsequently asked Chávez if the UFW was "getting pretty close to the end of the line," Chávez responded with customary confidence in higher powers as well as with uncharacteristic irritation: "I've answered that one fifty million times. It has nothing to do with contracts. It has to do with people and the people are here you know, and it's just a matter of time. . . ." Queried about what tactics would bring victory, he answered: "Exactly what we did five years ago."[14]

By 1974 promising signs indicated that Chávez's revolution was taking hold. A delegation of twenty-five church leaders, members of Congress, and labor leaders visited the Coachella Valley to talk with workers in the fields and hold a straw poll. Of about a thousand ballots the UFW received 795 votes, the Teamsters 80, and "no union" 78. Congressman Edward Roybal of California reported that "the workers were overwhelmingly in favor of Chávez. In fact, the first thing they said to us was 'Viva Chávez.'"[15] The UFW's primary arguments were that it—not the Teamsters—represented the workers, and that the Teamsters were an outside group.[16] Although the Teamsters had the contracts, Chávez asserted, he had the workers. He kept prodding the Teamsters to have an election because he knew he would win. The Teamsters continued to refuse.[17]

Also in 1974 Chávez found cause for optimism in the changing political climate in California, as Ronald Reagan—his long-time nemesis—left the governor's office and Jerry Brown—who had marched with the UFW in grape and lettuce boycotts—became governor.[18] Because of Brown's support the union was able to engineer the 1975 passage of the California Agricultural Labor Relations Act (ALRA), which gave migrant workers voting rights in union elections, and gave union members the secret ballot in elections, control over the timing of elections, and the right to boycott. The bill contained definite advantages for the UFW, creating a mechanism for conflict resolution between unions and growers and leading to the creation of the Agricultural Labor Relations Board (ALRB) to supervise union elections.[19]

In June of 1975, soon after the bill became law, Chávez embarked on a thousand-mile, fifty-nine day march through California's agricultural valleys to explain the bill's implications and its effects on the UFW and workers. The march began at Calexico on the Mexican border and worked its way north through the Imperial and San Joaquin valleys.[20] Because the UFW could not organize on the farms themselves, Chávez spoke at public rallies along the way about the UFW's victories and the advantages of the service centers and hiring halls.

The year 1975 brought other heartening news: the boycotts were succeeding. Gallo profits were said to be down 15 percent, for example, and many stores in the United States, Canada, and Europe stopped carrying lettuce, grapes, and Gallo wines. (By 1976, when the Giumarra company signed with the UFW, both Johnny Giumarra and Chávez spoke of a "mutual victory" based on "respect.")[21]

Although UFW membership had sunk to about ten thousand, the union's future again seemed bright.[22] Chávez predicted that workers would "flock to his union" if given a choice, and intensified his lobbying with the California state government for legislation to ensure that his union would be able to compete fairly with the Teamsters. In February, 1975, he attempted to reinvigorate the UFW by organizing a 110-mile march from San Francisco to Modesto, headquarters of Gallo wine, to publicize an ongoing boycott of Gallo products. The attention and the support the march received proved that the UFW still had broad public support and political clout.[23]

Throughout this period of disappointing betrayals and heartening victories, César Chávez's public address remained potent and at the center of his efforts. He now commanded a large audience as he preached his message to various audiences, including those with interests far beyond agriculture. In Washington, D.C., on November 4, 1971, he served as "chief speaker" at a fund-raising dinner for a lobbying group of some five hundred labor, religious, foundation, and anti-poverty leaders who represented about thirty anti-poverty organizations nationwide. According to the *Washington Post,* the forty-four-year-old celebrity orator had undergone few visible changes in his years of organizing; he "wore a blue cardigan sweater with a small hole in the back, striped shirt without a tie, dark blue cotton pants, and boots that looked as if they had just come in from a dusty field."[24]

"We are looking for a miracle, a leader who will do everything for us," Chávez warned his listeners. "It doesn't happen. The people have to do the work. One great thing that every person has is his own power, which some people call dignity." As proof, Chávez related how farm workers earned some 95¢ an hour when he started his unionizing efforts in Delano; as of the most recent contract, they were earning $2.40 per hour plus fringe benefits. During his twenty-minute address, reported the *Post,* "the patience of the man—who has worked for eight years, fasted, been jailed, separated from his family which includes eight children, and lived in poverty—came through." The humble and dedicated Chávez had in his life embodied his ideal of remaining part of "what he believes in most—'the people.'"[25] At the end of his address, the audience gave him a standing ovation.

Also in November, 1971, in Washington, D.C., Chávez sat with Congressman Mikva at the head table prior to addressing the Council for Community Action at the Sheraton-Park Hotel. His well-organized speech notes, written on stationary from the hotel, contained seven main points preceded by Roman numerals, with several numbered sub-points under each main point, some of which were further supported by lettered sub-points. Chávez modestly insisted that the people rather than their leaders were the most critical factor in a movement's success, and he argued that nonviolent actions and sacrifices would lead to organizing people who had the innate dignity that nurtures the hard work, patience, perseverance, and other qualities so valuable to acquiring power. His message was that he was "not discouraged," he wrote on the text margins to himself; and he ended with the topic heading, "Let's get back to the people."[26]

Chávez now received invitations to speak from throughout the nation and beyond. His speech at the National Council of Churches in 1974 demonstrated that he had formed an audience committed to supporting and following him as leader and embodiment of his union. Dorothy Rensenbrink, an observer who had heard Chávez speak many times, wrote for the *Christian Century* that she remained "puzzled at the power of such an uncommanding person to command so much loyalty from so many." The well-known Chávez enters the room almost unnoticed, she said; and "when he is announced, he appears suddenly on the platform as if he'd been hiding below it all the while." Compared to his earlier speeches, she noted, Chávez's delivery was "getting better—less sing-songy than when we heard him in the mid-'60s—and he lightly clutches the lectern. He speaks as though he is resuming a friendly conversation." On this particular day, she wrote, some listeners initially had difficulty following Chávez's usually clear message because they were unfamiliar with his subject. Nevertheless, she wrote, Chávez managed to fashion a deep identification that caused one listener to confess: "I am finally hooked by recognition. It is hard to describe why. It is not self-recognition, just a kind of kindred recognition; as it is with thee, so it is with me."[27] And if listeners identified with the man, they would be more likely to enact his agenda.

When speaking to other UFW leaders and organizers, Chávez continued to promote the establishment of kindredship or deep identification. After spending time with picketing unionists in and around Coachella, he told coworkers at UFW headquarters at La Paz of his hope that "someday . . . everyone in La Paz can go out and work with the workers, be there and touch . . . shoulders with them . . . let their flesh touch yours, let their spirit sort of be part of you, and let their complaints and their praises be part of your life." To see the worker who "understands his responsibility," he reported, "it's really fantastic."[28]

During an interview in 1975, Chávez reasoned that one problem previously plaguing movements comprised of poor people was that once the movement progressed and these people were no longer poor, they abandoned their cause. His own goal was reconstitution: to ensure that the poor who "made it" became "locked in to helping others."[29] Like his farm workers, poor people must take on reconstituted lives whereby the continuance of the struggle "becomes a responsibility. It becomes a part of their lives."[30] "We are working towards creating the new man, the new man in the fields, the man who will think of the common good, as you and I do, instead of the man who thinks of himself first," he told readers of a three-page letter he wrote on UFW stationary to farm workers and friends of the union in 1971. These "new men" would evince a "spirit of dedication and sacrifice" necessary for success. To accomplish the reconstitution, he warned, posed "a very large and a very complicated and a very mean problem of educating the workers."[31]

Chávez frequently asked that volunteer supporters also adopt new personae. For example, he appealed to a friendly audience of potential supporters to give a year of full-time work with farm workers, compensated by room, board, five dollars a week, and the reward of being part of a nonviolent movement creating social change: "We ask for even more now—not just your support, but your very selves!"[32] At a large rally in 1971 held to oppose the Vietnam War and protest the death of a Mexican-American reporter killed by police during an anti-war protest, Chávez carried forward his theme of reconstitution by declaring: "Individuals have to decide to give their lives over to the struggle for specific and meaningful social change," a struggle that could convert "their sacrifices and their suffering into a powerful campaign for dignity and for justice." Fusing his first and second personae, he concluded: "Perhaps we can bring the day when children will learn from their earliest days that being fully man and fully woman means to give one's life to the liberation of the brother who suffers. It is up to each one of us. It won't happen unless we decide to use our own lives to show the way."[33] He might have added that it would not happen without a skillfully crafted and presented rhetorical campaign to educate and win converts to become activists and to convince public opinion to offer crucial support.

Whether speaking to audiences familiar or unfamiliar with his message, Chávez remained fixed on his lifelong mission to educate them about goals, problems, and accomplishments of his union. After the successful grape strike, for example, he talked in an interview about how the fight with growers "has been won. I think the fight now is to convince the growers that the best thing for them to do is to sign with the union." During this period of negotiations with grape growers over contracts, he called for volunteers to join in the ongoing lettuce boycott and "for other work that has to be done. Some work is being ignored because we are concentrating on the boycott." He forecast that the successes in California would expand his union onto a national scale.[34]

In his rhetorical campaign Chávez continued to draw a vivid picture of the ongoing problems farm workers faced and then to propose specific ways of improving their lives. He communicated a portion of the harshness of their lives by explaining that workers were expected to travel from place to place "without job security, to the other side of the country in the hope of finding a job." They often found no employment; when successful in finding work, they were "paid a pittance for it. To go on hoping that they'll find a home. Most likely they wind up under a tree or under a bridge on a river bank."[35] In stark language he portrayed the never-ending cycle of migrant work:

To go with no money, save enough for the gas to get there. Risking all of the things that come from being poor and not having the security of a job and of a union. And they're asked that year in and year out and they do it. They do it because, you see, brothers and sisters, they're laborers. . . . Stoop labor. Ten hours, twelve hours. They do that and they do it willingly and you know what they do because of that great sacrifice.[36]

To capture the irony of farm workers' plight, Chávez frequently told a heartbreaking though common story. Farm workers produced immense amounts of food, enduring terrible exploitation and suffering many sacrifices to feed the nation and much of the world, but had no food for themselves or their families. "And that's the greatest, possibly the greatest shame that we have," he informed audiences.[37]

Despite setbacks in late 1971, when negotiations with uncompromising lettuce growers were broken off, and in 1974, when the UFW lost contracts to the Teamsters, Chávez reiterated that the workers would inevitably win because of their unflagging commitment to nonviolent means and a just cause. In 1971 he wrote to "friends of the farm workers" that growers had underestimated the strength of the farm workers' movement by not understanding that "farm workers are accustomed to suffering and to hardship."[38] In a one-page statement ending his twenty-four day "fast for justice" in Phoenix, Arizona, on June 4, 1972, Chávez acknowledged that his fast had been difficult for him but "was meant as a call to sacrifice for justice and as a reminder of how much suffering there is among farm workers." "In fact," he wrote, "what is a few days without food in comparison to the daily pain of our brothers and sisters who do backbreaking work in the fields under inhuman conditions and without hope of ever breaking their cycle of poverty and misery." One could easily be "discouraged about the injustice we see everywhere," he admitted, "but God gave all life and freedom to choose to use it" to bring about "a better and more just world for our children." It would take "hardship and sacrifice," but those who committed their lives to "nonviolent struggle for peace and justice" would "find that people will give you their hearts. . . . And in giving of yourself you will discover a whole new life of meaning and love." With sacrifice, nonviolence, and "work to spread the message," he forecast, "millions of people around the world will respond from their hearts, will support our efforts . . . and in the end we will overcome." "God," Chávez petitioned, "give us the strength and patience to do it without bitterness so that we can win."[39] For Chávez, rhetors who were persistent speakers could be certain, with God's help, of reconstituting audiences, of being reconstituted themselves, and of achieving personal happiness and union triumphs.

In 1974 Chávez maintained that "workers will struggle as long as it takes; they'll do whatever has to be done, legally and morally and unviolently; they'll stay with it until we win. That we know."[40] He continued to remind listeners that theirs was not a short-term struggle. Strikes had occurred in California since the 1880s, he pointed out, initially among Indians, Chinese, and Japanese, and then Hindus, Filipinos, Blacks, "Okies," Mexicans, and others who attempted and failed to organize unions. Times had changed, however, and a revolution was in progress. "It's like a great thirst," he said in simple prose, "and that thirst is not going to be abated, that thirst is not going to go away until the workers have a union that they can work with and they can work under and they can support and it's their union."[41]

In the fall of 1974 Chávez journeyed to Europe to promote his boycott. In Rome he met the Pope and addressed the Pontifical Commission of Justice and Peace, a group consisting of about two hundred religious leaders.[42] The quiet Chávez had become an orator of international note.

Chávez's rhetorical campaign so dominated his life that even the somber occasion of a eulogy became an opportunity to promote his themes. Juan de la Cruz was a sixty-year-old farm worker who was shot and killed on a UFW picket line on August 17, 1973. On the evening of August 20th, Chávez walked in a candlelight procession through the small San Joaquin town of Arvin to honor the martyr. In his short and pointed forty-one sentence eulogy the following day, Chávez began by depicting de la Cruz as "a simple and good man" whose spirit remained alive in the respect and love of his life shown by the thousands of people who had come to honor him. "What is there about the life of our brother, Juan, that produces such a response in us?" he asked rhetorically. He began his own answer with an account of the sacrifices made by early supporters of his movement. "With spirit like that," he said, "we had to win. No force on earth could stop us." "Juan de la Cruz is part of that spirit," continued Chávez, for the martyr had given himself fully to the union struggle since its earliest days: He had picketed, had worked on the boycott and had gone to jail, giving his all "so that all farm workers might some day be free." "His example of service and sacrifice reaches the spirit of each one of us," Chávez proclaimed. "His life and his deeds of love pull on our best instincts and cause us to want to give something of ourselves." The martyr had "not only given himself in life—but he has now given his only life on this earth for us, for his children and for all farm workers who suffer and who go hungry in this land of plenty." Consequently, Chávez told his audience, "We are here because his spirit of service and sacrifice has touched and moved our lives. The force that is generated by that spirit of love is more powerful than any force on earth. It cannot be stopped."[43]

Chávez had transformed the dead worker into "a martyr in a just cause," defining a second persona for all followers as he used de la Cruz's life and death as evidence and argument of the process and power of reconstitution. As Chávez told his audience in his conclusion: "We will give purpose and memory to his life and death by what we do. The more we sacrifice, the harder we work, the more life we give to the spirit of our brother, Juan de la Cruz." Chávez skillfully met the customary rhetorical demands of a eulogy, comforting the deceased's family and other listeners by showing that the deceased was a good man whose spirit and good deeds would live on through their influence on other people. Yet he had also skillfully told a story through which both de la Cruz and the message by which Chávez said he had lived afforded Chávez identification with his immediate listeners and those who would later read his message. Chávez thus extended his rhetorical campaign to convert an audience of mourners into reformulated believers—a cohesive group of activist supporters who would work hard and sacrifice for his righteous cause, find spiritual meaning in their efforts, be willing to forgo material gains while possibly exposing themselves to considerable risk, and so be assured of eventual triumph.[44]

Public address, Chávez told countless audiences, would remain the key to the UFW's success. On his long 1975 march to explain the California Agricultural Labor Relations Act Chávez answered a reporter's question on what the march had accomplished by stating: "Well I think it's gone very well, we've been able to talk to, by the time we get through with the march, about a hundred thousand workers." "We've been able to accomplish what we've set out to do," he added, "and that was to get the information about the [collective bargaining] law, to get votes for the union. . . ." When it was pointed out that the new law seemed to prohibit his union from going on farms to organize, Chávez further emphasized the importance he placed on discourse: "We're going to go anyway, rules or no rules, . . . because, if we can't talk to the workers it cannot be a free election, the workers must have the right to know our side of the story, so if the commission rules against us, we're going to go into the fields anyway, and risk arrest. . . ." In regard to those people who, a year previously, had believed that the UFW was doomed, Chávez explained that "they didn't understand the movement, they didn't understand the strength of the union, they didn't understand the following that we have with the people. . . . They never were right" because they lacked "the facts." Elections against the Teamsters were now inevitable, he predicted confidently, and "in those places where we can get to the workers and talk to them, I think we'll win. The places where we cannot talk to the workers, it's a different story. . . ." The story UFW advocates told workers was potent: Workers would create their own union, "be the masters of their own fate" in a "pretty social-minded union . . . a new kind of union" emphasizing service to workers and a "philosophy that workers must participate and run their own union. . . ."[45]

Chávez's confidence in his ultimate success allowed him rhetorically to convert setbacks into victories. Noting his opponents' surprise that he continued to struggle despite the union's difficulties, he quoted one of them as saying: "You know, we thought that when you lost the contracts last year, that was the end of the farm workers' union. But we are seeing now that nothing is going to stop the union until we sit down and negotiate with you." Chávez reasoned that "the growers made a bad mistake in taking those contracts away," because UFW followers had only gained determination to fight for the union that would improve their lives.[46]

The progress that workers had made under the UFW became evidentiary grist for Chávez's rhetorical mill. With his usual reliance on concrete facts, he reviewed gains in income: "In 1965 when we struck, those workers were getting 65¢ an hour; today, they are getting $2.30 an hour; and under our contract, they enjoyed some fringe benefits." Working through their own union, workers founded "their own medical plan—had vacations, better working conditions, better wages—many, many gains." Again showing that his ultimate goal was to educate the public, Chávez asserted that his biggest accomplishment was to raise the public awareness of "the awful conditions of farm labor. . . ."[47]

As his union persevered in its fight, Chávez stayed committed to enlisting support from other groups. In a 1968 letter to the National Council of Churches Chávez wrote of the ongoing struggle and then appealed for help: "You can help us survive and win new victories; but because of who you represent you can also help us stay true to our intention to serve our fellow farm workers." In 1970 he told another group of religious leaders of the union's essential connection to them: "We need it [your support]; but in the most basic sense you are part of us; our struggle for the poor is also your struggle; you belong with us."[48]

In a letter to "friends of the farm workers" on November 16, 1971, Chávez marshaled many facts to uncover the duplicity of lettuce growers and Teamsters in subverting the UFW's negotiations to settle its dispute with the growers. He cited dates, names of growers and fired workers, places of meetings, and several direct quotes by growers; he relied on transitions such as "Looking back, it is not hard to detect signs of bad faith by the growers," and numbered paragraphs to itemize such signs. He also combined rhetorical questions and his favorite rhetorical device, *anaphora* (the repetition of beginnings), as, for example, when he ended his three discussions of signs of bad faith with these identical words: "Would you call this good faith?"[49]

In a speech to "church people" gathered at the union's headquarters at La Paz in 1971, Chávez carried forward his themes that money alone was insufficient to organize people, and that he had succeeded by concentrating on that "1 percent" of his first audiences who "had the spirit and really wanted to do something." Recalling his appeals to potential organizers in his early years, he told his religious listeners that he had advocated the need to sacrifice and had told the vital core group that he himself had sacrificed and was poorer than they were. "When you sacrifice," he pointed out, "you force others to sacrifice." The need to embody your message and to identify with workers was what Chávez had learned in his experience, and it was, he claimed, the necessary ingredient to achieve success.[50] A one-page outline of an October, 1973, speech to a Christian group in Chicago includes a point about a "conversion of the entire church to a preferential option for the poor with a view to their full liberation." Jesus "was sent first to the poor," Chávez would remind listeners. When church followers acted out their "continuing thirst for justice" by working for the poor, they would "be satisfied" with themselves as reconstituted beings.[51]

Chávez continually sought to link his union with other labor groups. In a 1972 speech in Lattimore, Pennsylvania, commemorating the 75th anniversary of a 1897 massacre of miners who were trying to form a union, Chávez sought to tie together labor unions past and present, on farms and in mines. Laying out his organizational pattern immediately, he stated: "In this 75th year we come to Lattimore to honor the past—to pay tribute to the present and to organize for the future." He adapted to the occasion by comparing his union's struggle with the situation that the miners had faced. These martyrs—he wrote in his notes and manuscript for his speech—"if they could speak to us today they would tell us very plainly in the words of another labor martyr: Don't mourn for us—organize!"[52] "Only in preserving labor's past," he argued, "can we preserve labor's future." In this speech he spoke of the many ways in which his farm workers paralleled the miners, e.g., as immigrants and non-violent persons.

Chávez especially appreciated assistance from other labor groups. At a 1973 benefit given by the United Auto Workers (UAW), Chávez told an audience about how Walter Reuther had come to Delano to rescue the farm workers' movement in its early years, even citing specific quotes by Reuther from those dramatic days of confrontation with local police.[53] In a 1974 speech to the UAW he expressed gratitude for their public support and specifically for their $10,000 per week contribution to his union: "Without that money we'd be dead today. And we stand here today to tell you that we appreciate that."[54]

Maintaining his commitment to fight union battles on many fronts, Chávez redoubled his efforts to work in political and legal channels. The growers and their cohorts often engaged in extra-legal activities; and law-enforcement officials themselves unleashed violence against union members. In 1971 Chávez had reminded listeners that union members had been arrested over a thousand times in the previous five years in a variety of settings. In 1974 he statistically documented the extent of the violence: "The strike last year was a terrible bloody strike. Costly—we had almost five thousand people jailed; over two hundred people were beaten up and sent to the hospital. We had forty-four people shot and wounded, twelve people seriously and two people were killed."[55]

Farm workers were also harassed by private police forces and challenged by professional strike-breakers who went into Mexico to recruit illegal workers. "These are the new industries in California because of our struggle," Chávez lamented. "And because of that, the boycott must continue; the boycott must go on to be able to overcome, because we cannot do the organizing in the traditional way. . . ."[56] Perhaps the most despised new industries were those that signed up illegal workers brought into the country to break strikes. "If the illegals were taken out of the places where we are now striking," Chávez predicted, "the strikes would be over tomorrow." In 1974 he estimated that between sixty and seventy thousand illegal workers were in California, and he accused the federal government of knowingly allowing the practice.[57]

Worse still, Chávez charged, the federal government had moved far beyond passive cooperation with the growers by tolerating illegal workers. It was actively aiding growers through huge purchases of grapes that were then shipped to U.S. troops in Vietnam. Upon learning that the Department of Defense had purchased about eight pounds of grapes per soldier in 1969, the union demanded an end to this practice. In 1971 Chávez enlightened audiences on how the U.S. Department of Defense was also helping lettuce growers, particularly Bud Antle, a well-publicized target of the boycott. "Before the strike," Chávez instructed, "they were buying 8 percent of the lettuce from Bud Antle. . . . The first week of the boycott they went up to something like 15—they doubled it, but now they are buying between 35 and 40 percent of all the lettuce from Bud Antle. . . . They buy it by the pound." This lettuce normally was purchased by the head, at a rate that worked out to about 12¢ a pound, but the Defense Department paid "about 18¢ a pound" and did not submit to competitive bidding. To Chávez these practices were intentional, aimed at breaking the union boycott by providing markets for products that could not otherwise be sold.[58] To further publicize these unfair buying practices, Chávez and his followers picketed military bases.

In several states, growers backed legislation to restrict UFW activities. In Chávez's view, this tactic represented a desperate last attempt to halt the organizing of workers. Perhaps the most dangerous legislative challenge came in 1972 with California Proposition 22, which would have outlawed the boycott and would have allowed only full-time employees to vote in union elections. Both proposals would have severely limited the UFW's effectiveness. Chávez belittled the bill's provisions in his speech at Santa Clara: Should the bill pass, he said, "A grower, if he thinks there is going to be a strike, if he feels there's a threat of a strike, if he dreams there is going to be a strike, or if he just plain wants to think there is going to be a strike, he can go to the judge and get a sixty-day day injunction against the strikes at harvest time."⁵⁹ Since nearly all crops were harvested in a period of less than sixty days, the proposed law would have destroyed the effectiveness of any potential strikes.

Just before the 1972 election, Chávez warned listeners at Santa Clara University that because agribusiness was not succeeding through its traditional anti-union methods of ignoring or ridiculing the UFW—or accusing it of being comprised of Communists—growers were likely to increasingly employ the legal system against workers. Lacking much of the legislative protection afforded to other unions, farm workers faced "the awesome and total power that the growers have in small communities to get the courts to enjoin the union the moment there is a strike, or, the moment there is going to be a strike." Expanding this analysis in later speeches, Chávez spoke of the growers' influence over local district attorneys and sheriffs to enforce injunctions and use questionable acts to prevent picketing. Injunctions against strikers came easily, he said, because judges in most small towns, "with few exceptions, are owned by the growers."⁶⁰ Nevertheless, he reaffirmed, "even with all of that we continued to struggle, continued to fight and continued to have hope that we're going to win."⁶¹

Chávez criticized growers for unseemly acts in support of Proposition 22. For example, he said, when those who solicited the signatures necessary to place the proposition on the ballot had little initial success, they began misrepresenting the content of the proposal. Still guided by his millennial view of history and reform, Chávez assured his audience that the law would fail because it could not end the "turmoil in the fields. . . . The more repression we get, the more solidified we get and the more we fight."⁶² On election day the union and its friends defeated the proposition, a major victory for Chávez's cause.

But the growers were not defeated, and in fact found their most valuable collaborators from within the ranks of organized labor, signing pacts with the Teamsters as the UFW's three-year contacts expired. Still, speaking to an AFL-CIO audience in 1973, Chávez found a source of hope in his theme of the union as family. Teamsters were fearful that they would lose any confrontation with the UFW, he said. "We don't only take [on] the farm worker," he said they complained. "We gotta fight the wife, we gotta fight the kid, we gotta fight the grandmother, and the grandfather. . . ."⁶³

In a 1974 interview Chávez displayed his signature positive viewpoint and sought to minimize his losses: "Well, it is not completely correct to say that we've gone from fifty thousand to fifteen thousand [members]." Many workers who quit their jobs "and are working elsewhere . . . are paying dues to us, and some of them are on the boycott, some of them are on the strike." The UFW had lost some jobs but no support, he insisted, and had sponsored more strikes than in any year in its history—a strong testimony to the ongoing "concern, and the love, and the interest of the workers. . . ."[64]

Seizing the offensive, the long-time labor leader excoriated Teamster contracts for losing benefits that previous UFW contracts had won. The list of losses included the voiding of agreements that eliminated the use of labor contractors, instituted a hiring hall, placed restrictions on the use of some pesticides, and provided drinking water and portable toilets for workers. The Teamsters' pact actually cut wages from $3.00 an hour to $2.89 an hour. Such setbacks were not surprising, Chávez reasoned, for "the growers wouldn't invite the Teamsters in if it is going to cost them more money. They threw us out and got the Teamsters in because it is a sweetheart deal. It's cheaper for them."[65]

To communicate his disdain for the Teamsters, Chávez spun out a parable of three men (a Hindu from India, a Jewish Rabbi, and a Teamster) who were traveling through the countryside. When their car broke down, they went to the nearest farmhouse and asked for a place to stay the night. The farmer said he had room for two to sleep in the house and the third would have to spend the night in the barn. The Hindu volunteered to sleep in the barn, but he quickly returned because "there was a cow in the barn and thus his religion prevented him from staying there." The Rabbi went next but soon came back saying "he couldn't stay in the barn because there were pigs in the barn." When the Teamster went to the barn, there soon was "a commotion at the front door. The people opened the front door and the cow and the pig were at the front door."[66] Such humorous stories converted the Teamsters from a foe to be feared to a target of derision.

In 1975 Chávez backed the California Agricultural Labor Relations Act, a legislative proposal that, he said, had the simple goal of letting "the workers decide which union they wanted—a representative election bill."[67] The passage of that bill would mark a high point for UFW political influence, giving farm workers a tremendous boost (until 1982, when newly elected Governor George Deukmejian would lead a successful move to weaken the bill's provisions). During the 1976 political campaigns, Chávez took a clear stand on the nominees. At the Democratic National Convention he made a broad and brief nominating speech for Jerry Brown, seizing the golden rhetorical opportunity to reiterate many of his familiar themes to a large national audience. He focused on helping the needy and instructed on the importance of a rhetorical campaign led by those who could combine thought and character. It was necessary, he declared, to provide "people a sense of purpose," give "workers a voice," to practice the kind of sacrifice— working for people—that "brings meaning to one's life," and to select a leader who will "lead by example, by sacrifice." Chávez depicted Brown as such a leader, noting that farm workers had achieved nothing until they had been given a governor who "listened to us and gave farm workers an instrument—collective bargaining—so the workers can begin to deal with their own problems."[68]

Through shifting circumstances for the UFW Chávez's rhetorical discourse remained largely unchanged, still portraying the union as a family that could win over public opinion through its nonviolent fight. "We are doing it nonviolently because nonviolent action is superior to any type of action and more lasting," he lectured in 1971 to students at Sacramento State University; "You can fight nonviolently morally and legally and you can hope to get wide support from all of the interest groups and from all the people in the country."[69] Seeking to find—or create—activist followers in his audience of students and professors, Chávez questioned the usefulness of studying theory to the exclusion of action. Unless one applied theories to real-life problems, he declared, no one would be helped. As an alternative, he proposed that "if you are nonviolent and you go down into the gutter, into the ghetto, into the farm labor camp—into the farm labor community—and you do something then nonviolence has a real meaning."[70]

Chávez had by now fashioned a more sophisticated view of nonviolence. He believed in "militant nonviolence" as opposed to passive resistance, professing that "it is action" that "in some instances . . . requires more militancy than violence." He described how workers on the picket line had been nonviolent even in the face of violence against them: "Despite all this, the pickets have stood their ground and have fought back with aggressive nonviolence." In fighting back nonviolently, the workers wielded a proactive and moral tool. "Nonviolence is more powerful than violence," he taught. "We are convinced that nonviolence supports you if you have a just and moral cause. Nonviolence gives the opportunity to stay on the offensive, which is of vital importance to win any contest." Moreover, he added, nonviolence required more *machismo* [manliness] than did violence, for "true nonviolence is an impossibility without the possession of unadulterated fearlessness."[71] Thus manliness was best illustrated through nonviolence.

In a speech ending a fast, Chávez tied together the Mexican-American culture's emphasis on sacrifice, courage, manliness, and God: "I am convinced that the truest act of courage, the strongest act of manliness is to sacrifice ourselves for others in a totally nonviolent struggle for justice. To be a man is to suffer for others. God help us to be men."[72] In a speech before an audience composed largely of affluent Chicanos at an American Citizens' Club in Brawley, California, Chávez spoke in Spanish as he made clear that his struggle was "for better working conditions for all workers, black, brown, white or polka-dot." He then centered on the importance to Chicanos of eschewing materialism and of converting their machismo into a willingness to sacrifice for what justly should belong to them.[73]

Chávez's view of nonviolence had manifestly acquired new depth. His notes to a 1972 speech in San Jose honoring the fifth anniversary of a community organization that educated students to obtain jobs began by graciously recognized officers, priests, other distinguished listeners, and the organization's accomplishments. Then he set forth his evolving set of principles of nonviolence. "There is no such thing as defeat in nonviolence," he wrote, and nonviolent techniques do not depend on "the goodwill of the oppressor, but rather on the unfailing assistance of God." Yet God's will required humans' discourse: "In nonviolence the cause has to be just and clear as well as the means," and its "appeal" must be made to "the heart" rather than solely to the "brain." In characteristic form, his conclusion began with a reminder to himself to tell audiences that they and farm workers were "very close" and ended with his prompt to tell "a story."[74]

Chávez equated the failures of organizers with the failures of nonviolent tactics. "Nonviolence is so exact," he lectured, "that if you are a lousy organizer and if you propose nonviolence you are going to be discovered that you are a very nice guy, but oh so inefficient." "Violence," in contrast, "has the opposite effect. . . . You can be a lousy organizer even—if you promote violence nobody is going to question your ability to work as an organizer and to lead and to get things done." Violence often was proposed only after organizers failed: "They begin to advocate violence as the only way out," an admission that "as organizers and as leaders of men, we're failures." He acknowledged that violence sometimes succeeded, but argued that the best organization was done nonviolently after a tremendous amount of work: "The only way I know to organize is to work. If the troops work eight hours or ten or twelve you work at least one and a half times more than the ones you are asking to follow you."[75] Again, Chávez brings to mind the principle that rhetors who reconstitute listeners appear to be "like their audiences, only somehow more so."[76]

In 1975, one week after he had ended his Easter fast, Chávez repeated his theme. Hard work was necessary to make nonviolence succeed, he told an audience of readers of *Fellowship* magazine. "You have to train to be nonviolent just as a soldier trains to be violent," he insisted. "Nonviolence is people willing to reject violence and say, 'Okay, there's another way of doing it.' That way entails love, sacrifice, lots of work, some planning, and getting a real satisfaction from doing it."[77]

In 1974 Chávez's consistent advocacy of nonviolent boycotts expanded past grapes to include lettuce and white wines. He elaborated in the manner of a professor: "There is a little confusion about which lettuce to boycott and I would like to tell you that we're boycotting the western iceberg lettuce . . . the only lettuce that looks like lettuce so there's no confusion; it's a round head of lettuce."[78] Willing listeners must search for the union label, the emblem of the Black Thunderbird, he said, before purchasing lettuce, grapes, or wines. Such scrutiny would foil growers' schemes to circumvent the boycott. Gallo wine, for example, had "at least twenty labels. In some cases, the word Gallo does not appear on the label." To remedy the confusion, he advised: "If you don't see the name Gallo on the label you will read on the small print the words 'Modesto, California.' And if it says 'Modesto, California,' that's Gallo wine."[79]

"The boycott is having its impact," Chávez told many audiences, "and unless great changes take place, we think we are going to win." He even declared that the boycott "seems to be stronger than it was in 1970, when we first won."[80] Yet the seasoned rhetor also warned that the union must adjust its tactics whenever necessary. "The same things don't work forever," he declared authoritatively. "You've got to constantly . . . [be] inventing, thinking of new solutions, guiding yourself always by those things that are legal and are moral and are nonviolent."[81] As an example, he recited the details of a case where the picketing UFW could not gain access to workers to recruit them. Chávez had asked for suggestions from the membership. After some women who were strikers recommended that a vigil be held outside the fields as a way of increasing contact between picketers and strikebreakers, the union "set the vigil in an old station wagon and we celebrated a mass there . . . and when the workers saw that, they started streaming out of the camps," thus enabling union organizers to talk with them. "I spoke during the homily," Chávez recalled, "and the organizers the moment the sermon was over" distributed cards requesting a union election. Chávez claimed that the tactic contributed to the union's win in the subsequent election.[82]

As he laid out his case before varied audiences, César Chávez counted among his rhetorical resources his capacity to speak both in English and in Spanish. He understood the requirements for being rhetorically effective with two languages in a single address. In an interview he stated:

> But I'm really putting a message across: "Look, if I go too much in English, too much in Spanish, forgive me." And then I set the crowd so they'll accept. If I do a lot of Spanish, they'll accept—if I do a lot of English, they'll accept it. I got permission from them. I condition them really by using a little joke—an analogy.[83]

A 1971 speech in Austin, Texas, demonstrated how and why he used both languages, as well as his deft use of humor and analogy. His introduction, delivered in Spanish, contained this request for permission to speak in both languages:

Suddenly it is necessary to speak in two languages, and it appears that now is such an occasion. So we must use both languages—English and Spanish. A man was asking what difference there was between them and I said, "English is the language of business; Spanish is the language for angels and people in love." I'll start with business and end with the better part.[84]

The body of the address, delivered in English, thanked audience members for their courtesy in welcoming him to Texas, outlined his support for a strike at the Economy Furniture Company, asked people to boycott any business that sold furniture made by Economy Furniture, described the power of the boycott, and honored former Texas Senator Ralph Yarborough, a strong supporter of the UFW. Listeners heard his standard stories (described in chapter 6) about the little girl who wanted to buy boycotts and the little boy who said that Chávez invented grapes. Chávez urged Mexican Americans to unite to better their lives and appealed to them to support the union of the Economy Furniture workers. He concluded by explaining how unions could improve the lives of all people. He built a bridge to the last section of his speech with these clear and simple words: "I want to thank you very much for being here, and I want to say a few words in Spanish."

Aimed directly at Mexican Americans, the Spanish portion of the speech included a discussion of the need for unity among Mexican Americans as a group, an appeal for a return to traditional values, and a call for more emphasis on education. Here Chávez relied almost exclusively on folk sayings, stories, and aphorisms, a clear shift from his usual, broader mix of evidence and a revealing demonstration of his use of elements of the Mexican Americans' cultural and rhetorical conventions to increase his appeal. In his call for unity Chávez quoted a Mexican expression, "'In unity there is strength.' We recognize the need for organizing ourselves. Even little red ants are never alone, always in a bunch."

The potency of unity and organization surfaced more subtly in a Mexican anecdote about two cowboys, one well-known as an expert with a whip. As the two cowboys were out walking, one tested the skills of the whip expert by asking him to cut the fruit off a cactus—which he "did as though he were using a knife"; then a branch of a tree and "the man did a clean job of it"; then a fly's head, which he amazingly did, leaving his companion speechless. When the whip-wielder was challenged to kill a bee, he refused and said: "They're very organized; if I harm it I'll have thousands of its kind on me soon." In a rhetorical convention familiar to many Mexicans and Americans of Mexican descent, Chávez followed with a dicho to draw a lesson from the story or cuento: "That is how we ought to think; a wrong doing against any one of us is a wrong doing against all of us."

Still speaking in Spanish, Chávez next described how ideals in the Mexican-American community shifted as members of the culture became "super-consumers" and entered the race for material goods. He gave the example of his wife wanting to get rid of her "1970 model car because my godmother has a 1971 car"; in typical fashion he drew a moral from the story: "All these pressures are having an impact on our ideals and values. As long as we let it, we'll be victims of what we criticize." In the first of two additional examples of changing ideals in his community, he reminisced that when he had been young and working as a migrant, if one group's car broke down and "a car with Mexicans came they would stop immediately to help us poor Mexicans." Unfortunately things had changed: "But now with cars so new and big the Mexicans will rush by not noticing his brother in trouble." At the end of the second story he chastised listeners for ignoring the fact that young people were rejecting traditional values, describing how in previous generations people would never have considered putting their parents in nursing homes when they became old. Such actions violated the ideal that, "we have family unity and love as Mexicans." Individuals could not love their race unless that love began at home.

His conclusion started with an appeal to recruit young people. He reminded listeners that youths "are strong and can work day and night. They're not disappointed in knowing they are tomorrow's leaders. They need our encouragement and support." To portray young people as leaders, he narrated the story of how he thought his twelve-year-old son's hair was too long but the boy objected to cutting it. "I said I didn't speak that way to my father," Chávez recalled. "When I just could not get to him, he asked, 'How would you like it if I ate lettuce?' The discussion ended."

Following the story, Chávez glided seamlessly into a discussion of the need to educate youth. After telling listeners that he and other older people had faced many problems during their lives "because our education is not adequate," he spun out a story about an event in Mexico during the reign of President Lázaro Cárdenas. During a time of emphasis on education throughout the country, authorities found a small village in the mountains with no school so they built a schoolhouse and hired a "fourteen-year-old girl, who had two years of schooling, for the teacher." In a short time, the government dispatched an inspector to check on the students' education. Quizzing the students on Mexican history, the inspector asked them about Cuauhtémoc (1495–1525), the last Aztec ruler. (In 1521 Cuauhtémoc and his followers were conquered by the Spanish under Hernán Cortés. Cuauhtémoc was captured, tortured with fire, and hanged.) "Who can tell me who burned Cuauhtémoc's feet?" demanded the inspector. No one answered; but after the inspector insisted, one boy stood up and said: "Listen, Mr. Inspector, we are very poor but we are very honest. I guarantee you none of us burned Cuauhtémoc's feet!" Chávez then ended his speech with the moral that knowledge was crucial: "We must know everything; we must know who burned Cuauhtémoc's feet!"

Chávez's four pages of notes for a October, 1972, speech to a rally in Oxnard were also in Spanish. In this address he maintained his focus on history and higher purposes, his use of facts and calls for inclusion and nonviolence, his easy-to-follow organization and gracious manner. To adapt to his audience of Mexican Americans, he again spoke in Spanish and put more emphasis on stories as a proof and suffering as a theme.

After beginning notes of "Thanks" to Ray Huerta and other people and organizations including the "Finerman Clines Farms Urban Theatre," "Farm workers' support committee," and "Inter Harvest Strike," he reminded himself to point out that English was the language of "business," Spanish of "the little angels" and courtship. He then directed himself to use the "Story" in the speech; three stories respectively of "The muleteer," "The whip," and the "wasp," all standard stump cuentos that had appeared in his earlier addresses. The address presented a historical overview of his cause from 1962 through the Delano strike of seven years and discussed gains from general "economic advancement"—"contracts-loans-salary-conditions-worker's respect"—to particular victories such as the creation of a twenty-four hour clinic in Delano, a medical plan, and a day-care center for children. Specific facts included the "13 days" of the Inter Harvest Strike, the penalties of "1 yr. [in] jail [and] $5,000 fines" and the "58 members in 1971" who were jailed.[85]

Chávez's movement was "in favor of all races," he made clear to his Mexican-American listeners, whether "Mexican Cubans Puerto Ricans Blacks-Whites Arabic Portuguese." "We have suffered imprisonments, contempt . . . everything it takes in order to fulfill our mission," he reminded listeners, and would "fight until we free the people, the poor farm workers." The "revolution" would take place "without violence" by the means of strikes, boycotts, and "political campaigns with the purpose of ending exploitation." He made a notation to mention "the people's voice" and he featured a dicho from Benito Juárez in the closing section of his address: "Peace is the respect of another's rights."[86]

Chávez's rhetorical campaign of the first half of the 1970s reflected the many failures, successes, and challenges he and his movement encountered during the period. By 1970 he had become a national and international celebrity, and a hero with enormous credibility for many people. The UFW had won a series of startling victories over growers and in legislation. Chávez's all-encompassing commitment to discourse was perhaps best revealed by his explanation of his twenty-four-day fast in Phoenix in 1972: The fast was "not done out of a desire to destroy yourself, but it's done out of a deep conviction that we can communicate with people, either those who are for us or against us, faster and more effectively spiritually than we can in any other way."[87]

As a speaker Chávez had gained confidence, skills, and an expanded set of audiences. Yet while he deepened his message, he kept constant his fundamental rhetorical profile. He remained quiet and modest in delivery and manner, concentrating on presenting facts and arguments clearly to inform on whatever issue he addressed. Still dedicated to hard work, willing to sacrifice, and certain that God would ensure victory, he never stopped telling potential organizers that public address could transform audiences if those potential organizers joined him in his movement by embodying and communicating the message he gave them even as he embodied and communicated that same message. He portrayed many and wide-ranging audiences as possessing the possibility of becoming "new men"—farm workers as well as college students who could become volunteer workers or others who would contribute actively to his cause. Their altered self-definitions would include a newfound dignity, a heightened sense of responsibility, a dedication to hard work and willingness to sacrifice, a confidence in the ultimate triumph of their just cause, a valorizing of the spiritual, and—for the organizers—a commitment to discourse. They would find happiness in this transformation, he promised, and they alone held the key to his movement's success by reconstituting themselves and others into a powerful and unstoppable force for good.

Even the growers grudgingly and sometimes obliquely acknowledged Chávez's rhetorical power and influence. In 1973 one grower answered a reporter's question "Did Chávez do in your view some good along the way?" with a brief and general survey of the labor leader's range of effects: "Yes, I think we should give him credit, sometime maybe he awakens our conscience, of the growers, of the workers, shall we say of the American people, and . . . maybe a Chávez was necessary."[88] After the UFW victory over the Teamsters in 1975, an Arab farm worker attributed the win to Chávez's message that the Teamsters had no interest in workers' benefits, while the workers who supported the UFW did so because the UFW was for the workers. A more rhetorically minded observer might have added that Chávez's message also depicted the leader himself as a worker who embodied his union.[89]

Chávez himself attributed his crucial victory in securing a contract with

Giumarra to his movement's nonviolent means and just cause and to the "millions upon millions" of people who believed in and supported the means and cause.[90] It is safe to assume that many of these millions had heard or read Chávez's themes, arguments, explanations, appeals, and evidence, whether directly from him or from organizers whom he inspired and educated. It is also safe to assume that his message had persuaded many in his audience and reconstituted others. The need for listeners to understand the importance of rhetorical discourse remained crucial whether he spoke in Spanish or English, for—as he wrote in his brief outline of a speech given in English and Spanish to a rally of farm workers in Stockton in 1971—the "day when farm workers didn't say nothing is over."[91]

The first half of the 1970s concluded with triumphs for Chávez and the United Farm Workers. But the UFW had been clearly damaged by Teamster contracts, verbal assaults by enemies, and a conservative shift in public opinion that reduced its allegiance to most of the reform movements begun in the 1960s. During the 1970s the UFW also suffered from the legal decrees by courts and attempted legislation by anti-union political groups in California, Oregon, and Arizona that sided with the growers by placing restrictions on union picketing, boycotting, and recruiting practices. Chávez faced serious—but in his mind not insurmountable—challenges from hostile politicians, unfriendly jurists, and a more conservative public. As UFW prospects weakened, he resumed the grape boycott; later he also initiated boycotts on iceberg lettuce and Gallo wines. Critics saw the public as apparently indifferent to these tactics.[92]

While Chávez's rhetorical discourse in this period revealed a mature spokesperson at the height of his persuasive and personal power, his extraordinary commitment to public address created weaknesses as well as strengths in his union. Labor historian Cletus E. Daniel described the union's problem: "The challenge presented by the Teamster-grower alliance in the lettuce industry forced UFWOC [the United Farm Workers Organizing Committee] to divert precious resources into the reconstruction of its far-flung boycott network. It also distracted Chávez and his most competent aides at a time when the union was in the process of transforming itself from an organization expert in agitation into one equipped to administer contracts covering thousands of workers in the grape industry."[93]

Faced with declining membership, Chávez was forced to devote time to recruiting members and appealing for public backing rather than consolidating his past gains. Accordingly, he chose not to make the transition to full-time administration. He would not concentrate on developing structures to serve members and overseeing other operations; instead he would continue his widespread campaign to teach audiences of the problems, prospects, and needs of his union and movement. Chávez had never been comfortable when confined to managing anyway. "Another side of Chávez's personality," noticed *Time* magazine in 1974, "is becoming painfully apparent: his talents as a union administrator scarcely match his gift for inspirational leadership."[94] It was apparent to many observers that the union needed a full-time leader/administrator, a role that the overburdened Chávez could assume only partially and one that sometimes conflicted with his role as an evangelist and advocate.

Thus Chávez violated an essential principle of leadership in social movements, a principle Herbert W. Simons expressed concisely: "Theoreticians, agitators, and propagandists must launch the movement; political and bureaucratic types must carry it forward."[95] Because Chávez did not move with complete success to the next stage of leadership, his union would soon encounter added obstacles in reaching its potential.

Chapter 6

The Merger of Man and Message

Rhetorical Techniques of a Teacher of Truth

By 1975 César Chávez had created the rhetorical profile that would characterize his discourse until his death nearly two decades later. He had invented, developed, and tested this profile in his quest to create, sustain, and expand his union and its influence; and he had found ample proof of his message's success with audiences ranging from farm workers to college students. While he made some alterations in his rhetorical techniques to adjust to particular audiences, occasions, and issues—and to adjust to whether he was speaking in Spanish or English—his fundamental message, and the strategies and qualities that formed his rhetorical profile, remained consistent over the years.

Chávez's rhetorical consistency resulted both from his lifelong commitment to a worldview that privileged rhetoric and from his personal qualities and particular goals. Chávez always remained fixed on his central mission: to present ideas and facts clearly and to reach as many listeners, readers, and others as possible. He saw himself as a teacher of a message that God would bless with profound effects once that message educated a sufficient portion of the public. As we have seen, Chávez could not achieve the rhetorical identification required to reformulate audiences so that they would enact his agenda unless he himself embodied his substantive message of themes, arguments, and explanations. His success illustrates how well he achieved that embodiment.

As we have shown in previous chapters, Chávez's experiences convinced him that such rhetorical reconstitution required him to embody his cause and message while preaching his substantive themes; accordingly, he lived the life he asked others to adopt. His heritage and life alone did not create his persona, however, for he also used his own discourse to communicate a self-portrait: union organizer as teacher of truth.

Thus far this study has concentrated on Chávez's early life, on his rhetorical worldview, and on his substantive message as he responded to historical contexts and challenges from 1962–1975. We now draw from Chávez's discourse through 1975 to summarize his rhetorically constructed self-portrait. We discuss how both his tireless speaking and writing and his particular ways of using language, organization, and evidence contributed to his embodiment of his substantive themes and consequently to the merger of thought and character that allowed him to reformulate audiences. We also review how he used the second persona to intensify the identification that produced reconstitution.

When discussing two areas of Chávez's speaking in this analysis, we also refer to his rhetorical career after 1975. To document the extent of his speaking and the format for his rhetorical performances, we cite his speaking tours, which took place at different times through the end of the 1970s. In addition, in order to underscore career-long similarities and differences in his preparation and thus in the speech delivery that reflected that preparation, we draw examples from throughout his life on the stump.

Chávez's message and manner remained largely consistent whether he spoke in English or Spanish. His speechwriter and press aide Marc Grossman claims that the labor leader's "substance" was the same in his speeches in either language, a comment supported by our analysis of Chávez's Spanish-only speeches. One notable modification he made when speaking in Spanish was to tell more *cuentos* (stories), cite more *dichos* (sayings), and talk more of sacrifice—three conventions familiar and appealing to Mexican-American audiences. On many occasions, Grossman said, Chávez switched languages during a single speech, sometimes advising: "For those of you who are bilingual, I apologize, you'll have to hear it twice."[1]

Chávez's hand-written speech outlines for his bilingual addresses contain notes to himself about language choice. He often wrote "Spanish" next to the last section of the speech; sometimes he wrote "English-Spanish" or "Change to Spanish" at the top of the outline.[2] Chávez explained to an interviewer that early in his career he would only switch in one direction, from English to Spanish, but had later learned that he could be more flexible: "'Look,'" he'd say to an audience, "'if I go too much in English, too much in Spanish, forgive me.' And then I set the crowd so they'll accept. If I do a lot of Spanish they'll accept. If I do a lot of English, they'll accept it. I get permission from them."[3]

Chávez often immediately translated his ideas from Spanish to English or English to Spanish. On some occasions, such as the speech ending his fast on March 10, 1968, he spoke in both Spanish and English, delivering the message in both languages as a means of relating personally to his audience, especially when speaking in Spanish. As Winthrop Yinger commented about Chávez, "It is their speech, in their tongue. He knows that many farm workers do not yet speak English fluently or have difficulties with it. He likewise seems to realize that by translating his ideas into a native language he makes meanings not only more personal but more precise and clear (some things get lost in translation)."[4] Chávez believed that those who only spoke Spanish should receive his message directly. Once during a government hearing he "testified in Spanish so as to protest the fact that none of those conducting the hearing spoke the language. (The only Spanish-speaking person on the government side of the table was a Cuban translator.)"[5]

Whether using Spanish or English, Chávez spoke in a calm and unobtrusive manner. Audiotapes, videotapes, and films of his speeches consistently demonstrate his low-keyed vocal style and a manner that seemed professionally calm and reasoned rather than charismatically supercharged and emotive. Chicano activist José Ángel Gutiérrez related that Chávez

> usually spoke in Spanish. He spoke in English to staff, non-Mexican audiences and reporters, and on college campuses. He was bilingual and bicultural. He didn't have an eloquent, grandiose, or verbose speaking style. He was plain-speaking and monotonal. Rarely did he raise his voice to make a point or command attention.[6]

Richard Griswold del Castillo and Richard A. Garcia described Chávez in a way that summarizes the perceptions of other close observers: "He was not an emotional speaker. He convinced . . . through his sincerity, humility, and command of the facts about the struggle between the farm workers and the growers. His low-key approach was disarming in an age of radical and flamboyant rhetoric."[7] Chávez's modesty and occasional lack of confidence were real: He became "at least a little nervous" before speaking in public throughout his life despite his vast experience and striking successes as an orator.[8]

The calm modesty and quiet humility he displayed in his speaking infused many aspects of his life. For example, he told celebrating listeners after the signing of contracts in 1970 to be humble in victory—even as he refused to take credit for or gloat over the triumph. Evidence of his unwillingness to take responsibility for his union's successes—or even to acknowledge his own stature as a hero—appeared often in his discourse. To one interviewer's question of what he wanted people to know about him, Chávez responded typically: "About myself? I don't know. I have never thought about it. It really isn't important."[9] When another interviewer pointed out to him that most people attributed the UFW's successes largely to his own contributions, Chávez reacted characteristically: "And so people go around and give you a lot of credit. . . . I can't take the credit."[10] His modesty also surfaced in his refusal to accept honors and awards. On May 1, 1971, he wrote a letter declining the offer to be Grand Marshall for a parade in the Latin American Fiesta: "It was an honor to have been asked. But as you know, I refuse this kind of focus upon myself. Our Union is a movement of our people and it is to them that the glory must go."[11]

To reach his goal of informing audiences, Chávez often made his addresses brief. Short speeches, he believed, would be more easily understandable. "If you can't say in ten minutes what you have to say," he declared, "then you shouldn't say it." Early in his career he timed himself to make sure that his speeches were brief; and throughout his life the great majority of his talks did not exceed twenty minutes.[12]

Chávez preferred a format where he could give a short talk and then respond to questions. "That is when I'm at my best," he said. By calling for questions from an audience, he uncovered its interests and then adapted his presentation appropriately. To him, the "hardest thing is to know what the people [want to] hear, what are their main interests." His audience analysis often drew from his informal surveys before speeches, a time in which he asked about issues and personalities in order to appeal to the interests and passions of his listeners.[13] His desire to teach the truth was accompanied by his understanding that messages must be adapted to audiences to be effective.

When addressing farm workers, Chávez's habit of also holding informal dialogues *after* his more-formal talks met important needs of listeners. At many speeches he had dozens or even hundreds of exchanges with individual farm workers who asked questions ranging from the personal to the political. He took notes on questions he could not answer, directing his staff to obtain necessary information and make sure the farm workers received it. Convinced of the need to identify with listeners, he made it a point to look them directly in the eye during his one-on-one dialogues, giving them his full attention even if they only wanted to introduce their children to him or tell him about personal problems. His policy was to take questions until there were no more. Not surprisingly, after speeches to farm workers he was frequently exhausted.[14]

Because he spoke so often, Chávez usually had little time to prepare for a particular address. "My speeches are mostly off the cuff," he confessed. "Once in a while I can prepare. I have like a [standard] lecture. The speech is a lot better when I can prepare. I mean they're more thought out."[15] In the early years of the union Chávez spoke from a text only in formal testimony or for governmental agencies or other special occasions. That lack of formal preparation added to his appearance as a casual and spontaneous rhetor. "It is true that he confers with officials and intimate advisors before giving a major address," wrote Yinger, "but these sessions seem to be designed to stimulate relevant ideas rather than polish a style or produce a written manuscript."[16] Yet it would be wrong to conclude that Chávez filled his many tours and even his addresses at special occasions with impromptu and spontaneous speeches. Instead, he customarily prepared a standard address that contained his major ideas, arguments, explanations, and evidence; and he employed a standard outline for each speech on a particular tour, revising his address slightly for different audiences and occasions.[17]

By the mid-1970s Chávez typically spoke from note cards or from outlines on sheets of paper. His speeches were gaining polish through his stylistic schemes and especially through the use of anaphora, whereby consecutive sentences began with identical or almost identical words and phrases. Major addresses now were written down in detailed outlines; for some of his most important talks, Chávez worked long hours with Grossman through several revisions. On a few occasions— the first being his 1984 Commonwealth Club speech in San Francisco, which we analyze in a later chapter—he would read a complete text to his audience.[18]

By the 1970s Chávez was nationally known so the union scheduled him to reach as many people and audiences as possible. Chávez explained his role as that of attracting attention to the UFW's cause: "I'm good press, right? I'm good press and that's my forte. I mean, I know how to deal with the public, with mass media. I've learned it by instinct. I never went to school."[19] Thus he would put in long days filled with appearances, talks, and interviews for television, radio, and print media—all to spread the message of his union and cause.

To carry out his frequent canvasses of California and neighboring states in the 1970s and indeed throughout his career, Chávez needed physical stamina to match his extraordinary commitment. In 1972, for example, he made exhausting tours through California to defeat Proposition 22, the grower-backed initiative to outlaw the boycott; he toured in 1976 in support of Proposition 14, the bill to guarantee the funding for the Agricultural Labor Relations Board and access for farm organizers to workers. By 1979 the 52-year-old Chávez was still making made twelve-to-fourteen separate appearances each day; at each, Grossman recalled, Chávez appeared intellectually sharp.

These demanding days frequently would leave him physically exhausted. Fortunately for the UFW, he functioned well on little sleep, usually about four hours a night; unfortunately for Chávez, he did not like to fly so almost always traveled by the slower means of automobile—or on foot. Because he rarely owned a car, he typically was driven by supporters or colleagues. He stayed in hotels or motels only infrequently. In rural areas he typically spent nights in farm workers' homes; in cities he stayed with supporters.

One of Chávez's most physically draining tours took place in California in 1975, where he and supporters completed a thousand-mile march in fifty-eight days in order to inform workers of their newly won rights under the Agricultural Labor Relations Act (ALRA), in particular a new law guaranteeing secret-ballot elections for farm workers. Chávez himself walked from San Ysidro near the southern border of California to Sacramento and then back to farm workers' headquarters in Keene. At the end of each day's walk, he always went to a supporter's home or motel to shower, shave, and put on clean clothes. He then was driven to a rally where he delivered a speech.

Speaking from the back of a flatbed truck, at the front of an auditorium, or in whatever venue was available, he addressed audiences of hundreds and sometimes thousands in his 1975 speaking tour, usually speaking in Spanish but sometimes in Spanish and English. Often his speech would be preceded by a fifty- five-minute film, "Fighting for Our Lives," introduced briefly by Chávez and shown on a bed sheet if he was to speak from the back of a truck or on a screen if organizers had found an auditorium. His message would change little from stop to stop, always focusing on the new laws and their effects.[20]

Chávez's rhetorical qualities were appropriate for his message and goals. Yinger explained that as a farm worker, "Chávez himself [is] a quiet, almost shy man who has retained a simplicity that is rare in such a public figure." That simplicity "reaches into the everyday experience and language of the farm worker." Yinger found that Chávez's speaking aimed to involve, to relate, rather than to impress.[21]

Chávez's speeches were inevitably well organized, a quality clearly revealed in his outlines. Here he numbered and lettered his points, in some cases including a number or letter or Roman numeral before virtually every sentence and fragment in the speech so as to have an indented set of headings on his outline.[22] In other outlines, he grouped together several consecutively numbered sentences and placed other topic sentences in orderly but unnumbered form, or he numbered all headings or sections and indented most or all supporting topics.[23]

Chávez's simple and straightforward manner was immediately evident in his addresses. He ordinarily avoided flowery or dramatic openings in favor of moving directly into the substance of his speech. Such an approach, noted Yinger, suggested "simplicity, directness, and purposeful candor."[24] On many occasions Chávez began by reviewing the major ideas of his address. For example, he opened his address at the University of Santa Clara in 1972 with the following statement: "We're pleased to be here this afternoon to spend a few minutes with you; to talk to you about the farm workers; to talk to you about the problems that are everyday occurrences in California."[25] More often, however, Chávez began by briefly acknowledging special listeners, including speech organizers, officials, and distinguished guests, and thus built identification by demonstrating respect for the listeners who were most respected by that audience. For example, in a speech to a labor group he began: "Thank you very much, Brother McDermott, Brother Woodcock, Brother Mazey, Officers and Delegates to this twenty-fourth Constitutional Convention. . . ."[26] Many of his speech-note outlines started with a list of the dignitaries to acknowledge. In his various renditions of his standard speech during his speaking tours of the 1970s and 1980s, the primary way in which Chávez adapted his standard outline to his particular audience was to add a few or several listeners to recognize.[27] This practice of acknowledging distinguished guests reflects the values of graciousness and formality in the Mexican-American rhetorical tradition.[28]

Chávez's most formal introductions occurred in his carefully prepared speeches before prestigious groups such as congressional committees. Hence his first words to a Senate labor subcommittee: "My name is César E. Chávez. I am Director of the United Farm Workers Organizing Committee, AFL-CIO, a labor organization whose office is Post Office Box 130, Delano, California, 93215."[29] Even these formal openings were brief so that he could quickly move into his main ideas.

Chávez's introductions combined graciousness, directness, and informality to create an intimate bond with many listeners. His speech at California State University, Sacramento, in 1971 illustrated his approach. He began in this forthright manner: "Thank you for having me here and thank you very much for being— giving me the opportunity to be with you for a few minutes. I . . . thank all of you or at least that part of you which didn't eat grapes for about five years so that farm workers can have a contract in the grape fields."[30] Similarly, in a talk before a labor group he said: "We want to especially thank the many locals, too numerous to count, of your great Union which have been assisting us in the boycott, the CAP [Community Action Program] Council, and all of the men, women, and rank and filers and officers of your great Union, for the tremendous support we have gotten throughout the ten years of rough going for our Union."[31] Even in formal settings such as congressional hearings, however, he might open on a gracious note such as this: "It is indeed a privilege to address this body, so many of whose members have distinguished themselves over the years by their genuine concern for the welfare of farm workers."[32]

In his speeches and often in his written discourse Chávez ensured clear understanding of his message by relying on clarifying and pointing techniques such as transitions, previews, and summaries. His speech at the University of Santa Clara on October 26, 1972, is a model of how he sought clarity. Before the speech Chávez had to resolve a problem caused by a labor dispute on campus. Thus in his introductory words he carefully explained: "Before I came here I met with the

Chicano brothers and sisters and they were airing their complaints to me that they have against the administration and it reminded me so much of the complaints that farm workers have." He then expressed his hope that the university and its workers could resolve their differences. The next section of the address began with this attempt at clarification: "Now I talked with my brothers and sisters and they told me that there will be picketing out there and I told them that if they were picketing this session I would not speak here because I'm not one to cross picket lines." He then spoke of the workers' grievances, even though he admitted that he did not thoroughly understand them. He concluded with a summary to ensure that his audience understood his point: "What I am saying is to all of you who do not feel the grievance, to all of those of you sitting there who do not understand what the grievance is, take a little time and find out."[33]

Chávez's quest for instant intelligibility often took the form of specific statements telling his audience what he wanted them to understand. In an essay to farm workers and union friends in 1971, he began: "I'm writing this letter to you with two thoughts in mind: . . . ." He started his second paragraph with this clear forecast: "To summarize some of the basic problems, as I see them: . . . ." Later in the three-page letter he declared: "I began this letter by saying that I was certain we could accomplish these goals. Let me tell you why I think these goals can be accomplished."[34] At Santa Clara Chávez discussed the attitudes of agricultural employers in California and their unwillingness to deal fairly with workers, and immediately made his point of emphasis clear and personal: "And this is what I want to talk to you about." Speaking to a labor group he used the same technique: "I want to tell you that we're asking all of you to boycott grapes, to boycott lettuce, and to boycott the yellow wines." Later in that speech he reemphasized his ideas and divulged a rhetorical goal: "You see, it is very plain and clear."[35]

Chávez provided abundant transitions to help the listener better understand his ideas. In his testimony before Congress in 1969, for example, he directed listeners with these and similar statements: "I also must add here. . . ," ". . . another example . . . ," "As I said before. . . ," and "I would like to say, for instance. . . ."[36] A speech at City College of New York in May of 1968 reveals his reliance on personalized previews. Early in the speech he forecast: "But I'd like to tell you a little about the power that the growers have in the West and California in particular." He followed with a statement that divided the next section of the speech into three parts: "In my opinion there are three things that make them very powerful"—land, water, and cheap farm labor. Next he introduced an example in the following manner: "I remember a long time ago, talking with a farm worker . . . and he told me a story, and I'd like to tell it to you." He used similar personalized introductory statements before other parts of the speech, as when he stated: "You may wonder, and may ask, 'Why is it that you have to boycott to win your strike?'"; "I've been asked many times, 'What are you really, a union or a civil rights movement?' and I say, 'both'"; and "If you were to ask me which are the most important items in the drive to organize workers, it would be very easy, I would say." He introduced his ideas on union organizing by stating, "I'd like to tell you very briefly some of the things we did."[37] In his speech at the Montopolis Community Center in Austin, Texas, in February of 1971, Chávez characteristically directed his listeners from topic to topic with the following clear transitions: "And I'm asking you to do a couple of things"; "I'd like to tell you two short stories"; "I want to tell you one more thing:"; "Let me relate a Mexican anecdote about two men"; and "Friends, let me close by just saying. . . ."[38]

Chávez's conclusions ordinarily were as brief and simple as his introductions. Some of his speeches contained no discernible conclusion—the speech simply ended;[39] others concluded with a brief statement like, "So we thank you for being here. I have a few moments and if you have questions I would like to answer."[40] In speeches after 1975, Chávez's conclusions are frequently longer and sometimes written out in full. For example, his "Wrath of Grapes" boycott speech (1986) concluded with this statement:

My friends, the wrath of grapes is a plague born of selfish men that is indiscriminately and undeniable poisoning us all. Our only protection is to boycott the grapes and our only weapon is the truth. If we unite we can only triumph for ourselves, for our children and for their children. We look forward to hearing from you soon.[41]

The language of Chávez's public statements also reflected the man and his worldview. His desire to be intelligible appeared in the simplicity of his style and in his stylistic efforts to ensure the understanding of important points. "When I do public speaking," he once related, "I want to make it simple, just very simple."[42] To ensure easy comprehension of his central ideas, Chávez relied upon several rhetorical means. His most characteristic qualities were anaphora, rhetorical questions, restatement, personal language, and simple words. He also occasionally added irony and antithesis.

A passage from one of Chávez's speeches illustrates the simplicity, clarity, personal manner, and restatement of his explanations:

I have been asked to discuss some of my thoughts on community organizing. Labor organizing, as I know it, has a lot of community organizing in it. When you read of labor organizing in this country you can say there is a point where labor "is organized." But in community organizing there never is a point where you can say "it is organized."[43]

He often repeated or restated words or phrases, as with the word "victory" in the following passage:

> The greatest victory [was] not only for the membership of the union, the leadership of the union, [was] not only for the employers because I think that in signing contracts it was definitely a victory for them, but [was] also a victory for all of mankind and particularly for all of us in this country. . . .[44]

Anaphora continued to be a signature stylistic element in Chávez's discourse throughout his career. For example, Chávez made his point before one audience in this manner: "People who are hungry have no spirit, have no strength to fight. People who are hungry don't care who makes decisions for them, so long as their families don't starve. . . . People who are hungry have to eat first." In sentences displaying his penchant for personal, clear language and well-crafted anaphora containing antithetical balance, Chávez summarized his request to the Catholic Church for help:

> We don't ask for more cathedrals. We don't ask for bigger churches or fine gifts. We ask for its presence with us, beside us, as Christ among us. We ask the church to sacrifice with the people for social change, for justice, and for the love of brother. We don't ask for words. We ask for deeds. We don't ask for paternalism. We ask for servanthood.[45]

In his outline for a speech commemorating the seventy-fifth anniversary of a massacre of striking anthracite coal miners in Lattimore, Pennsylvania, Chávez compared his farm workers to those miners by lining up seven consecutive sentence fragments:

—they too are immigrants
—they too—have strange sounding names
—they too—speak a foreign language
—they too—trying to build a union
—they too—face hostile sheriffs and recalcitrant employers
—they too—had powerful employers
—they too—are nonviolent, as these men were

• • •

His conclusion—again in anaphoric form—expressed his desire for strength and unity in the ranks of labor:

—Let there be only one voice
—Let there be only one Lattimore
—Let there be peace
—Let there be justice
—Let there be love
AMEN[46]

Chávez's use of anaphora added impact to his ideas and description. For example, he told a gathering of the United Auto Workers:

> We know that the workers are committed to the struggle. We know that they're willing to sacrifice. We know that they have determination. But we also know that this determination comes because of unions like the UAW who are still with us for so many years.[47]

In a variation of anaphora in a speech in 1970, Chávez began two consecutive sentences with "We would hope," followed by two consecutive sentences beginning with "You know"; later, five sentences began with "We know," followed by consecutive sentences beginning respectively, "In 1966 when we started," "When we signed," "I'm sure," "And I'm sure," "I'm sure," and "We know."[48]

Another of Chávez's stylistic signatures was the rhetorical question. His penchant for anaphora sometimes took the form of such questions. When discussing how the UFW had lost contracts to the Teamsters after UFW contracts had expired in 1973, Chávez posed the following series of questions:

> How could it be when there were no elections held? How could it be when the workers didn't know what had happened? How could it be when we were in negotiations with the growers? How could it be when we had been struggling with those workers for about ten years?

He then continued, "We were an incumbent union; we had a contract with the growers. That's the way the contracts were taken away from us."[49] His comments underscored his main idea and strongly emphasized the unfairness of the actions by the Teamsters and growers.

Chávez's most notable, and perhaps his most conscious, use of irony occurred when he described how farm workers worked so hard and suffered so much in difficult conditions to succeed in producing the food for the world, yet they could not afford to feed themselves and their families. In several speech outlines he wrote the word "irony" beside his topic heading of the farm workers' inability to feed themselves.[50] Before a Denver audience in 1967, he had this heading: "Irony of farmwk. in America—He toils fields—plants—cultivates—picks—packs—harvests—to make America the best fed nation in the world. Yet when [his] children gather around his table it['s] empty."[51]

Chávez's syntactical strategies included varying the lengths of sentences. In some addresses, lengthy sentences preceded brief ones in an attempt to punctuate his points. For example, he said:

> Community organization is very difficult. You can't put it in the freezer for a couple of years and they thaw it out and you're in business again. Or even a month.[52]

While simple, clear, and at times emphatic language communicated his ideas directly, Chávez typically relied on his abundant evidence—examples, statistics, and anecdotes—to substantiate his claims with concrete facts and personal accounts. Audiences would expect such heavy use of evidence from a rhetor with Chávez's faith in informing the public. Richard A. Garcia explained that "Chávez liked to give facts" so that each member of the audience "could read the truths of oppression from the litany."[53]

A speech Chávez gave on the grape boycott is representative of his litany of information. Specific data explained the economics of the strike: "When we started the strike . . . the wages were between $1.00 and $1.05 an hour, and in some cases, 90¢ an hour, 95¢ an hour, very few cases $1.10." He then outlined what the union had accomplished: "Our minimum wage in our contract here is $1.75 an hour and they go for what we call common labor, $1.75 minimum in those cases where they pay a minimum hourly plus an incentive rate. They average around $2.15 an hour." Furthermore, he continued, the workers now had paid holidays, a health and welfare fund, a grievance procedure, and seniority rights. After presenting his facts, he offered his analysis of what the information meant to his listeners: "According to people who are very well-versed in labor matters, most of the old timers in labor tell us that what we got and what we're getting in our first contracts took their unions twenty or thirty years to accomplish."[54]

The labor leader lined up an array of specific data to illustrate the problems workers faced in the fields. When discussing the harmfulness of pesticides, for example, Chávez turned loose legions of statistics. A study by Dr. Lee Mizhari of the Salud Clinic in Tulare County, California, tested 170 children from sixty farm worker families and discovered "pesticide levels which can only be described as epidemic." Chávez cited precise findings: "On 29 children tests, 32 of the reported values have fallen outside normal limits. Dr. Mizhari has informed me that as a practicing physician he would be greatly worried if he found ten percent of reportedly normal children outside normal limits. In this case he is frightened."[55] Chávez complemented Mizhari's figures by reciting a raft of facts from a study by the California state director of public health, Dr. Thomas Milby, on incidents of pesticide poisonings:

> . . . of the 774 workers who filled out the questionnaires . . . 469 of the workers had worked in the grapes and 295 had not worked in the grapes. Among the 774 farm workers, the following symptoms caused by pesticide poisonings were reported: Eye irritation, 548; nausea or vomiting, 141; unusual fatigue, 145; unusual perspiration, 159; headaches, 309; dizziness, 115; skin irritation, 249; difficulty in breathing, 188; pain in the fingernails (some workers lost their fingernails), 52; nervousness and/or insomnia, 122; itching in their ears, 12; nose bleeds, 25; burning and sore throats, 51; swollen hands and feet, 7; loss of hair, 4; diarrhea, 2.[56]

Chávez usually made his statistics personal through specific examples, such as examples of people harmed by pesticides. In the address above he introduced his examples by stating that workers "are becoming very concerned, very aware of the poisoning, and they are now referring to it in Spanish as *la muerte andando,* walking death." He followed with the case of Gregorio Sisneros, who was directed by his employer to use twice as much pesticide in a water solution as the manufacturer had recommended. After spraying the solution, Sisneros became ill, was taken to a doctor, and "confined to his home and unable to work for some days. Since then he has been sensitive to chemical spray and has become ill several times." Chávez also told of Beatrice Roman, who "developed trouble breathing, sore throat, difficulty in speaking, and stomach pain" after working in recently sprayed fields; Abelardo Hernandez who ate some grapes from the vines where he was worked and then began "to vomit and bleed from the nose"; and María Serna who developed, "as a result of the spray residue on the vines, skin rash, eye irritation, and hands swollen so badly that her ring had to be cut off." After giving these and other examples, Chávez restated his claim that such problems could only be solved through a union contract.[57] Often on his speech outlines Chávez wrote "reminds me of a story" or "tell a story" to prompt him to add a human element to his talk.[58] The last point on his Lattimore outline was prompted by the word "story"; and at a rally in Stockton in 1971, he wrote on his outline: "Exploitations best told in story of Filipinos."[59]

In Chávez's call to boycott Gallo wine, he combined examples with humor:

> There are two ways to find out if you're drinking Gallo wine. If you don't see the name Gallo on the label you will read on the small print the words Modesto, California. And if it says Modesto, California, that's Gallo wine. And another way to find out if you're drinking Gallo wine is to drink the stuff and if you get sick, that's also Gallo wine.[60]

He added: "Among the labels that are made by Gallo is the one called Ripple and there's a button out and it's very popular these days. The buttons say simply, 'Nixon Drinks Ripple.'"[61] Chávez frequently repeated two stories that demonstrated the effect of the boycott. One featured a family who heard him speak in New York City. On the morning of the speech the father told his six-year-old son that they were going to church to hear Chávez: "The father asked the little boy if he knew who I was," Chávez narrated, and "the little boy said sure he knew who he was, 'everybody knows—he invented grapes.'" The other story also related the experiences of a family who strongly supported the grape boycott and often discussed the farm workers' struggle. One day the mother and her four-year-old daughter were shopping when "they came upon a huge display of grapes in the store and as she was going by [the display] the little girl stopped her and was pulling her dress and she asked 'Mommy, when can I have some boycotts.'"[62]

Although he used statistics and examples more frequently than other forms of evidence, Chávez occasionally quoted authorities to back up his claims, as demonstrated in his citations of medical doctors above. In testimony before a Senate labor subcommittee in 1969 he quoted these words from George Meany, president of the AFL-CIO: "The United Farm Workers Organizing Committee already has awakened the nation's conscience. Even more important, it has demonstrated to farm workers across the country that they can obtain first class membership through self-organization."[63] In his speech at an anti-Vietnam war rally at Exposition Park in Los Angeles in 1971, Chávez began by quoting seven sentences from the *Los Angeles Times* reporting how a mother reacted to her son's death in Vietnam by throwing his medals for heroism against a statue.[64] In many of his early speeches he cited the Environmental Protection Agency, the *New York Times,* and politicians such as Robert Kennedy and Gandhi to support his points.

Chávez frequently included dichos or cuentos in his public address to make his point concrete and in many instances more emotionally moving. Listeners and readers could thus identify with his stories of people like them; and Chávez could embody his substantive theme that God's plan would ensure that Mexican Americans who had the will could share in the success, and even be a part of the leadership, of their protest movement. Anecdotes and aphorisms have been a common communication form in Mexican-American culture; and Chávez often found rhetorical proofs in Mexican history.[65] His use of a form popular to Mexican Americans helped to demonstrate for audiences that a Mexican-American farm laborer like Chávez could retain his culture and still become a celebrated national leader—truly a miraculous feat in the eyes of some listeners who saw a conspiracy of seemingly unbeatable forces aligned against farm workers. Chávez himself consequently represented the evidence that God did indeed plan to lift to victory those Mexican Americans who spoke for justice.

Chávez learned many dichos from his mother. "When I was young I didn't realize the wisdom in her words," he acknowledged, "but it has been proved to me many times since. Today I appreciate the advice, and I use quite a few of the dichos, especially in Spanish." For example, he shared her consejos on not fighting: "No, it's best to turn the other cheek. God gave you senses like eyes and mind and tongue, and you can get out of anything." His other sayings on the same subject included, "It takes two to fight, and one can't do it alone"; and "It's better to say that he ran from here than to say he died here."[66]

Chávez's standard stories inevitably contained a message he believed important enough to repeat in many texts. One example is the fable he related on a number of occasions of a farm worker, whom he called Juan García, who died and was denied passage through heaven's pearly gates because he had no horse. When he left to find a horse he encountered his former employer who also lacked a horse and therefore could not enter heaven either. The employer proposed that both could enter if the grower rode on Juan's back. Upon reaching the pearly gates, the grower was instructed to tie his "horse"—the farm worker on his hands and knees—outside and enter. Chávez then laid bare the point of the story for his listeners: "And this is what happened to us. . . . We've been kept out of society too long." Farm workers could only enter society through collectively bargaining in order to gain their rights.[67]

Chávez added to his solidarity with listeners through generalized epithets and polarization. Committed to nonviolence and the allied idea that nonviolence entailed love of one's enemy, he characteristically avoided name-calling and invective against individuals but instead attacked the corporations, large institutions, or governmental agencies that blocked or fought farm workers. He attempted to polarize audiences by structuring the contest between the farm workers and the corporations as a fight between the "rich and poor," contending that his adversaries had many powerful friends in the federal and state governments, in public relations firms, banks, the legal system, and other groups. In sharp contrast, the farm workers had abundant moral resources: "We are poor. Our allies are few. But we have something the rich do not own. We have our own bodies and spirits and the justice of our cause as our weapons."[68] Chávez had a clear purpose for using polarization. In his view, rhetors for his revolutionary reform must construct a "solid wall of opposition in order to have an impact. . . . If your opposition is unclear and undefined, it's like making an impact on a bowl of mush."[69]

Another way Chávez identified with workers and others was through his use of personal pronouns. He often employed "I" to refer to himself and "we" or "us" when referring to the union or to workers, thereby personalizing his message, his relationship to his audience, and his persona. The following passage demonstrates this point:

> And I am reminded when I say this that there are many little stories, but I want to share a couple of them with you because it seems to me these two, that I want to share with you, most clearly indicate the depth of the support that we had from the American people and from other people around the world for a grape boycott and strike.[70]

In the quote he began by talking about himself, using "I," but switched to "we" when talking of support for the union. The "I" emphasized his personal approach to his audience, the "we" his attempt to build the family so important to him and to emphasize that farm workers' triumphs required the efforts of his followers and himself together. One of the most striking cases of his use of personal pronouns occurred in a speech to striking furniture workers in Austin, Texas, where he said the words "I" or "we" 108 times.[71]

The consistency in technique and content in Chávez's speeches confirm that his conception of the place and power of public address in the service of a just reform did not change throughout his career. As Chávez called for followers in a moral crusade that would require leader/rhetors to educate audiences about the facts and arguments of his cause, and as he promised that God's plan would guarantee success if rhetors effectively presented the moral case to the public, he embodied the very qualities needed to enact his message. He thus displayed the rhetorical techniques necessary to educate audiences to a divinely sanctioned message of truth: to increase the intelligibility of his themes, arguments, and explanations, his addresses were short, to the point, painstakingly clear in organization, worded in simple prose, and filled with clear previews, reviews, and transitions. Moreover, his speeches were calmly delivered by a modest man and thus focused the audience's attention on the substantive message rather than on the speaker; put forward claims backed by the ample evidence needed to inform listeners; and were optimistic and ubiquitous, again showing a faith in their ultimate success and a commitment to inform audiences. Too, he spoke and wrote ubiquitously, engaging in exhaustive tours that further melded the man with his theme of the need to communicate in order to advance the will of God and the cause of farm laborers. He thereby projected the persona of one who trusted and was dedicated to God's plan to educate the public.

Chávez further identified himself with his own substantive themes as well as with his audiences by living the life of an activist farm worker/leader who was motivated by noble rather than material concerns; by using personal language, repetitive and parallel form, and rhetorical questions that engaged audiences and linked him to them and to his message; and by skillfully adapting to the needs and conventions of Mexican-American audiences, talking in their customary forms, and embodying his pledge that they could become successful leader/rhetors. His high regard for his farm-worker audiences surfaced in a comment he made to Grossman: Out of respect for his listeners, he said, he would shower, shave, and be sure to wear clean clothes before going to address his audiences; and while speaking he sought never to read a text or fix his eyes on his outline but instead would look directly at his listeners and give them his full attention. The reason for his respect for his audiences was perhaps best expressed by Chávez's answer to the question of why farm workers had so much affection for him: "The feeling is mutual."[72]

By communicating a second persona that followed naturally from his substantive message and matched much in his first persona, Chávez magnified his invitation to his audiences to enact his agenda as they identified with him. Whether addressing farm workers or college students, Anglo union members or the general public, Chávez invested his audiences with qualities and attitudes that would allow them respectively to become UFW organizers, volunteers in his movement, or less-active but nevertheless vocal supporters of his cause.

Chávez fulfilled the requirements of our model of reconstitutive discourse extraordinarily well, reciprocally merging its three major elements and therefore multiplying and deepening the lines of identification with his audiences. From oft-overlooked means of identification such as his text's organizational patterns (which linked his persona to his substantive message and second persona), to his more noticeable incarnation of his message and second persona through his own life of perseverance, hard work, and other qualities, Chávez merged himself, his message, and his depiction of his audience to a startlingly high degree. His rhetorical reformulation of personae and substantive message would be tested by daunting challenges; we examine them in our next two chapters.

Chapter 7

Triumphs and Defeats in the Ongoing Quest

"To Enable Common People to Do Uncommon Things"

T he years from 1976 until 1983 were a time of transition and change in the structure and workings in the United Farm Workers, a gyrating journey filled with daunting challenges, heady successes, and major failures. In these unsettled times, with the national mood becoming more conservative and less idealistic, the UFW would undergo awkward internal changes even as it faced outside exigencies that threatened everything it had accomplished. Some of César Chávez's closest coworkers would become openly critical of his leadership style and join an internal revolt. Meanwhile, opportunities accompanied difficulties. Toward the end of the period new UFW resources offered Chávez possibilities for expanding his audience. As a leader and rhetor, how would Chávez respond to these challenges to his rhetorical means and message? Would he modify his rhetorical profile? If so, in what way and why that way? To answer questions such as these, this chapter and chapter 8 briefly trace the history of Chávez and the UFW to the end of Chávez's life and carefully examine a sizable sample of his continuing rhetorical crusade.

In 1975 the first elections held under provisions of the California Agricultural Labor Relations Act (ALRA) yielded an even split between the UFW and Teamsters. The UFW contested many of the Teamsters' gains on the grounds of fraud; sociologists Patrick H. Mooney and Theo J. Majka argue that the union had many early successes because California Governor Jerry Brown had appointed a pro-UFW Agricultural Labor Relations Board (ALRB) to oversee implementation of the legislation.[1] Opponents of the ALRA unleashed a "textbook example" of the use of power to undercut troublesome labor laws and bust unions, engaging in illegal activities such as the burglarizing of union offices and the use of spies in the UFW as well as bringing lawsuits and legislative action to weaken the law and deny funds for the ALRB to function.[2] The UFW counterattacked by getting Proposition 14 on the ballot in 1976, a bill proposing that the ALRB be adequately funded and that union organizers be given free access to workers on farms. Though the bill was supported by Governor Brown and President Jimmy Carter, anti-union opposition united to defeat the proposition.[3]

Although the union failed with Proposition 14, it acquired both members and contracts in the following years. Because of the UFW's successes under the ALRA, in 1977 the Teamsters signed a "pact that effectively ceded jurisdiction over agricultural labor to the UFW."[4] The elimination of the Teamsters problem removed one of the UFW's largest obstacles to success. By 1978 Chávez's union had over 100,000 members, its largest total ever, and Chávez called an end to the general grape and lettuce boycotts. Only selected labels, he announced, would be boycotted in the future.

Ironically, the UFW's external successes came at a time of growing internal problems. Amid ongoing questions about Chávez's abilities as a manager, growers claimed that they could not work with such an unprofessional union. The UFW's staff changed so often that few mastered their jobs. "A Union today," wrote the *Nation* in 1977, "must have accountants, experts in management, lawyers, personnel officers, researchers. Inevitably, once a union is securely established, many of its important activities take place in courtrooms, in meeting rooms, at desks in offices."[5] Lacking the necessary complement of experts, the UFW could not consolidate its gains.

In 1977 Chávez moved the union headquarters from Delano to La Paz, a former tuberculosis sanitarium located near Keene, California, in the Tehachapi Mountains. Critics charged that the move separated the leadership from the members. The *New Republic* said: "In their move to the hills Chávez and the UFW vanguard removed themselves from the concerns of the rank and file, and developed the besieged mentality typical of distant, distrustful leaders."[6]

A host of criticisms of Chávez gave credence to the *New Republic*'s unflattering depiction. *Newsweek* reported that Chávez was accused of acting unprofessionally by requiring staffers to work "long hours six days a week for subsistence wages," directing coworkers "to try vegetarianism and meditation," advocating "yoga and holistic medicine," participating in "weird rites of faith-healing which included using candles, incense, and music to cure everything from headaches to ulcers," and instituting a variation of the Synanon encounter program with sessions "peppered with vile language and sexual accusations." Opponents charged that his strange and sometimes bizarre actions led to a discontented work force and demoralizing work environment.[7]

Another set of criticisms leveled at Chávez maintained that he centralized power in himself. Associating the UFW's "administrative chaos" with Chávez's "personality and social philosophy," the *Nation* charged that the "magnetic, autocratic" Chávez had exerted "dynamic and imaginative leadership" that brought him "nearly absolute control of the union. . . . Authority is seldom delegated; members of the executive committee are not free to act without his permission." Even the volunteers who did most of the UFW's work, the argument proceeded, were controlled completely by Chávez.[8] Chávez allegedly had transformed the union's "top leadership into a family cartel"—and indeed the UFW's national executive board included his brother, sister-in-law, and son-in-law. When a group of dissidents challenged the executive board, Chávez removed them from their offices. They then successfully sued to have their positions returned.[9] One damaging consequence of the internecine struggles, according to Mooney and Majka, was that "much energy was turned inward in what proved to be a spectacularly unsuccessful attempt to resolve internal differences. Energies that could have focused on winning elections and contracts were instead directed to a bitter internal struggle over power and loyalty."[10]

Disgusted, demoralized, or defeated as a result of internal politics and policies, many veteran leaders left the UFW between 1978 and 1981. Among those were Gilbert Padilla, one of the union's founders and its secretary-treasurer; Jerry Cohen, chief legal counsel and director of the legal office for seventeen years; Marshall Ganz, the union's chief organizer; Jessica Govea, director of the union's health service program; and Eliseo Medina, former member of the union's executive board.[11] When most of Cohen's coworkers also resigned from the union, the UFW found itself without an experienced legal staff to negotiate contracts. Mooney and Majka note that the effects were soon evident: "Several former ALRB officials . . . agreed that the demise of the well-coordinated legal staff in the union was a decisive factor in slowing down the momentum of farm unionization under the aegis of the ALRB."[12]

The move to La Paz brought improvements in addition to problems. Expanding its communication capabilities, the UFW purchased computerized mailing equipment that could send out a million appeals a week to supporters and union members.[13] Chávez acquired assistance from public-relations experts to help him to refine his message as well as to communicate it to the public.[14] He also broadened his appeal and influence by starting a "Chicano lobby" to help Democratic candidates and improve the lives of urban Hispanics, by supporting his son Fernando's election to the presidency of the Mexican-American Political Association (MAPA), and by establishing a network of Spanish-language radio stations to beam his message to more listeners. Such actions furthered his plan, according to the *New York Times,* "to consolidate the union's role as the most influential Hispanic political force in the state."[15]

In April of 1976 Chávez told readers of the *Los Angeles Times* that current defeats had not eroded his faith in his rhetorical means or millennial ends. In a verbal trek across recent history he reported that after the UFW had won 204 of 327 elections and represented 68 percent of the workers involved, agribusiness had counterattacked by cutting ALRB funding. He had then lost faith in the legislature, he admitted, and had gone directly to California voters through the Farm Workers Initiative (Proposition 14) that would strengthen the ALRB. At this point in the article, he expressed his customary confidence in what he acknowledged would be a difficult campaign: "But the growers have money, and we have time. We will match their millions with our bodies, our spirits and the goodwill of the people of this state."[16]

The dimensions of Chávez's worldview surfaced in his April, 1978, essay honoring the memory of Martin Luther King Jr. "This observance of Dr. King's death," he began, "gives us the best possible opportunity to recall the principles with which our struggle has grown and matured."[17] Chávez proceeded to lay out many of his animating convictions: God gave human life; "nonviolence is more powerful than violence" and "supports you if you have a just and moral cause"; audiences "faced with a direct appeal from the poor struggling nonviolently against great odds . . . will react positively"; and "the American people and people everywhere still yearn for justice. It is to that yearning that we appeal." Mirroring the growing frustration of many civil-rights activists in an increasingly conservative and passive period, however, Chávez confessed that the never-ending injustice suffered by farm workers left them all with "feelings of frustration, impatience, and anger," and he speculated uncharacteristically that if nonviolent tactics failed, "our only alternative is to turn to violence." But he rejected the use of violence because "one of two things will happen: either the violence will be escalated and there will be many injuries and perhaps deaths on both sides, or there will be total demoralization of the workers." Further addressing the effects of recent defeats, he added that "although we would like to see victory come soon, we are willing to wait. In this sense time is our ally. We learned many years ago that the rich may have the money, but the poor have time."[18]

Among Chávez's longest addresses was his opening-day report to the delegates of the Fourth Constitutional Convention of the UFW, on September 1, 1979. His twenty-four page, single-spaced text opened with typical organizational clarity and simple language: "Our report is divided into two parts: How far we have come and where we are going. We will deal first with the past." Well-organized, replete with evidence, and easy to understand, the speech's first section contained twenty-five headings and twenty-two underlined sub-headings to guide auditors through a broad and deep history illustrated and documented by many concrete and in some cases detailed examples and stories of defeats, difficulties, and triumphs, including an extended discussion of ALRB General Counsel Walter Kintz, who "demoralized farm workers and encouraged grower lawlessness," and of his successor "San Jose lawyer Harry Delizonna," who "was either unable or unwilling to enforce the statute." The early 1976 performance of the ALRB emerged from a forest of statistics: "By early 1976, out of 327 secret-ballot elections decided, the UFW had won 204 and represented 68.8 percent of the workers involved. In the Imperial Valley, the scene of the most recent balloting, the union took 16 out of 22 decided elections by winning 4,349 of the 5,004 total votes." Chávez included short as well as lengthy explanations of issues the UFW had faced and of related topics ranging from the support given by President Jimmy Carter and AFL-CIO leader George Meany to the union's opposition to the bracero program; and he marshaled a mass of statistics, descriptions of studies, and other evidence of UFW accomplishments and difficulties, for example pointing out that "Despite Delizonna's incompetence and anti-farm-worker bias, UFW election victories have mounted steadily since the board was reactivated. Our union has won clear victories in at least 39 out of 54 elections held since December, 1976, and represents well over 79 percent of the farm workers at ranches where balloting took place."[19]

Section II of the speech, "The Future," was divided into sixteen headings and argued that leaders must "infuse the membership with excitement, hope, mission and promise, and define exactly the goals, objectives, programs, policies and procedures that will enable them to completely assume the burden of leadership and administration." Chávez delineated beneficial results of such a leadership/management pattern, strongly underscoring the need for strong leadership and briefly summarizing a set of difficult union issues ranging from the use of volunteers to the effects of U.S. immigration policies.[20]

In his address Chávez implicitly and explicitly projected a second persona that mirrored his first persona. Those who identified with him would commit themselves to create clear messages backed by plentiful facts, assured of eventual success by calling attention to ideas and information rather than to themselves as speakers or writers. In the middle of the report Chávez defined his followers more directly by relating that "our movement would have perished long ago had it not been for the selfless support from so many good people from across America and around the world." "The assistance and support we have enjoyed from the labor movement, the church, minority and student groups, and many others," he added in a delineation of his core audience, "has been a real source of inspiration to all of us." Of particular help were "young people throughout the nation who have worked, sacrificed, and suffered with us on the picket lines and in the jails. Men and women with high ideals and disregard for personal wealth and ambition," and volunteers who have "worked side by side with the farm workers." In contrast were some volunteers who "have come with their own political and social values." These potential troublemakers, unlike "those men and women of good heart and clean minds who have stood with the farm workers through good times and bad," would need to bow to the views of the workers or would not be welcome.[21]

Again emphasizing the continued importance to his cause of effective communication, Chávez claimed that "as news of the farm workers' struggle has spread, interest and support for the movement has developed in many nations." He specifically noted meetings with a list of influential people from Mexico, including President José López-Portillo, and visits with "some 100 labor leaders" in the Philippines.[22]

Chávez's informative report illustrates his commitment to teaching through a careful and clear presentation of facts, arguments, and explanations in support of his cause. He concluded by using anaphora to underscore the solidarity, broader mission, and significance of the UFW:

> The challenge before us is plain: to carry on the struggle to build one national union that will unite all farm workers regardless of race, sex, creed, or nationality; one union that will bring farm workers the blessings of union democracy and collective bargaining; one union to liberate farm workers from the pain and suffering that enslaves so many of our people in this rich country; one union that will form a powerful force for dignity and justice for all poor people in American and around the world.
>
> One brotherhood; one people; one union.
>
> Viva la Causa![23]

Although Chávez's published essays and conference reports reached many readers and listeners, he devoted most of his rhetorical energy to his continuing campaign of public speaking. His notes and outline of a speech given to the Department of Health, Education, and Welfare (HEW) in Washington, D.C., on March 21, 1978, reveal that he relied on his customary rhetorical means and standard message before this U.S. governmental audience.[24] Twenty-one large note cards contained a detailed outline typed in capital letters that used five levels of subordinating symbols: Roman numerals, capital letters, numbers, small letters, and numbers preceded by a parenthesis. Chávez completed his outline by adding many handwritten comments. His explicit purpose was to show that lessons learned by his union could be applied to the broader task of helping the people whom HEW served.

Chávez opened by announcing his goal: To "use [the] occasion to address [an] issue close to [his] heart: Being of service to people."[25] At the very beginning of his "experiment" in Delano, he recounted for his listeners, he had committed himself to "key principles": workers themselves would have to organize, form the union, and pay for it; they then must lose their fear; outside money would not bring success; and because he and his fellow-organizers would steadfastly believe that workers could be organized, the responsibility for and any failures related to building the union must be assumed by its organizers. He claimed to draw from ten years of prior research on organizing, for he related that as a Community Service Organization (CSO) organizer during these years he had "talked to many people; read everything" and learned that when outside sources took over nascent organizing movements, the movements failed. He divided the listeners he approached in his early Delano campaign into three categories: "95 percent kind, smiled; 5 percent asked questions; 1 percent really interested." He said that he'd concentrated on the 1 percent, those most easily converted into effective organizers.[26]

After identifying potential organizers, Chávez presented his method to reconstitute them from fearful workers into dedicated organizers. Projecting his own persona, he told how he endured "constant ridicule, no income, [and] no paycheck," yet won the "hearts" of people as he formed the "nucleus of leadership." He said that the experience had reformulated his character, that he had "felt free" by learning to discipline himself to live without income. He had found he could not be "free or happy" until he devoted all of his time to changing the outrageous conditions facing farm workers. By following the principle of requiring supporters to "participate" by giving their "time and money," a principle Chávez illustrated through stories of farm workers—such as the man in McFarland who gave $3.50 for "a dream" when he only had $5 to buy groceries for his family— Chávez "ingrained in them [a] spirit that kept us going for five years." This spirit would be essential to sustain reconstituted followers who would soon leave their homes to travel across the country organizing the boycott, all for only $5 per week and room and board in supporters' homes. "With this spirit," Chávez summed up, "hundreds of farm workers and supporters" made the boycott a "potent weapon for nonviolent change." Additional examples of such sacrifice and service showed that these qualities alone, rather than money, led to power. It was "by their example," he instructed, that they "inspired hundreds of thousands to join [the] struggle."[27]

Chávez's extended analysis of the advantages of nonviolence—a pertinent topic during a period when many supporters were tempted by frustrations, defeats, and radical leaders to turn to violent means—would be repeated many times. Chávez reasoned that nonviolence was moral, for human life is a "very special possession given to man by God" that no one had the "right to take for any cause." Violence, although often more effective than nonviolence in temporarily achieving just ends, leads to one of two results: It "escalates," causing many "injuries and deaths," or it demoralizes workers. In contrast, nonviolence has positive effects: Proponents can seize the offensive rather than merely react; masses of participants can be part of the effort; and if opponents use violence to counter nonviolent means, "millions who have consciences and [would] rather see [a] nonviolent solution" will give support. Moreover, violence brings victories with "strings attached": proponents either suffer from feelings of guilt or must take in "extremists" who will seize control of the struggle; and victories are short in term, with more violent actions sure to follow. History demonstrates these principles about violence, he professed, pointing to workers who died in violent revolutions, people who lost their land in return for nothing, and others who had heard the "call to arms with many promises" but later faced the "most vicious type of oppression." To practice nonviolence successfully, however, required a "clear understanding of what we are doing": Participants must realize that "poverty" and "exploitation" are "not more important than one life"; that adherents must be "nonviolent by nature"; and that violence appears because of frustration from confronting "seemingly overwhelming odds." Beneath Chávez's appeal for nonviolence was his long-held assumption about his rhetoric and its audience: "people will respond to [the] poor struggling nonviolently against great odds," for the "American people still year[n] for justice."[28]

In a clearly stated transition employing rhetorical questions, Chávez converted his story of the farm workers' history into a blueprint for HEW. His note cards read:

III. Does our story have anything to say in terms of how we serve people in [the] U. S.?

A. Does it mean anything to people outside [the] movement who are also concerned about [the] poor and homeless?; Can it relate to broader problems of society—problems you in HEW face in everyday lives?

I. We think it does.[29]

• • •

Chávez quickly pointed out the application of his principles: By "example, by sacrifice, by love, but not by money," HEW could meet the needs of those it served. He repeated his point, "But you can't do it with money," at the end of three subsequent sentences to magnify the need for HEW to sacrifice, serve, and meet its obligations to help the poor in ghettos, the addicts of alcohol and narcotics, those who needed health care, as well as the "Chicano, Filipino, Puerto Rican, and other migrants [who] travel the southwest." To carry out the HEW charge, workers must possess a "tremendous sense of mission." He might have added that reconstitutive discourse and personal examples were essential elements in instilling that sense of mission.

Chávez's address to an audience at a union-organizing convention in Pharr, Texas, on February 25, 1979, demonstrates both his traditional and newly added rhetorical qualities and substantive arguments.[30] Again Chávez ensured a clear message, using clear, easy-to-understand language. The following familiar techniques guided listeners through his many arguments and explanations: rhetorical questions, such as "What are the Imperial Valley farm workers fighting for?"; transitions, such as "Our farm workers struggle can be divided into four distinct phases: . . . ; and clarifying summaries, such as, "This is what we have won in California; and this is what we want in Texas." And once again he rested his case on a mass of facts, especially statistics and examples. He illustrated paltry wage increases by noting: "Since 1970 farm-worker wages in the California-Arizona vegetable industry have gone up from $2 per hour to $3.70 per hour in the contracts which have expired. An 85 percent increase. But consumer prices went up 71 percent in the same period. And the farm workers are earning only 13 cents more per hour in real wages, adjusted for inflation, than they earned eight or nine years ago." He immediately added that "In 1970 lettuce workers earned 40¢ per box piece rate. Today, under the old contracts which have expired, they continue to earn 57¢ per box. But in real earnings, they are making 6.4¢ less per box today than they earned eight or nine years ago." For examples of martyred UFW supporters, he referred to Rufino Contreras, whose life and tragic death he discussed in several paragraphs; Nan Freeman, "an 18-year-old supporter . . . crushed to death on a UFW picket line in Florida"; and Juan de la Cruz and Nagi Daifallah, "brutally murdered during massive grape strikes." His lucid explanations were broken into easily understood parts, as when he delineated the committees that would be necessary for a union to form in Texas or listed the nine objectives of his union.[31]

Several new themes and arguments of this period appeared in his talk in Pharr. One of his new topics—a discussion of farm-worker suffering that would focus on the value of human labor as opposed to the value of capital producing "the fruit of the land"—he introduced with rhetorical questions: "We wonder what is the worth of a man? What is the worth of a farm worker?" Adapting to the prevailing dearth of idealism, a desertion by many of his top-level cohorts, criticisms of his autocratic control, and other new challenges facing his union, he articulated what was becoming a second new theme in his discourse: "The union will be strong and united because its members and worker leadership is strong and united. We must infuse the workers with excitement, hope, mission and promise, and define exactly the goals, objectives, programs, policies, and procedures that will enable them to eventually assume the burdens of leadership and administration."[32]

This speech developed a second persona that fit Texans being exhorted to take the dangerous path to become effective unionists. Chávez defined his audience in clear terms: While California farm workers had reached the third of four "stages" of union development, a stage where opponents are worried and offer "stern opposition," Texas farm workers were in the first stage, where union efforts begin, ridicule comes from all sides, and many workers are afraid and believe success is impossible. Thus Chávez sought to offer hope, motivation, persuasion, and in some cases reconstitution to listeners fearful for their welfare and doubtful about success.[33]

Early in his text, when discussing the death of Contreras and the worth of a man, Chávez painted a vivid picture of those who ""torture their bodies, sacrifice their youth, and numb their spirits" to produce the wealth that feeds "all of America and much of the world." These people, the working "men, women, and children who are the flesh and blood of this production, often do not have enough to feed themselves." Such sacrifice was well known to his listeners. For them, he taught, "true wealth is not measured in money or status or power. It is measured in the legacy that we leave behind for those we love and those we inspire." Thus "Rufino still lives because those of us who mourn him have rededicated ourselves to the ideals for which he gave his life: . . . to build a union that will, someday, bring justice to all farm workers." It is a "mission to finish the work . . . , knowing that true justice for ourselves and our opponents is only possible before God, who is the final judge." As incentive for his potential recruits, Chávez itemized a long list of improvements his union had brought to workers in California; to make their task easier, he delineated the steps necessary to create an effective union; but he clearly prepared them to withstand material difficulties, mitigated only by spiritual ideals and a close bond with those who preceded and would follow them.[34]

A new theme of the value of modern management techniques appeared in his address at a dinner meeting of the United Church Board for Homeland Ministries, United Church of Christ, in October of 1981.[35] Here he candidly reported on the difficulties he was facing in the early 1980s. He began with a gracious expression of appreciation, praising the church as his foremost supporter among churches "year after year" including recent years when many of the liberal churches "have gone on to the next cause." After reprising numerous specific events in the church's work for the UFW, he previewed his upcoming discussion: "Let me now take a few minutes to bring you up-to-date on our movement." In an extended analogy, he compared his movement to a developing nation: The UFW was shifting its focus from a "highly public struggle" to managing, planning, and administrating; was "besieged with problems and adversaries"; and needed "professionals from the outside like doctors, computer programmers, and management experts." Chávez covered in detail a new organizing structure in the union, promised to keep the original ideals and emphasis on "organizing poor people who are mostly black and brown," and professed to be motivated by "our faith in God and our choice to follow His son." Chávez concluded by admitting that resisting violent means was growing ever more difficult, that handling internal strife was not easy, and that he wished to continue his close cooperation with the United Church of Christ even though many church members might be willing now to "let this particular relationship slide."[36]

A text containing fragmented as well as complete sentences encapsulated Chávez's short address in 1982 to a graduating negotiations class for UFW members. He focused on the need to learn from the failures of the past, to see the future in optimistic terms, and to shift emphasis from individual to team leadership. His themes revealed his assessment of various setbacks in recent years, his increasing study of management theory, his recognition of the criticisms of his overly controlling style of leadership, and his enduring belief in eventual success.[37]

He began by proclaiming, "Throughout the long history of the world true progress [is] only made when leaders [are] willing to take risks, to depart from past practices, to chart a new course." It had not been "an easy task," he admitted, for "there are many who fear change" and take "security from stability, no matter how false it may be." Yet the negotiating school represented "a conscious decision by the national executive board to depart from past practices and chart a new course." The principle underlying this change held the key to Chávez's rhetorical purpose and attendant definition of his audience: "Our purpose is to enable common people to do uncommon things." His conclusion summarized his second persona for his audience of union activists and represented his understanding of the rhetorical powers possible in appeals to the fundamental Mexican-American values of pride, sacrifice, hard work, and dignity:

> In a real sense today's ceremony symbolizes the passing of the torch to a new generation, born in the movement, hardened by the struggle, disciplined

through many difficult and demanding battles, and firmly committed to the principles of sacrifice and servanthood that has built our union and kept the movement strong and vibrant.

> Justice, not Charity
> Dignity, not Mercy
> Servanthood, not Service.[38]

When casting his message in written rather than oral form, Chávez did not fundamentally change his rhetorical tactics or tone. In a fund-raising letter, for example, he described the living conditions for farm workers as being improved for some but still harsh for most. For the fortunate workers, Chávez could report: "Now many farm workers earn decent pay, have medical and pension plans and protection from dangerous pesticides. They earn enough so they don't have to migrate anymore with their children; their kids go to school and they can afford to live in decent homes instead of rotten camps." And he added proudly that these workers lived better because the UFW "boycott persuaded growers to back an historic law in California allowing farm workers to organize."[39] Yet his statistics documented that the number of such fortunate workers was small: *"But only about twenty percent of California farm workers enjoy these protections. For the rest, poverty and abuse are daily facts of life."*[40] Chávez communicated a vivid picture of that poverty through the use of imagery:

> Thousands of farm workers live under savage conditions beneath trees and amid stenchy garbage and human excrement near tomato fields in San Diego County which uses the most modern technology. Rats gnaw on them as they sleep, they walk miles to buy goods at inflated prices and carry water from irrigation pumps.[41]

In his letter Chávez stayed faithful to his practice of proving the farm workers' privation with statistics, numbers, stories, and vivid images. He marshaled this mass of evidence: 800,000 children worked in fields with their parents; 30 percent of the garlic harvesters in California were children; 53 percent of migrants dropped out of school to work; the average migrant child took three years to move from the third to the fourth grade; malnutrition among children was ten times the national average; the life expectancy of a farm worker was 49 years as compared to a national average of 73 years; families made an average of $2,475 a year; and farm work was the third most dangerous occupation in the country. After the problem was laid out clearly came the customary lesson to be learned and exhortation for action to be taken: "Where farm workers are organized, these injustices soon pass into history."[42]

During the turbulent period from 1975 to 1983, and in the midst of an increasingly media-savvy campaign, Chávez's public address stayed true to the approach and methods that had brought him earlier successes. Despite the increasing inhospitality of public opinion to his cause, and conservative political swings in 1980 both nationally (reflected in the election of Ronald Reagan as U.S. president) and in California (with the election of George Deukmejian as governor of California), Chávez's rhetorical worldview so controlled his life that he steadfastly maintained confidence in the power, methods, and substance of his rhetorical campaign. He continued to maintain his fundamental rhetorical profile, although he did adjust it to add new explanations, evidence, arguments, and directives pertinent to changing circumstances. On occasion his discourse revealed the difficulties of these days, as when he hinted at a threatened retreat from nonviolence and when he took the sting from any immediate lack of progress by retreating to the claim that time was on the side of farm workers.

Perhaps as a remedy for the spiritual emptiness that many people felt in a period of lapsed idealism, Chávez's first persona placed heavy emphasis on the happiness that comes with giving oneself to a worthy cause. Auditors who identified with him were also defined to be like him: They would find true wealth not in material possessions or rewards but in the living out and legacy of a good life; and they would lose their fear, find fulfillment, and endure sacrifices by following Chávez's example—an example that extended to being a rhetor who spoke the facts clearly and persistently and with confidence of success. In short, Chávez's first and second personae worked reciprocally to persuade some and reconstitute other audiences in his quest "to enable common people to do uncommon things." But the injustices he had fought for so long would continue to plague farm workers and force him to extend his unending rhetorical quest through the next and last decade of his life.

Chapter 8

The Difficult Last Decade, the Unfinished Last Boycott

"To Encourage a Multitude of Simple Deeds"

After the zenith years of the early 1970s, and following the momentous defeat of the Teamsters in the middle 1970s, César Chávez and his union would never again see so many major goals within their grasp. The last half of the 1980s and early 1990s were particularly difficult. Factionalization within the union and Chávez's inability to make the transition from advocate to bureaucrat internally weakened the United Farm Workers; the union lost most of its contracts and saw its membership further decline; the mass media, a longtime ally, now openly criticized Chávez for causing the UFW's internal problems. Richard Griswold del Castillo and Richard A. Garcia note that segments of the press "blamed the declining fortunes of the UFW on the contradictory nature of Chávez's leadership," contrasting "his advocacy of democracy in union organization . . . with the increasing role of the Chávez family in top positions" in the union's hierarchy.[1] Problems extended into the political realm, too. The favorable climate that had developed in the late 1970s, when the national government was headed by Jimmy Carter and the state government by Jerry Brown, dramatically changed with the elections of Ronald Reagan as president and George Deukmejian as Governor. Reagan had strongly opposed the UFW during his years as governor of California and remained hostile as president; nor would his successor, George Bush, be a friend of labor or of the UFW. Such political opposition contributed to legislative and legal difficulties. As Patrick H. Mooney and Theo J. Majka note, for example, the 1986 Immigration Reform and Control Act allowed a virtually inexhaustible supply of cheap labor to be brought into the country; and in the early 1990s the UFW was forced to devote its money, time, and energy to fight expensive and sometimes successful lawsuits filed by growers, a process that further distracted Chávez from other duties.[2]

By 1984 the hostile actions of Governor Deukmejian and other Chávez opponents had reshaped the Agricultural Labor Relations Board (ALRB) to the point that Chávez could no longer count on its support. After Deukmejian vetoed legislation to create a compliance board under the state Agricultural Labor Relations Board, companies did not have to sign contracts even if Chávez successfully organized their workers. Forced to rely on his own resources, Chávez decided that he had no choice but to return to a tactic effective in the past: the boycott. A new boycott was justified, Chávez proclaimed, because "the law that guarantees our right to organize has been shut down. . . . It doesn't work anymore."[3]

Chávez announced what would turn out to be his last major boycott on June 12, 1984. Its purpose, wrote Matt S. Meier and Feliciano Ribera, was "to protest excessive and negligent use of dangerous pesticides by growers and to call attention to the emasculation of California's Agricultural Labor Relations Act."[4] Because the UFW had initiated more than fifty boycotts over the years, the public could easily be confused about which products should be boycotted or why they were being boycotted. Chávez thus characteristically embarked upon still another educational campaign, this one to convince the public to honor the boycott. His campaign would use the new tactics and technologies he had instituted at La Paz; as Meier and Ribera note, he "hoped to reverse declining national support for unionism and the loss of UFW contracts by using direct mailing and computerized lists."[5] Chávez described his strategy and goal: "We will use modern techniques of direct mailings, media advertising, and other means of once again bringing together liberals, church groups, workers, and others to support us until the full meaning of the California labor law is restored and provides protections workers must have."[6] According to the *New York Times,* strategically targeted consumers who were likely to participate in a boycott received "carefully written appeals . . . followed by opinion polls to determine if they are having the desired effect." If found ineffective, the appeals were rewritten.[7]

Complementing his extensive use of technology, Chávez continued a broad campaign of communicating through varied means. He completed extensive speaking tours for the boycott, often following his talks by showing a film titled "The Wrath of Grapes." This film described "cancer clusters" and an extraordinarily high incidence of children's cancer and deformity found in several farming towns.[8]

When the boycott did not elicit the attention granted to earlier efforts, Chávez reinstituted another traditional tactic. In July and August of 1988 he undertook a thirty-six day fast in an attempt to energize the boycott. While well-publicized, the fast seemed to accomplish little of practical use.[9] Though the boycott sputtered, Chávez directed it until his death five years later, and consistently argued that it would be successful. "In political campaigns you race against time to get your message out," he instructed, "and you are always dramatically outspent. With boycotts, time becomes your ally. In the end, it can be a more powerful force than all the money that special interests can muster."[10]

The boycott did result in some victories. In 1989 Vons, a California supermarket chain, stopped selling grapes in sixteen markets in California that served mainly Mexican Americans. On the East Coast, five supermarket chains—Red Apple, Gristedes, Sloan's, Man-Dell, and Co-op—suspended sales the week of July 3–9 to show solidarity with the UFW. Those actions did not significantly lessen grape sales, however.[11]

In an article in the *Nation,* Frank Bardacke offered an unfavorable description of the state of the UFW at the time of its founder's death: "The UFW was not primarily a farm worker organization. It was a fund-raising operation, run out of a deserted tuberculosis sanitarium in the Tehachapi Mountains, far from the fields of the famous Delano, staffed by members of César's extended family and using as its political capital César's legend and the warm memories of millions of aging boycotters."[12] Several years earlier, labor historian Cletus E. Daniel had elaborated eloquently on contradictions in Chávez's leadership:

> . . . a sincere devotion to democratic unionism that is undermined by a tendency to regard all internal dissidents as traitors at best and anti-union conspirators at worst; a professed desire to make the UFW a rank-and-file union governed from the bottom up that is contradicted by a strong inclination to concentrate authority in his own hands and those of close family members; a commitment to professionalize the administration of the UFW that is impeded by a reliance on volunteerism so unyielding as to have caused many of the union's most loyal and efficient staff members to quit.[13]

Even such critics tempered their evaluations with noteworthy praise. Daniel stated that Chávez should not be judged on the same basis as other union leaders because he tried to promote changes "more fundamental than those attainable through collective bargaining and other conventional avenues of trade union activism."[14] "When measured against the magnitude of his proposed enterprise," Daniel reminded readers, "and against his extraordinary achievements on behalf of workers who were among the most powerless and degraded in America prior to his emergence, Chávez's real and alleged deficiencies in guiding the UFW across the hostile terrain of California's industrialized agriculture in no way detracts from his standing as the most accomplished and far-sighted labor leader of his generation."[15]

In this chapter, more so than in prior chapters, we probe deeply into the primary source of Chávez's accomplishments—a source heretofore largely overlooked by Chávez's critics as well as his biographers. We examine speeches that include many of his most carefully constructed and widely celebrated; a personal letter he wrote to supporters; and two statements issued on his long fast in the summer of 1988. For the first time we analyze a large group of his press releases and newspaper articles. To complete our chronicling of Chávez's lifetime of public address, we illustrate and explain consistencies and changes in his rhetorical profile, and offer description and analysis of his rhetorical interaction with audiences in considerable detail.

The fall of 1984 was perhaps the most ominous few months Chávez's movement had ever faced, with Reagan, Deukmejian, and their respective Republican political regimes popular in the opinion polls and antagonistic to the UFW and its interests. In California, Proposition 39 would reapportion the state in a way that reduced the political influence of Hispanics and liberals; and Deukmejian appointed ALRB members who were unfriendly to UFW interests and blocked implementation of collective-bargaining measures. The first two speeches we analyze reveal Chávez's rhetorical response to these troubling issues and times.

Chávez prepared carefully for his featured address before delegates and press at the UFW's seventh constitutional convention, in Bakersfield, California, on the first weekend in September, 1984. His press aide Marc Grossman worked closely with Chávez on this address, typing drafts to capture the leader's ideas, style, and manner. By this time Grossman knew intimately the rhetorical profile of Chávez and frequently produced drafts of speeches or essays for Chávez to review and revise. For this address, Chávez wrote comments on drafts to make final changes in wording. We examine the last draft of this address, ten double-spaced typed pages, to illustrate Chávez's standard rhetorical profile and identify changes in that profile.

Chávez began by acknowledging the difficult period: "There is a shadow falling over the land, brothers and sisters, and the dark forces of reaction threaten us now as never before." "The enemies of the poor and the working classes hold power in the White House and the Governor's Office," he warned. Immediately displaying his proclivity for anaphora, nine of the next ten paragraphs—eight of which consisted of one sentence each—began with "Our enemies" and then detailed the federal government's various attacks on a broad spectrum of farmworker interests ranging from a new bracero program, money for segregated private colleges that "close their doors to blacks and other people of color," tax cuts for the wealthy and new taxes on the poor, cash to wealthy growers for not growing crops, and military support for Central American dictators who engage in "the brutal murder of thousands of dark-skinned, Spanish-speaking farm workers."[16]

A simple transition from the federal to the state government introduced Chávez's next section: "The same dark forces of reaction that dominate the government in Washington also dominate the government in Sacramento. Governor Deukmejian is a lackey of Ronald Reagan." A list of protections won by farm workers' contracts followed, again in anaphoric form, citing child labor, bad wages and living conditions, sexual harassment of women workers, unfair and discriminatory hiring, and dangerous pesticides. "Where we have organized, these injustices soon pass into history," he proudly claimed. But now the governor had made sure that the law that guaranteed such protection was not being enforced. "What does all this mean for you and for other farm workers?" Chávez asked in a rhetorical question that served as a transition; he followed with six anaphoric and fact-filled statements, each beginning with "It means . . . ," to spell out the new dangers to free elections, organizing, speaking, negotiation, and money and contracts for sixty-three hundred workers owed $72 million dollars in back pay and thirty-six thousand farm workers waiting for contracts for which they voted. Duplicating the same stylistic pattern, Chávez asked a rhetorical question and then proceeded with five consecutive sentences in anaphoric form, including one about "the family of René López, the young farm worker from Fresno who was shot to death last year because by supported the union . . . because he spoke out against injustice . . . because he exercised his rights under the law."[17]

The last half of the address primarily discussed proposition 39, the "Deukmejian Reapportionment Initiative." As a reminder to broaden his appeal, Chávez wrote this comment in the margin of the text: "The same Governor Deukmejian who is working to deny a better life to farm workers is also working to deny all Hispanics in California the right to full participation in the political process." It was exactly this growing Hispanic influence, he warned listeners, that prompted Deukmejian and growers to propose Proposition 39, because they feared Hispanic political power. As Chávez said, "Deukmejian and the growers have looked into the future—and the future is ours!" The growth of the Hispanic population assured that "history and inevitability are on our side," he asserted; in "twenty and thirty years from now—in Modesto, in Salinas, in Fresno, in Bakersfield, in the Imperial Valley, and in many of the great cities of California—those communities will be dominated by farm workers and not by growers . . . by the children and grandchildren of farm workers and not by the children and grandchildren of growers." Nourished by "the values we cherish," in contrast to "the things they [growers] hold dear," farm workers who take pride in their families will triumph over growers who take pride in their money. And one day soon "when our children are the lawyers and the doctors and the politicians . . . when we hold political power in this state," history will shift course. That day "may not come this year. It may not come during this decade. But it will come, someday!" Until then, however, much work was required: "Our duty is clear. We must stand up and defend our rights as free men and women. We must defeat Proposition 39! We must unite with our Hispanic brothers and sisters who don't work in the fields by joining together in this noble crusade."[18]

The Bakersfield speech and the next one we examine show that Chávez had not changed his rhetorical profile, but that he had broadened his substantive case to include many public issues that affected farm workers and to introduce as major themes two new substantive points: the growing power of numbers of Hispanics to ensure victory in the future, and the pressing need for patience for the day when that victory would come. Even as he lost some measure of faith in political means to achieve his movement's triumphs, however, Chávez remained convinced of its inevitable success and in the need to speak effectively as the means to that success.

On November 9, 1984, Chávez spoke at the Commonwealth Club of San Francisco. This carefully crafted and lengthy address was the first speech—excepting those given as convention reports—that he read word-for-word before an audience. He labored as hard on this address as he had for any in his life, Grossman remembered, and took the text through several drafts before completing it.[19] The speech reflects his standard rhetorical profile, with substantive content matching closely—even using identical language at some points—many points he made in Bakersfield. It was an expanded version of his earlier address at the Comstock Club in Sacramento; and large sections of it, even many of the same phrases and sentences, appeared in a much briefer address in the *Los Angeles Times* on June 23.[20] The Commonwealth address demonstrates his rhetorical profile in its most polished form.

A concrete and shocking example opened the speech: "Twenty-one years ago last September, on a lonely stretch of railroad track paralleling U.S. Highway 101 near Salinas, 32 bracero farm workers lost their lives in a tragic accident." The unlicensed and dangerous bus, which had been converted from a "flatbed truck," had been hit by a "freight train," he said; then he disclosed that no one, not even their employer, knew the names of the dead workers. "Today," he extrapolated, "thousands of farm workers live under savage conditions—beneath trees and amid garbage and human excrement—near tomato fields in San Diego County" and suffer a long list of abuses he then itemized. Completing his introduction by presenting a statistic-laden rendition of conditions endured by farm workers, he turned first to children: Some as young as six years old were being forced to work, some 30 percent of garlic harvesters in Northern California used "under-aged children," 800,000 under-aged children worked in harvests across the U.S., and babies born to farm workers had a 25 percent higher infant-morality rate average, a ten-times higher malnutrition rate, and a life expectancy of thirty fewer years compared to national averages.[21]

The speech's body was divided neatly into two sections: The first chronicled the history of Chávez's farm workers' movement, intermingling Chávez's own history with reasons why the growers so feared the union; the last section, about a third longer than the first, centered on twin topics introduced with characteristic simplicity and clarity: "Two major trends give us hope and encouragement."[22]

Perhaps as a means to capitalize on one resource that had remained potent in the UFW's arsenal of rhetorical weapons in this period of setbacks, Chávez referred more than usual to himself and his own life. His persona had now become a major source of appeal for many audiences. "All my life," he divulged, "I have been driven by one dream, one goal, one vision: To overthrow a farm-labor system in this nation which treats farm workers as if they were not important human beings." Although "that dream was born in my youth," he confided, "I'm not very different from anyone else who has ever tried to accomplish something with his life. My motivation comes from my personal life," specifically from experiences such as watching his parents suffer as migrants, being subject to racism himself, and feeling the pain of others. He spoke of his "anger and rage—emotions I felt forty years ago when people of my color were denied the right to see a movie or eat at a restaurant in many parts of California"; and the feelings he had "later, in the '50s" when he "experienced a different kind of exploitation" in urban communities where Mexican Americans "were dominated by a majority that was Anglo."[23]

Chávez emphasized the power of teaching as central to who he was and what he had accomplished. He declared that "people like me had to develop the skills it would take to organize, to educate, to help empower the Chicano people"; he therefore "spent many years—before we founded the union—learning how to work with people." "Political awareness among Hispanics was almost non-existent" during this early period. "But deep in my heart," he said, "I knew I could never be happy unless I tried organizing the farm workers. I didn't know if I would succeed. But I had to try." Consequently he and others began the UFW, "always something more than a union," to attack injustice—"*not* by complaining; *not* by seeking hand-outs; *not* by becoming soldiers in the War on Poverty. We organized!"[24]

Once the UFW had achieved successes, "the message was clear: If it could happen in the fields, it could happen anywhere—*in* the cities, *in* the courts, *in* the city councils, *in* the state legislatures." Chávez did not "appreciate it at the time, but the coming of our union signaled the start of great changes among Hispanics that are only now beginning to be seen." Since that time, the inveterate orator related, "I've traveled to *every* part of this nation. I have met and spoken with *thousands* of Hispanics from *every* walk of life. . . . from *every* social and economic class"—and one thing he had often heard from them and from many others: "the farm workers gave them *hope* that they could succeed and the *inspiration* to work for change." Near the speech's end Chávez reiterated the UFW's contributions: "For nearly twenty years, our union has been on the cutting edge of a *people's* cause . . . ; regardless of what the future holds for farm workers . . . our accomplishments cannot be undone."[25]

Chávez's persona demonstrated his lifelong dedication to a just cause that he understood deeply through his own searing personal experiences, his deep concern for others, his willingness to do what was morally right regardless of the chances of success, his commitment to discourse and a life of acting out that commitment, his hard-earned understanding of the issues and people of the movement, his personal modesty, and the successes of his movement. Listeners who identified rhetorically with this noble and impressive man might discover and enact their own qualities of dedication to a just cause, willingness to work and even to sacrifice and suffer for that cause, commitment to speak out in ways to educate others, faith in ultimate victory, and pursuit of the goal of justice rather than personal gain or acclaim. For the wealthy and powerful listeners at the Commonwealth Club, and for the broader audience who heard the speech on the radio or read reports of it, the enactment of Chávez's agenda could take many forms ranging from voting for pro-farm-worker acts to boycotting grapes.

Chávez extended his audience and movement to include urban Hispanics through a series of three closely related statements employing his signature stylistic devices of anaphora and rhetorical questions:

How could we progress as a people, even if we lived in the cities, while farm workers—men and women of our color—were condemned to a life without pride?

How could we progress as a people while farm workers—who symbolized our history in this land—were denied self-respect?

How could our people believe that *their* children could become lawyers and doctors and judges and business people while *this* shame, *this* injustice was permitted to continue?[26]

• • •

The union's survival, he pointed out, proved to all Hispanics that "we were overcoming injustice. That we were empowering the least educated among us; the poorest among us."[27]

Turning to charges that the UFW had lost power and stature, Chávez invited his listeners' tacit participation through still another rhetorical question: "If we're so weak and unsuccessful, why do the growers continue to fight us with such passion?" His answers, most in anaphoric form, cited many areas of the union's contributions, both to farm workers and to Hispanic pride, strength, and accomplishments. Thus Chávez clearly tied union fortunes to the fortunes of Hispanics, culminating in his claim: "Our union will forever exist as an empowering force among Chicanos in the Southwest."[28]

Chávez's reliance on anaphora and similar techniques of parallel structure dominated the style and form of this address and communicated the interconnectedness of many of his points. His text, twenty-seven pages in length, was in large print and double- and triple-spaced. On nine occasions it contained three sentences or three clearly separated clauses where one word or a set of words began his thoughts. Four times he used anaphora in four consecutive sentences or clauses; twice for five sentences or clauses (in one instance where other sentences came between the anaphoric statements); once with six parallel statements that varied the restated words but slightly; and once with ten sentences or clauses where he also added epistrophe, that is, ending four sentences with identical phrases. In most instances, the anaphoric words were underlined in his speech text to remind him to provide vocal emphasis and timing in order to add further drama and impact to his comments.

The second section of the body of the speech unveiled Chávez's plan to return to "a *tried and tested* weapon in the farm workers' nonviolent arsenal—the boycott!" After the passage of the ALRB in 1975 in California, he recounted, farm workers had discarded the boycott, which had been so effective in the early- and mid-1970s, to work on winning elections under the new law; and the progress had been impressive in "*overcoming* poverty and injustice . . . , in *overcoming* miserable wages and working conditions, in *overcoming* sexual harassment of women workers, in *overcoming* dangerous pesticides which poison our people . . . and poison the food we eat." Noting that Deukmejian, backed by growers, allowed the law to be broken, Chávez asked rhetorically, "What does all this mean to farm workers?" His reply consisted of ten consecutive statements, each beginning with "It means . . . ," that listed the wide range of losses. Referring to the disastrous effects he had cited, he again asked rhetorically, "Are these make-believe threats? Are they exaggerations?" and then responded in anaphoric form with three sentences that began with, "Ask the farm workers" who respectively had lost contracts, jobs, and endured threats of physical violence. The mounting drama culminated in his horrific final answer: "Ask the family of René López, the young farm worker from Fresno who was shot to death last year because he supported the union." It was this recent history, he said, that was forcing the UFW to return to the boycott, a means once supported by seventeen million Americans according to a Louis Harris poll he cited.[29]

Reemphasizing the role of rhetoric in his worldview, Chávez delineated the audience for his new appeal as Hispanics, Blacks, other minorities: "Our allies in labor and the church," and "*also* an entire generation of young Americans who matured politically and socially in the 1960s and '70s." "If you were young, Anglo, and on or near campus during the late '60s and early '70s," he instructed, "chances are you supported farm workers." This audience, he pleaded perhaps with a touch of nostalgic hope, is "still inclined to respond to an appeal from farm workers. . . . The union's mission still has meaning for them."[30]

In a surprisingly candid revelation, Chávez identified not only his target audience but some of his new rhetorical strategies. He declared: "Only today we must translate the importance of a union for farm workers into the language of the 1980s" by raising issues of protection against sexual harassment in the fields rather than of the right to organize, and by speaking about the right of everybody to eat safe food. "I can tell you that the new language *is* working," he assured listeners, "the seventeen million *are* still there"; only today they respond to a "high-tech" appeal using computers, direct mail, and advertising techniques that have revolutionized business and politics.[31]

Chávez's last major point, the growth of Hispanic influence, rested upon persuasive statistics: south of the Sacramento River in California Hispanics constituted more than 25 percent of the population, a figure that would top 30 percent by the year 2000; 1.1 million Spanish-surnamed people were registered to vote in California, 85 percent of whom were Democrats; and the two hundred Hispanic elected officials in 1975 had grown to over four hundred by 1984. To the growers' charge that farm workers caused their problems, Chávez spun out a long set of sentences and paragraphs set in anaphoric form. "The growers *only have themselves* to blame," he would repeat, for their "sins" in unjustly treating "entire races of dark-skinned workers," the environment, food, consumers, and the political and legal systems.[32]

"The chickens are coming home to roost," Chávez announced confidently, "and the time to account for past sins is approaching"; "We have looked into the future and the future is ours!" With "history and inevitability . . . on our side," in "twenty or thirty years" farm workers and their children and grandchildren would dominate "*in* Modesto, *in* Salinas, *in* Fresno, *in* Bakersfield, *in* the Imperial Valley, and *in* many of the great cities of California." Connecting the UFW with the new majority, he reminded his audience that his union had represented this movement and these people for "twenty or thirty years;" that its "accomplishments cannot be undone"; and that *"the day will come"* when fair economic and political rewards will accrue, "the day will come" when politicians do the right thing by our "people out of *political necessity* and *not* out of charity or idealism."

Chávez's retreat from his earlier confidence in a fair-minded political system was accompanied by his new timetable for justice: "That day may not come this year. . . . That day may not come during this decade. . . . But it will come, someday!" He concluded by promising that "when that day comes," it will fulfill a passage from the Book of Matthew: "'That the last shall be first and the first shall be last.' And on that day, our nation shall fulfill its creed . . . and that fulfillment shall enrich us all."[33]

While his speech to the Commonwealth Club was carefully written out, Chávez more commonly spoke from an outline such as the one for a breakfast address to an Hispanic audience on September 26, 1984. Scribbled on the text are hand-written names of those whom Chávez planned to acknowledge in his introduction. His message does not emphasize farm workers but relates directly to his immediate audience and to contemporary political elections by carrying forward his recent focus on political issues, Hispanic problems, and increased Hispanic influence.

Chávez's rhetorical tactics largely duplicated those in his major addresses of his last decade. He employed anaphora, as illustrated on page one with his repetition of "still exploited, . . . still plagued . . . still living in poverty." He used techniques to ensure clarity, as indicated by his transition "and it's because of four really bad issues on November 6 ballot that we're meeting this morning," followed by "four propositions that vitally affect Hispanics," each positioned in the left margin to stand out as main points. He provided many statistics, examples, and other facts; and he finished with a clear set of action steps asking listeners to participate by providing their names as supporters, helping in registering voters, boycotting grapes, and become dynamic rhetors by following his directive to "speak out in meetings, conferences" and "let me know of forums I can address." This rhetorical campaign would utilize the new media capacities of the UFW through its direct mail appeals to registered voters, with for the first time "Chicanos writing to all Chicanos in state."[34]

Chávez's ten pages of notes on October 7, 1984, written in Spanish, offer several important insights into his substance and methods when addressing Mexican-American audiences in the language of their forebears' homeland. His audience seemed to consist of many workers not in the UFW. In response to new threats to take away gains made by his union, he focused on his long-standing commitment to nonviolent means, higher motives, and the goal of justice. And he once more filled his speech with facts, promoted the boycott as a tactic, and favored anaphora and rhetorical questions in his style and form. Yet he also adapted to his audience's ethnicity, with his large number of *dichos* and *cuentos,* his many appeals to sacrifice, suffering, and penance, and his dramatic references to the image of blood, a powerfully motivating image in Mexican and Mexican-American history and culture.[35]

Chávez's first sentence pointed out that all farm workers' agreements "should recognize that our sacrifices have helped a lot." Several subsequent sentences urged all farm workers to understand that their struggles were bound closely to the UFW's struggles and that unaffiliated workers could help his union's effort. The assistance was especially important in the current "negative reaction" threatening the UFW, for "the exploitative and racist forces are against the justice, they oppose the decent people that ask for justice." Laws that formerly protected farm workers were no longer enforced, but farm workers were "not scared" of the reactionary "bullshit and scum" that "run the agrarian life . . . ."[36] Although his attempts to remove fear among farm workers were common throughout his rhetorical career, he had never before used such vulgar and derogatory language in the many texts we have studied.

Enlisting specific events to illustrate his points, Chávez informatively reviewed a set of Teamster meetings and actions relating to contracts and to ALRB policies and laws. After noting for listeners that Teamster President Jackie Presser—like all Teamsters' presidents "for the last forty years"—had been prosecuted for "racketeering, theft, and more," Chávez promised to fight on and asked recognition for some of his colleagues in the fight: the union's board members, Frank Ortiz, Arturo Mendoza, the Vegetable Division's Arturo Rodríguez, Grape Division's Oscar Mondragon, and Multicultural Affairs' Dolores Huerta.[37]

In his fight, the strike and boycott remained "the preferred weapons . . . and they'll continue to be used until we reach justice." Such tactics had brought improved salaries, a pension, medical plan, transportation, employment office, and other gains for workers. Workers had not forgotten how to use such time-tested tactics. As Chávez said in a dicho: "This is what we have to say to the ranchers—'Don't look for three legs in a cat because they'll find four.'" He added what he labeled a "Spanish saying, 'They paid more for the nuts than for the broth,'" to illustrate his claim that ranchers would face a boycott and allied campaign as damaging to them as the one in 1979 if they persisted in trying to undo farm workers' gains.

"The ranchers should know," Chávez wrote in one of nine sentences that began with the same or only slightly modified words, "and if they don't know it they better learn that all our sacrifices, our sweat, tears, and blood have a focus, a very important ideal. This ideal is an impulse toward sacrifice, it is the ideal of justice." Chávez reified the point in his reference to the ranchers' need to learn that the tears and "the blood that has been shed for [martyred farm workers] Nagi, Juan, Rufino, and René was not done in vain." The benefits farm workers had earned, he restated to underscore his appeal to values and images deeply embedded in Mexican-American culture, came through "so much sacrifice, sweat, tears and blood." To his question of "How can this happen if all these benefits were earned through strikes, boycotts and campaigns?" he answered: "Everything we have has cost us a lot of sacrifice," had been hard earned, and would not be returned.[38]

On October 25, 1985, Chávez again spoke to a group of Hispanics, the Chicano Employee Association of Los Angeles County. His substantive message and rhetorical manner paralleled his addresses before non-Hispanic audiences. He focused on the state of his movement, particularly Governor Deukmejian's many efforts to defeat it, and the history of and need for his latest boycott. His reliance on concrete facts and faith that a moral message would animate audiences emerged immediately with his first statements: "Twenty years ago last month long-suffering men and women in the vineyards surrounding Delano—120 miles north of here—struck out against a hundred years of humiliation and oppression." The grape workers' use of the boycott became "a powerful statement against poverty and injustice" that "touched the hearts and consciences of millions of Americans who never worked on a farm" and led to historic union contracts with growers. In the remainder of his address he again linked farm workers to Hispanics and then to all Americans, pointing out with typical clarity: "It's not just farm workers who're threatened by agricultural poison," for "Hispanic kids in McFarland, near Delano, are contracting cancer at alarming rates." Water was contaminated "in dozens of other San Joaquin Valley cities and towns"; and "there is nothing more important that we as farm workers share in common with the consumers of America than the safety of the nation's food supply which we both depend upon."

Even in this short address Chávez featured transitions and anaphora to guide listeners and dramatize his points; e. g., "Like Ronald Reagan, George Deukmejian also left a legacy of nonenforcement. Deukmejian's legacy . . . can be seen. . . . It can be seen. . . . It can be seen. . . . But Deukmejian's legacy of nonenforcement can also be seen . . . . Deukmejian's legacy can also be seen . . . ." Easing into his customary rhetorical mold, Chávez cited specific statistics such as those from opinion polls on who supported or would support boycotts respectively in the 1970s and the present; and presented his concrete and often-used examples of René López, the 21-year-old farm worker killed in 1983 for voting by "two grower goons hired to harass farm workers . . . *after* Deukmejian's men failed to take action against armed guards who were threatening workers with guns"; and of Juan Chavoya, "thirty-two and the father of four young children," who died after working in a field in San Diego County just sprayed by dangerous pesticides. Chávez's ending, optimistic as ever, was directed at his immediate audience: "With this boycott weapon in our nonviolent arsenal—and with the unselfish support our union cause continues to enjoy from the House of Labor—we shall win in the end. You can count on it."[39]

Chávez wrote a widely distributed letter in the mid-1980s that conformed to and complemented the message in his speeches and made clear his belief in using technology to spread his ideas. Focusing on the failure of the ALRB, he offered statistics and examples to persuade readers that Deukmejian's actions had reduced the effectiveness of the law and thereby had severely curtailed the rights of workers. While uninvestigated cases filed by farm workers had increased from 392 in 1982 to 1,073 in 1984, complaints against the growers by the state had declined from 137 in 1981/1982 to 24 in 1983/1984. The percentage of worker accusations that had been dismissed by the Agricultural Board had grown from 46 percent before Deukmejian to 90 percent in 1984; and funding for the law had decreased by 30 percent even as "the best prosecutors were driven out and replaced with grower loyalists." In addition, "farm workers, many who are illiterate, must prove complex labor law theories before their charges are investigated. Dozens of cases are dismissed on narrow technical grounds before evidence against growers is even examined."[40]

To add impact to his allegations, Chávez offered examples that included a case of favorable treatment received by Abatti Farms, Inc., at the hands of the governor's appointees. State officials flew in an Abatti Farms airplane to a settlement meeting with farm workers who were owed ten million dollars, "money workers lost because Abatti broke the law." Rather than granting workers the money they deserved, "Deukmejian's men offered to 'settle' the case for 10¢ on the dollar."[41]

The anti-union climate created by Deukmejian resulted in thousands of workers being fired from their jobs, "victims of intimidation, threats, and physical violence." Chávez cited his often-used story of René López, a striker at the Sikkema Dairy near Fresno, who was killed because he led a strike that resulted in workers voting on unionization. "René cast his ballot on September 20, 1983," Chávez recounted, and "was shot in the head by two strikebreakers—violent men imported by the grower to suppress the workers. René was the fourth UFW member murdered by growers in ten years." Such examples put a human face on Chávez's charge that the hopes of thousands of other workers "for a better life are being dashed because Governor Deukmejian won't enforce the law that protects them."[42]

Moving flexibly to meet the new threat, Chávez blamed the failure of the ALRB for forcing union members to return to past tactics. "When the law was passed in 1975," he instructed, "we took down our boycott to work with the law. Now that Deukmejian and the growers are closing the law off to us, *we must take up where we left off in 1975 by boycotting growers who violate the law and refuse to recognize their workers' rights.*"[43]

The veteran rhetor's ongoing commitment to discourse motivated him to write this letter. He expressed his intention that nearly one million people a week would receive his message, an ambitious goal that required him to make a rare request for direct financial donations from his public family. Continuing to enact his commitment to farm workers, he wrote in a personal appeal for money: "All of us in the movement work as volunteers for $10 a week plus room and board. We stretch each dollar to compete with the growers' wealth."[44]

To reach the million Americans each week, Chávez augmented his traditional methods with a sophisticated direct-mail campaign. In his letter he described and justified this new means of communication in practical terms: "We are also mailing appeals to hundreds of thousands of people across the country. We are using computers and direct mail techniques to reach millions of people quicker and more effectively. (Why should only agribusiness and the right wing make use of the new technology?)"[45]

In 1986, increasing his attention to expanding his audience to include consumers, Chávez frequently gave a standard speech that contained several primary themes: consumers as well as farm workers were being poisoned by pesticides; consumers must therefore join into a coalition with farm workers to oppose Deukmejian and his agribusiness allies; the boycott had worked in the past and would work in the future; and rhetorical discourse was working effectively to ensure victory for his cause. To add to his audience of supporters, he was now obviously increasing his efforts to wed the interests of consumers and farm workers. Long-tested rhetorical tactics put his signature on his standard text: His easy-to-understand message that relied on plentiful facts and lucid arguments that were organized clearly and enlivened frequently through anaphora, transitions, and rhetorical questions.[46]

The opening two paragraphs of a representative standard speech contained his twin themes of the potential of rhetorical discourse and the promise of the boycott:

• • •

I am speaking to you about our Wrath of Grapes Boycott. Because I believe our greatest court, the court of last resort, is the American people. And I believe that once you have taken a few moments to hear this message you will concur in this verdict along with a million other North Americans who are already committed to the largest grape boycott in history.[47]

Once he had declared his faith in the power of his discourse to move the American people to boycott, he asked consumers to join forces with farm workers: "I see us as one family. We cannot turn our backs on each other and our future. We farm workers are closest to food productions. We were the first to recognize the serious health hazard of agricultural pesticides to both consumers and ourselves."[48]

The speech's body briefly covered farm workers' history and problems but placed major emphasis on dangers to consumers. Chávez introduced new evidence into his rhetorical campaign by quoting a recent *New York Times* article that "virtually everyone is exposed to pesticides"; and warnings by Environmental Protection Agency "experts" that pesticides were being discovered "in a growing number of food products," were now known to cause cancer and birth defects, placed in markets after insufficient or fraudulent testing, and had contaminated water in twenty-three states. Consumers thus faced serious dangers, a charge Chávez developed further through his customary pattern of presenting a clear transition leading to concrete evidence: "Let me share some frightening facts with you. Last July, the *New York Times* and a national television reported that nearly one thousand Californian, Pacific Northwest, Alaskan, and Canadian consumers became ill" from eating watermelons tainted with Aldicarb, a pesticide prohibited from being used on melons. Moreover, five toxic poisons legally used on grapes, according to a study he cited, were as or more dangerous than Aldicarb. He next delineated and briefly discussed "five major threats to your health that cling to the California table grapes": Parthion, Phosdrin, Captan, Dinoseb, and Methyl Bromide.[49]

After quoting the statistics and experts cited above, Chávez introduced his third and most moving form of evidence: "Statistics and new articles do not relate the real cost, the human anguish that originates from poisons on our food. They do not tell the tragedies I personally learn of daily." To heighten the impact of the anguish and horror he had witnessed, Chávez presented seven consecutive questions to introduce examples of dead, dying, and deformed children and adults who were poisoned by exposure to pesticides. These questions respectively began with the words, "how can I explain" to a maimed child "what statistics are important to . . ."; "what headline can justify . . ."; "how do we comfort . . .";

"what report can be cited . . ."; "what court will hear the case . . ."; and "what excuse for justice will we offer . . ."; the four children and widow of a farm worker "murdered" by pesticide poisoning.[50]

To prevent the growing tragedy from recurring, auditors must become rhetorically active by adding their "voice to our demands for decency." Specifically, they should support a ban on the five most dangerous pesticides, a testing program for poisonous residues on grapes with results made public, and free elections for farm workers to decide on contracts that would limit use of dangerous poisons. "Until these demands of decency are met," he promised, "we will carry the message of the wrath of grapes boycott from state to state."

"California's Governor Deukmejian and agribusiness," Chávez predicted with customary faith in the rhetorical potency and potential of his message, "cannot withstand the judgment of outraged consumers who refused to purchase their tainted products." "Even now," he claimed, "every month over a million grape consumers like yourself receive our message"—and these converted listeners "in turn have reached out to their friends and relatives to help build the foundation of a growing coalition of decency." Thus "consumers and farm workers must stand together as one family if we are to be heard." Chávez finished by asking for financial contributions, giving his "personal pledge that every cent of your contribution will be spent on the Wrath of Grapes campaign bringing this crucial message into every home in America, because this message is the source of our combined strength."[51]

Speaking to students at University of California's Boalt Law School on May 24, 1986, Chávez tailored his standard appeals to his audience. He began with quotes from George Bernard Shaw and Robert F. Kennedy to introduce his first section, four handwritten pages in which he challenged those who would soon graduate to engage in the "risk-taking" of working for humanitarian causes rather than for a "large corporate firm." The next section, four additional pages, related how "some twenty years ago a small band of your unreasonable men and women lawyers" founded the UFW legal department, "a kind of a domestic legal Peace Corps." They discovered challenging, intellectually stimulating, satisfying, and interesting work that made a "contribution to the noble profession [that] fills law books with UFW cases." To this point in the address, Chávez had attempted to enhance his case by quoting sources and appealing to circumstances very familiar to his audience.[52]

Referring to his own long crusade, he noted in his last section that even in the difficult political times under Richard Nixon and now under Reagan and Deukmejian, his cause had survived. And even though many said that today's college students sought only the rewards of "gross materialism," he saw an America with very different values—"values of justice and fair play . . . which our movement has successfully appealed to over the years through our boycotts." He then returned to his standard address, duplicating its substance and style by beginning with "our court of last resort—the American people"; moving through his quotes from the *New York Times* and listing of poisonous pesticides; citing examples of the victims of pesticides, expressed through his usual questions and anaphoric form; and calling for the customary actions and promising the standard rhetorical campaign. Only his concluding paragraph was entirely created for his audience of students: He cited Gandhi on the sin of "possessing 'knowledge without character'" to bolster his invitation to students to join him in advancing "the cause of a more just society."[53]

In 1987 Chávez delivered an address to the striking Pecan Workers in Arizona that showed how he adapted his message to a specific occasion and to a specific audience. Finding solidarity and support with the workers of the Santa Cruz Valley Pecan Company, Chávez told strikers: "We are proud to stand with you on this picket line." "Together," he promised in a section replete with anaphora, farm workers and picketers would send a message to owner Richard Walden,

a strong message. A message to stop trying to bust the union. A message to sit down and bargain in good faith . . . . A message that we won't stand for his cheap wages, harassment, unsafe jobs and unhealthy conditions. A message that we will not continue making him rich with our sweat. And a message that the farm workers will support the boycott and that he won't be able to sell his damn pecans.[54]

Chávez helped to weave together the tight connection of himself, strikers, and his movement by using the personal pronouns "we," "us," and "our" over thirty times in this short speech.

Chávez's expanded list of topics included many specific rights of workers and far-reaching national and worldwide concerns for justice. He discussed numerous damaging actions of Reagan, Walden, the newly formed NLRB, and consultants like Robert Deeny and Juan Garza who implemented anti-union and anti-strike tactics, men whose abuses he itemized and then summed up as seeking to "reduce workers to mere industrial tools instead of human beings." Despite such formidable opposition, Chávez subscribed to an optimistic version of the future. For example, in various places in his address he said, "We are confident of your victory"; "Together we will win this critical battle. Together we will stand till victory"; "We cannot turn our backs on each other because we all share in the same future"; and, in his conclusion, "Our unity—our solidarity—and our faith in justice shall prevail until the day comes when Richard Walden will negotiate a just contract and we can return to our job with dignity. Secure in our job and in our union. . . ."[55]

Another of Chávez's 1987 addresses shows how he adapted his message to the format and medium of televised talk show questions and answers. Interviewed in Michigan on a public broadcasting channel, he emphasized two themes: tying the needs of consumers for healthy food to the needs of farm workers for a ban on pesticides and a commitment to proper sanitation in the fields; and revealing that agribusiness-controlled immigration and particularly the bracero program in order to create a surplus of workers and thereby depress wages and other conditions for farm workers.

The rhetorically sensitive Chávez easily adjusted the public address he employed in platform speeches to his format and medium in Michigan, maintaining his customary substantive themes and rhetorical qualities. In answers to particular questions he provided a raft of facts and historical examples for his claims, appearing as well prepared as in his formal speeches. He also mentioned his "argument" or advocacy several times, communicating once more his faith in reasoned discourse to fair-minded audiences and even assuring that "right thinking people know" that agribusiness was harming the entire nation, consumers and farm workers. Chávez used clear summaries, as when in a summary to one answer he cited "those two reasons" for the bracero program—keeping cheap labor and retarding unionizations; emphasized the need for strategic communication, citing "five" groups or audiences in Michigan he was targeting for his boycott; and demonstrated his typical optimism by answering questions about recent defeats for the labor movement with an explanation of how labor historically gained support, unity, and energy when under attack. A new theme in this electronically mediated message stressed that housing was essential for farm workers, because workers gain independence when they own their homes.[56]

Despite advances in technology, expanded themes to include urban Hispanics and most consumers, and more realistic appraisals of the inherent justice of the political system, Chávez entered the 1990s aware that the boycott he initiated in 1984 was not attracting the attention and support he sought. Nevertheless he continued undeterred on his rhetorical crusade, announcing in 1991: "It's looking very good. . . . It's looking like the beginning of the end." As Griswold del Castillo and Garcia wrote: "Into the 1990s, Chávez exhibited the same qualities of character that had brought his success in the earlier struggles. He was tenacious in his leadership," and still believed his boycott could be won. The recipe for success, wrote the two historians, included a motivating rhetorical ingredient: "If history was to be a guide, the success of the boycott would be assured mainly through the hard work of hundreds of dedicated volunteers inspired by the vision put forth by the UFW's leader. César Chávez never gave up on the farm workers."[57]

Chávez's optimism seemed unwarranted. In 1991 shipments of grapes increased by 2 percent over 1990; and a spokesperson for Safeway stores reported with considerable accuracy: "The boycott is not working. . . . We buy on the basis of customer demand . . . and, as for grapes, the demand has always been there." Moreover, many of Chávez's long-time coworkers and previous supporters, including religious leaders who worked in previous Delano strikes, also declined to endorse his latest and last boycott. Many others, including some of his strongest political allies, were unaware of the boycott.[58]

In the last several years of his life, even while in a weakened physical state after his last fast, Chávez maintained his demanding campaign of public address. In 1992, for example, he led walkouts and protests by workers in the Coachella Valley and the San Joaquin Valley.[59] To chronicle and explain his rhetorical campaign during his final several years, we will turn first to a sample of sixteen of Chávez's statements written between April, 1989, and September, 1992. These statements were almost always one-to-three double-spaced pages in length and were distributed before his public appearances or as opinion essays in newspapers or books. Because they reached many readers and formed an important part of his public address, they help to reveal the contour of his rhetorical profile as he faced new issues toward the end of his career. They also illustrate the place of his press releases in his discourse.

The sixteen statements indicate that Chávez continued his quest to broaden his audience, for he adapted his message to a wide variety of issues and occasions. In a release before his speech in Sacramento with the Rev. Jesse Jackson at a large protest against proposed state cuts in funding for schools and other areas, for example, Chávez tied public education to race and his union by showing that "the majority of children in our public school are minority . . . from poor and working-class families" such as farm workers.[60] At the dedication of a school named for him, he focused on his movement's relationship to education and outlined its broader goals and history.[61] Near Delano he discussed cancer clusters in communities in that area, charging that agricultural pesticides caused that cancer and reviewing UFW efforts to combat pesticide use.[62] In releases in 1992 he appealed directly to feminists and their sympathizers by lamenting the frequent sexual harassment of women who were farm workers by the growers' managers and supervisors.[63]

In many releases Chávez connected his movement to urban areas and all consumers by focusing on the dangers of farm pesticides. Each abuse, he reminded, had been fought by the UFW.[64] During the widespread aerial spraying of the medfly in California, he charged that urban areas were now subject to direct and dangerous pesticide sprays in a manner similar to that suffered by farm workers.[65] In a statement released to the press before he spoke in Hong Kong, Chávez documented the terrible effects of pesticides on farm workers and consumers in the United States and warned of similar dangers to those in Asia who ate products imported from California.[66] At times he bound his movement to the hopes of all minorities, describing African Americans and Asians as well as Hispanics as sharing UFW challenges, goals, and gains.[67]

At the heart of his press releases resided a fundamental substantive message that had changed little from Chávez's earlier years: Greedy growers treated farm workers unfairly with disastrous results to people and products; Chávez's union was part of a just cause and thus would inevitably succeed;[68] broad participation was the key to his movement's success; rhetorical appeals to the public—"to spread the news"[69]—were necessary; and nonviolent means, and especially the boycott, were crucial tactics.

The difficulties and defeats suffered by his movement also influenced his message. He often mentioned the setbacks his union had encountered and difficult challenges it faced, and sometimes complained that the miseries endured by farm workers were worse than when he himself was a migrant in the 1930s and 1940s.[70] Perhaps because he had not achieved some of his goals, and by 1991 had faced nine years of unfriendly conservative political regimes in California and the nation, he spun out two new and interrelated arguments he had elevated in importance earlier in the decade: (1) His movement would triumph because it had time on its side, or as he said in finishing an op-ed article submitted to the Bakersfield *Californian:* "Time is our ally. In the end, it will prove a more powerful force that all the money the grape growers can muster";[71] and (2) Hispanics and allied minorities would eventually win by their sheer numbers, for they would soon be a majority and thus owned the future, where in "twenty and thirty years" they would dominate "the great cities and valleys of our state. . . ."[72]

Combining his argument of numbers with his theme of inevitability, the ever-optimistic Chávez forecast: "We have looked into the future and the future is ours! Asians and Hispanics and African Americans are the future in California. That trend cannot be stopped. It is inevitable."[73] Perhaps disclosing the reason for his emphasis on these new arguments, he admitted that he had been unable to influence political institutions to bring him success—and thus appeals must be made directly to the public and especially to the public of ethnic minorities, college students, and the now grown-up idealistic and supportive student generation of the 1960s and 1970s.[74] By featuring a line of argument based primarily on growing numbers of minority voters, he implicitly acknowledged his retreat in his commitment to his moral case as sufficient to convince the entire public and thereby to ensure victory.

To communicate his themes, Chávez stayed in his role as a teacher of truth who sought to educate audiences through clearly expressed facts and ideas. He put forth ample statistics to document his claims and added examples to put a human face on those statistics and claims. His two-page statement in September of 1989 on cancer clusters exemplified this element of his profile well. He first cited a cancer rate in McFarland "800 percent above the expected rate" and in Earlimart about "1200 percent" above; next he related how "the Ramírez's daughter, Natalie, lost one kidney to a malignant tumor. Now cancer threatens her remaining kidney. Her four short years have been filled with sickness and pain from extensive chemotherapy and other treatments." A "quarter billion pounds" of pesticides were used in California yearly, he added. He then provided examples of "The Caudillos—Jaime and Mari," whose three-year-old son Jimmy died of leukemia; and of María Quihada, whose child was afflicted. In this release he also cited evidence from the National Academy of Sciences on pesticides and cancer and warned of the dangers of the pesticides DDT, Aldrin, and Dieldrin.[75] In later releases he combined the statistics noted above with additional statistics and added new examples such as Miriam Ramírez, the deceased daughter of her father Gonzalo; farm worker José Campos, dead from Parathion poisoning; María Robles who had leukemia; and Felipe Franco, Ramona's nine-year-old child born without arms and legs. When he discussed five-year-old Johnnie Rodríguez, son of Juan and Elia, dead after "a painful two-year battle with . . . neuroblastoma," he confided: "I keep a picture of Johnnie Rodríguez. He is sitting on his bed hugging his teddy bear. His sad red eyes and cherubic face stare out at you. The photo was taken four days before he died."[76] To make his larger point, Chávez concluded: "Johnnie Rodríguez was one of 13 McFarland children diagnosed with cancer in recent years; and one of six who have died of the disease. With only 6,000 residents, the rate of cancer in McFarland is 400 percent above normal."[77]

In each of the examples, Chávez mentioned the parents who were farm workers exposed to pesticides. In each case he also explained clearly the process of spraying by growers. In some releases he added a detailed explication of scientific studies of cancer, for example showing that a State of California study on leukemia and home-used pesticides compared 123 children between 1980 and 1984 to find a 3.8 times increase in likelihood of cancer if parents used household pesticides once a week or more, 6.5 times if parents used garden pesticides once a month or more, and 9 times if the mother used the garden pesticides.[78] Whether he discussed the effects of the grape boycott, the state of public schools, or the dangers of imported U.S. produce in foreign countries,[79] Chávez customarily provided telling statistics and examples to educate his audiences.

Chávez's prose style remained designed primarily for clarity. In short paragraphs, with clear language and necessary transitions, he told his story. As our examples above illustrate, he wrote in a personal, concrete, and easy-to-understand style, frequently referring specifically to himself, his colleagues, and various particular farm workers, politicians, and other people as well as to specific legislation, studies, and other topics. To further ensure clarity, rhetorical questions or other obvious verbal guideposts led readers to his points—e.g., "But grape workers in California face other forms of oppression."[80] Sometimes he began his release with a question or questions, as when he wrote: "Some people may ask, Why should the farm workers be concerned about the condition of public schools in California? Let me answer them: Who do you think are in the public schools today in California?"[81]

Even without Chávez's transitions or rhetorical questions, most readers would have little difficulty following a message expressed in a form constructed for easy comprehension. Most releases contained at least one series of short paragraphs linking closely related ideas, with one or more summary statements or subject sentences capturing his central idea. Examples of Chávez's use of a subject sentence are in the first essay cited in our sample, where he finished by stating: "Carcinogenic pesticides must be treated as guilty until proven innocent. That means their use must stop—now";[82] in essays from the middle of our sample, where he wrote: "We're here to tell the pesticide traffickers that we will no longer tolerate being sprayed in silence";[83] or when he began an essay: "Farm workers are demonstrating today because state health officials are treating child cancer clusters in agricultural communities as a public relations problem instead of a public health problem"; and in the latest release in our sample, where he ended: "Please give the grape growers an incentive to halt the use of these poisons. Don't buy or eat California fresh grapes. Don't let the grape growers use Hong Kong as the dumping ground for the grapes they cannot sell in America."[84]

Chávez's analogies, metaphors, dichos, and anaphora dramatized his points. In several releases, he began by saying: "Years ago, miners carried birds with them to warn against poison gas. They hoped the birds would die before the miners. Farm workers and children are today's canaries. They demonstrate the effects of pesticide poisoning before anyone else."[85] In several other essays he stated: "You can't fool Mother Nature. In time, insects can outfox anything we throw at them."[86] He used anaphoric parallel structure in a few essays; e. g., "We must say 'no' to suspending Proposition 98. . . . We must say 'no' to cutting essential services. . . . We must say 'no' to making our children and their teachers scapegoats for the budget crisis."[87]

The releases contributed to Chávez's persona primarily through his reliance on facts and understanding that indicated his deep knowledge; his emphasis on clarity of instruction and on faith in eventual rhetorical success thereby showing the consistency of man and message; and his self-portrait as a modest servant in God's plan for the world rather than a seeker of material gain or glory. On a few occasions Chávez displayed more obvious efforts to develop his persona. To show the fidelity of his facts and his commitment to his cause, he noted that "the National Academy of Sciences has finally verified what we have said for twenty years";[88] and he told both the readers of the *Sacramento Bee* and residents of Delano of his careful and committed research with these words: "I studied this wanton abuse of nature. I read the literature, heard from the experts about what pesticides do. I talked with farm workers, listened to their families and shared their anguish and their fears. I spoke out against the cycle of death."[89]

Chávez's speeches during this period followed closely the profile of his press releases, differing primarily only in their greater length and hence fuller development of his points. In many cases he used the same examples, statistics, and even the same precise wording of points in both written and spoken discourse. We now examine texts of three representative speeches, each delivered to a very different audience, to illuminate the primary features of his spoken discourse at the end of his career.

Chávez's first public speech following his debilitating thirty-six day fast in Delano in the summer of 1988 to protest the use of pesticides in farm work, was in March of 1989, at Pacific Lutheran University in Tacoma, Washington. He worked unusually hard on preparing this speech, going through several drafts with his press aide Grossman in order to make clear his intent in the fast and perhaps to find the rhetorical mix for capitalizing on the attention given to the fast. Along with his Commonwealth Club speech in 1984, this speech is among those on which he worked the hardest.

The nineteen-page typed text, organized into three distinct sections, thoroughly covered the use and effects of pesticides. The structure of the first third was anchored by sets of rhetorical questions, each set followed by an example. Chávez began with the questions that had begun one of his press releases from the period: "What is the worth of a man or a women? What is the worth of a farm worker? How do you measure the value of a life?" He followed with a stark and detailed example of Johnnie Rodríguez, complete with several quotes from the young cancer victim's parents, Juan and Elia, on how their son played in the fields and drank the water that had been sprayed. Chávez quoted Johnnie's father: "Once your son has cancer, you hope it's a mistake, you pray, Juan says. He was a real nice boy. He took it strong and lived as long as he could." Chávez inserted himself into the heart-wrenching story of pesticide use, just as he had in his press releases: "I keep a picture of Johnnie Rodríguez. He is sitting on his bed, hugging his teddy bear. His sad eyes and cherubic face stare out at you. The photo was taken four days before he died."[90]

Other parts of the first one-third duplicated the organizational structure of questions followed by examples. In his fact-filled refutation of Deukmejian's claim that no evidence proved that pesticides on grapes and other products harmed consumers or workers, he began: "Ask the family of Felipe Franco. Felipe is a bright seven year old"—but unlike other children, "he was born without arms and legs." His statistic-laden rebuttal to the claims by the pro-grower Table Grape Commission and the Farm Bureau commenced with: "Ask the family of Juan Chabolla." He completed this section by using two identical patterns of asking the respective questions, "What does acute pesticide poisoning produce?" and "What are the chronic effects of pesticide poisoning of people, according to scientific studies?" He then listed the effects, followed respectively by a single dramatic word, "Death," and "Cancer."[91]

The middle section formed around answers to the question, "Who will protect farm workers from poisoning if it isn't the farm workers' union?" He began his answer with, "The Environmental Protection Agency won't do it," and then moved to respective discussions to prove that "the law won't do it," the agrichemical industry won't do it," and even the universities and doctors would not help. In each case he depicted the powerful influence of agribusiness over those who might help farm workers.[92]

The last and longest section covered other aspects of the history, nature, and effects of pesticides, governmental attempts to regulate their use, and special dangers to consumers, now grouped with farm workers as victims of agribusiness. Many paragraphs again began with questions. Consumers and farm workers alike, he argued, suffered and will suffer from the poisons in the food, ground, water, and air. Any "acceptable" level of exposure recommended by "growers, the chemical companies, and the bureaucrats" must be challenged by the question, "Acceptable to whom? Acceptable to Johnnie Rodríguez's parents? Acceptable to Felipe Franco? Acceptable to the widow of Juan Chabolla and her children?" After having thus connected his first and last sections, Chávez concluded his address by discussing his fast and offering directions for supporting his cause.[93]

Chávez's language contained two well-used images, the canary in the mine and the picture of Mother Nature whom no one could fool. He included several references that seemed particularly appropriate to the college students and professors who formed most of his audience, quoting Oscar Wilde, citing Darwinian evolution, noting the *Wall Street Journal's* lament about industry trading quick profits for long-term jobs, urging his young listeners to reject forty- and fifty-year old policies that did not work, and mentioning the horrors of sexual harassment in fields and pollution of the environment. In an attempt to belittle the growers' claims that pesticide use benefited farm workers, he referred to the Vietnam War's analogous claim of destroying villages to save them. His prose was clear, to the point, crisp, and filled with short summaries such as: "There can be no toleration of any toxic that causes cancer, still birth, deformed bodies."[94]

Chávez explicitly added qualities to his persona in several ways. Enhancing his image while identifying his movement and himself with his audience's values and interests, he declared that "there is nothing we care more about than the lives and safety of our families," a concern that outweighed other union goals; and "There is nothing we share more deeply in common with the consumers of North America than [concern for] the safety of the food all of us rely upon." He pointed out that as long ago as 1967 his union had won a contract that led to the initial ban on DDT and other deadly sprays in the U.S.

Confiding how he had been "ashamed" of his initial lack of feeling for inflicted and endangered farm workers and their children, he recalled that he had "studied this wanton abuse of nature. I read the literature, heard from the experts about what pesticides do. I talked with farm workers, listened to their families, and shared their anguish and their fears." When he had completed his research, he became an advocate: "I spoke out against the cycle of death." He disclosed how he went past words in order to dramatize his case, undertaking a "thirty-six-day unconditional, water-only fast" designed "to purify my own body, mind, and soul" as an "act of penance for our own members who, out of ignorance or need, cooperate with those who grow and sell food treated with toxics."[95]

From his own suffering and action, Chávez found qualities he embedded in his second persona. His fast, he explained, "was also for those who know what is right and just," "for those who know that they could or should do more—for those who, by not acting, become bystanders in the poisoning of our food and the people who produce it." Therefore to end the injustices he so carefully documented required not only action by unionists and himself but by his audience. "The answer lies with you and me," he insisted; "It is with all men and women who share the suffering and yearn with us for a better world." He provided specific directions for those willing and wanting to be persuaded or reconstituted: "So I ask of you, take the pledge: boycott grapes. Join the many hundreds who have taken up where my fast ended—by sharing the suffering of the farm workers—by going without food for a day or two days or three." He finished by quoting the prophet Micah from the Old Testament: "'What does the Lord require of you, but to do justice, to love kindness, and to walk humbly with your God.' Thank you. Boycott grapes."[96]

Chávez's second persona depicted listeners as impelled to support his case if they sought justice or felt the pain of the honest, hard-working farm workers and their children who were struck down by dangerous pesticides. If his audience identified with him and his message, they would adopt his qualities of commitment and action and be transformed into individuals who enacted their better qualities by boycotting and otherwise supporting the UFW in its just cause. He also subsumed his listeners into his movement by arguing that the standard of protection they would want for their family matched that sought by farm workers.[97]

Two-and-one-half years after speaking at Pacific Lutheran, Chávez gave an address in Washington, D.C., in which he developed in detail the anti-politics theme that had emerged in his recent discourse. He began by recalling that "One year ago next month, many good people in California were disappointed by the election-day defeat of Proposition 128, the statewide Big Green environmental initiative"—an initiative supported by the UFW that would have ended "cancer-causing agricultural poisons." This electoral failure reflected "profound voter frustration with incumbent politicians," for "only a handful of the twenty-eight ballot measures in California were approved last November." The election taught "an important lesson for reformers: electoral politics isn't the only medium of change."[98]

Rhetorical discourse remained the essential tool, though the public and not the politicians must be the primary audience. Chávez explained: "Direct confrontation, making grass-roots appeals—principal tactics of the environmental and other popular movements of the 1960s and '70s—are still viable alternatives in the 1990s." Through such methods, he noted, he and his movement had battled for many years; and he could now see that his faith in political solutions and politicians had been misplaced. Social change would come less and less from politicians or even the "political process," avenues controlled in California by "agribusiness, chemical, timber, and other monied interests." Even when right-minded people entered politics, they became "mired in political gridlock" as wealthy interests blocked progress.[99]

The voting process itself posed difficult problems. In California the middle class in particular and voters in general—"so much older and whiter and wealthier and more conservative than the population as a whole"—controlled elections; and that controlling class remained far apart from the poor minorities who comprised his movement with non-English-speaking minorities facing an "intimidating" process even to register to vote.

Chávez did not give up on the large middle class, but instead attempted to meld its interests with those of farm workers through a set of claims relying on anaphora for dramatic effect. After introducing this series with, "Issues of concern to the middle class are also disregarded if change threatens the rich corporate special interests that dominate political fundraising," he related: "So politicians don't ban the most toxic agricultural pesticides" because of cancer and deformed babies of farm workers; "So they don't imperil millions of dollars in agribusiness and chemical-company profits today because some day, some consumers might get cancer; So they allow all of us—who place our faith in the safety of the food supply"—to eat such dangerous food. Chávez found the legislative process "incapable of accomplishing anything meaningful" on "issues that affect ordinary people—health care and education, unemployment and insurance reform."[100]

In a characteristically clear transition and statement of his main point, Chávez proposed confidently: "There are solutions. But they are not to be had through public policy, which requires that you place your fate in the hands of the politicians. Solutions can be achieved through public action—taking matters into your own hands by taking your case directly to the people." His solution, one that expressed his customary faith in discourse, possessed advantages: "The polls never close, your supporters can vote more than once, and you don't need a majority to win."[101]

The remainder of the body of his speech concentrated on the boycott, demonstrating its power through many statistics and examples including an extended example of Vons' southern California stores that were "losing millions of dollars." Success in the boycott rested on rhetorical processes rather than on the legal system in which his movement had wrongly placed its "faith"; consequently, he pointed out, "we turned to our court of last resort: farm workers are again asking the American people to boycott California table grapes." His core audience rested on a "base of support . . . among Hispanics, African Americans, and other minorities—plus allies in labor and the church" and also on an "entire generation of Americans who matured politically and socially in the '60s and '70s." These audiences accounted for his early successes and must be rallied again.[102]

As in his other discourse in the last years before his death, he used the vastness of time to banish discouragement over recent setbacks:

When we win isn't important. The rich have money—and the poor have time. We don't have to win this year or next year or even the year after that. We'll just keep plugging away, day after day, until the boycott takes its toll. We will never give up. We have nothing else to do with our lives except to continue in this nonviolent fight.[103]

• • •

Chávez's concluding comments began with a clear transition underscoring the advantages of time to a rhetorically based campaign: "Which is the last point I would make for those who seek change: In political campaigns, you race against time to get your message out—and you are always dramatically outspent." But in public action and boycotts, time is on your side. Clearly defining the audience, and identifying it with himself as well as with his thesis in this speech, he restated and repeated much of his conclusion at Pacific Lutheran: "The answers lie with public action, not public policy. The answers lie with you and me, and with all men and women who yearn with us for a better world." Chávez's persuaded or reconstituted listeners would not be isolated or small in number but would be part of a response to "a calling for millions of decent people in thousands of distant places to heed through a multitude of simple deeds the commandment set out in the book of the Prophet Micah, in the Old Testament: 'What does the Lord require of you, but to do justice, to love, kindness, and to walk humbly with your God. Thank you. And boycott grapes." Chávez had defined not only his audience but implicitly his commission and himself: He must communicate far and wide the well reasoned and fact-filled explanations and arguments that formed the "calling" that would bring justice.[104]

Chávez's rhetorically constructed first persona participated in a reciprocal relationship with his second persona and substantive message. He had told listeners how he and farm workers had fought against injustice for forty years and how he had spoken out against injustice for so long; and he had embodied his faith in facts and reason and a moral case through his own fact-filled, well-argued, and clearly presented case. His image also drew from well-known stories of his sacrifice and hard work for justice, his indifference to material gain, and his exhausting fasts and marches. Thus through his rhetorical efforts and personal life he projected a self-portrait that contained the qualities he wanted audiences to emulate: He appeared as the committed battler for justice who possessed faith in a just cause and would carry out acts to help the poor and deserving in their struggle with the rich and powerful. If he successfully identified with audiences through his first persona, he could more easily formulate them into the mold he had built in his second persona. Although he recognized the political defeats of the last years, his answer was to engage in direct action and extend the time-line for success—but never to lose his deep faith that inevitable success would result from the rhetorical campaign of a teacher of truth.

In a speech to a very different audience than those to which he usually spoke, Chávez addressed the Building Industry of Northern California on the evening of November, 1991, in San Jose.[105] Characteristically, he spoke not in a "flashy" manner but in one described as "genuine and from the heart." Earlier that day in a radio interview, Chávez's soft-spoken and low-key manner had prompted a similar description of his delivery from the President of the BIA: "If you didn't know who he was, it was easy to lose him in a crowd."[106] In his evening speech Chávez talked more than usual about his own life and about issues in housing, sharing his past with a friendly audience with whom he had long worked to provide affordable homes for California's farm workers and other low-income families. In the speech he nevertheless stayed true to the form, style, method of evidence, and other features of his standard rhetorical profile.

Chávez began by personally identifying himself with the site of his speech, describing how San Jose seemed like home to him because his "family often called this place home when we became migrants after the bank foreclosed on my father's small Arizona farm during the late 1930s." He recounted the difficult life he had lived as a youth in the San Jose barrio Sal Si Puedes, and sketched his early career in the CSO where he battled segregation, police brutality, and a host of other social evils facing Hispanics. Although Sal Si Puedes had been replaced by a freeway, he related, nearby today's "farm workers are living in caves and crude shacks, under trees and bridges, and in wretched labor camps" amidst dangerous conditions and no sanitation. "These savage conditions are often the rule and not the exception" in California, and thus the UFW had stayed on its long battle against "injustices." Relating his main point directly to his audience, he claimed that the "denial of housing that is decent and affordable" contributed to many of the problems facing Hispanic farm workers; "affordable, entry-level housing" would help resolve the problem.[107]

In his by-now-expected fact-filled and optimistic rhetorical manner, Chávez provided examples in five valley communities where his movement's tax-exempt service center had built affordable homes of high quality for farm workers and other poor people. He cited precise prices, averages, numbers of lots in subdivisions, and percentages of tenants who lived in his subsidized housing developments and earned very low incomes; and he followed with the "typical example" of Steve Padilla and his family who went from "a small, rat- and cockroach-infested two-bedroom apartment" without carpeting, central heat or air, to a "three-bedroom apartment with wall-to-wall carpeting, central heat and air, dishwasher and garbage disposal"—and at "30 percent less rent."[108]

After reviewing national achievements of his labor-movement housing programs, he turned to his organization's current project in Hollister, California, to build a "105-lot single-family housing project" for "five hundred low-income farm workers" in an area where land cost average some "$100,000" an acre. The BIA could help in the Bay Area market where only "about 10 percent" of residents, or all those households earning more than $70,000 a year, can afford the median-priced house of $268,000.[109]

Chávez introduced his conclusion with a series of questions cast in parallel structure and employing his favored stylistic device:

> Should owning a home of your own be the dream all Americans can work toward—except farm workers and Hispanics and other working families, rural or urban?
>
> Should home ownership be everyone's right—except farm workers and Hispanics and other working families?
>
> Should all people be able to work for the day when they can purchase a home—unless their skin is brown or black, or they work on a farm or factory?[110]

Following his reminiscing about his experiences when he left the Navy after World War II to find his and others' families denied home ownership because they were farm workers, he concluded by challenging the BIA to join his movement's efforts to reverse such discrimination.

After the speech Chávez patiently answered each question from his audience. Listeners left the speech "very impressed," the President of Shea Homes declaring: "What so impressed me about Chávez was that he was such a genuine character. There was nothing phony about him."[111] When the address and questions had ended, at 10:00 P.M., Chávez and his aides drove five hours back to UFW headquarters in La Paz.

The last sample of discourse we will study consists of his statements on his fast of 1988. Here Chávez adapted his form and message to the emotional and personal setting of his fast. Though he did not alter his fundamental message or essential manner, his remarks were briefer, less factual, more personal, and more focused on personae than those in his speeches or essays.

On July 19, three days after he had begun his fast, he issued a one-and-one-third page statement from Delano. He began by confiding that "a powerful urge has been raging within me for several months," one that he could no longer resist and that led him to fast. Calamitous setbacks of the past year "precipitated the fast, including the terrible suffering of farm workers and their children, the crushing of farm worker fights, the denial of fair and free elections and the death of good faith collective bargaining. . . ." While the fast "is first and foremost personal" and "directed at myself . . . for the purification of my own body, mind, and soul," Chávez disclosed, "the fast is also a heartfelt prayer for purification and strengthening for all of us—for myself and for all those who work beside me in the farm worker movement, whatever the work we do." The pain of suffering farm workers and children, working in poisoned fields, dying and deformed from cancer, led him to ask rhetorically: "Do we feel their pain deeply enough? I know I don't—and I am ashamed." He felt pain too because some workers still cooperated with "those who grow and sell the poisoned food we all eat," and many people still shopped at stores that sold grapes or ate at restaurants that displayed them. Connecting himself to his audience, he asked, "What have we done, you and I?" and he answered for his part that he would fast as "an act of penance for those in positions of moral authority and for all men and women activists who know what is right and just, who know that they could or should do more, who have become bystanders and thus collaborators with an industry that does not care about its workers."[112]

The course for the fair-minded who identified with Chávez was clearly marked: "It is my fondest hope that our friends, everywhere, will begin a great movement of non-cooperation with supermarkets; that people will resist, in a myriad of nonviolent ways, the presence of grapes in the stores where they shop." He finished by relating his study and experiences that had convinced him of the "plague of pesticides" and by forging one final tie among himself, his audience, and the agenda he wished readers to enact: "I pray to God that this fast will be a preparation for a multitude of simple deeds for justice, carried out by men and women whose hearts are focused on the suffering of the poor and who yearn, with us, for a better world. Together, all things are possible."[113]

At the close of the fast he issued another statement, one that he requested be "shared with you" by a colleague who read it because "my heart is too full and my body too weak to read this message for myself." He again asked rhetorically if "we carry in our hearts the plight of the farm workers and their children," felt their "pain" or knew their "heartaches" when loved ones died of cancer"? to which he answered: "I know I didn't. And I was ashamed." He reiterated many points made in his first statement, noting his recent in-depth study of pesticides and their effects, the cooperation of unionists and others with growers and supermarkets that sold grapes, the penance he undertook for those in power and those "who know what is right and just" but "could or should do more," and the boycott that should be followed. His final sentences melded himself with his audiences: "The answer lies with you and me. It is for all of us to do more. We will demonstrate by what we do and not by what we say our solidarity with the weak and the afflicted." Again he ended with his prayer that "this fast will encourage a multitude of simple deeds."[114]

In his conclusion, and indeed throughout his statement, Chávez explicitly sought to share his shame, suffering, and action with his audience of well-meaning auditors. If they saw the injustice he saw and identified with him, they must enact the simple acts he requested. His appeal reflected the tradition of suffering and penance that comes directly from the cultural orientation and attendant rhetorical tradition of Mexican Americans. The appeal in these statements, however, has broad allure to many audiences, for it binds personae in a way that impels action, redefines listeners and readers, and gives them a set of concrete actions. Just as Chávez purified his guilt over the heartbreaking poisoning of people by suffering in his fast, so audiences who felt the injustice and pain and felt the shame for abetting the poisoners could remove their guilt and be purified through the simple act of boycotting grapes.

Chávez's last decade and a half featured important changes in his rhetorical profile. He extended his rhetorical reach by incorporating much more direct-mailing as a channel for his message; added stylistic polish, in part as a result of Grossman's influence; and broadened his audience through new themes and images that appealed to the growing constituencies of health-conscious consumers and non-farm worker Hispanics. In rhetorical retreats that reflected changing political and social conditions, he reconfigured his central claim that his moral case would inevitably swing public opinion and change conditions: He placed less faith in political institutions and more in the general public and extended the time-line for when success would occur. Capitalizing on his increased stature, his own persona occupied a larger place in his set of appeals; reordering his audience to reflect recent history, he singled out the generation that matured during the idealistic 1960s and 1970s as an important segment of his potential coalition. Yet perhaps more significant than these and other changes, to the end of his life he continued to rely on the rhetorical profile that characterized his entire career. This profile not only reached back through his history, it reached across the various forms and formats he employed—even extending, as we have shown in this chapter, to his written statements or addresses to audiences of homebuilders.

Chapter 9

Conclusion

L ooking back over the life of César Chávez, one could marvel over his accomplishments not only because of their enormity but because he seemed so initially ill-fitted to achieve them. By traditional standards, Chávez lacked the personal qualities necessary to be a successful leader or charismatic advocate; and his opponents had financial and political resources that he and his movement could not come close to matching. Indeed, he appeared to be the wrong person, in the wrong place, with the wrong group of potential followers, against the wrong opponents, at the wrong time.

The perspective a student of rhetoric and public address can bring, however, yields a very different interpretation of Chávez and his career. A rhetorical perspective illuminates both how he reached his lofty goals and why he adopted his particular means to pursue those goals. It also allows us to understand both how and why Chávez lived the life he chose.

In previous chapters we examined the issues Chávez raised and conditions he faced; studied his response to those issues and conditions; documented, explicated, and analyzed his rhetorical efforts; and reviewed the history of his life and movement. To explain how he achieved his unprecedented successes, we attempted to uncover the foundations of his interrelated worldview and theory of reform rhetoric and to show the effects of that worldview and theory on his discourse. More specifically, we applied our reconstitutive-discourse model to demonstrate how Chávez's thought and character merged into a message that rhetorically informed, persuaded, and reformulated audiences. Our analysis of his discourse went far beyond that of any previous study and provided special insights from Chávez's own handwritten comments on speech texts, outlines, and speech notes. In our conclusion we review some of what we have learned about Chávez and about rhetorical discourse.

• • •

Although he would remain by nature a quiet and shy man, César Chávez was superbly prepared to be an advocate for his cause. He arrived in Delano in 1962 as an experienced orator/organizer who had conscientiously practiced and studied the art of spoken discourse and had compiled his own set of principles of effective discourse for a cause to which he had already committed his life. Chávez's version of rhetorical theory drew from his own experiences as a speaker and organizer as well as from his keen observations of other speakers and his reading about history's great reformers. As a youth he had seen and suffered from the injustices done to farm workers and Mexican Americans and learned from—and was inspired by—relatives and acquaintances who were protesters; later at the CSO he methodically established and honed his rhetorical skills.

Thus when Chávez burst into the consciousness of the general public, in the early years of what would be an exhausting lifelong campaign of speaking and organizing, he was more than an accidental beneficiary of the opportunities of the times, more than a product of the militant climate of social movements and rhetorical protests of the 1960s. He possessed a unique blend of experiences, training, skills, understanding, and outlook that equipped him formidably to advocate his cause. An historical study of Chávez can reveal his accomplishments, life, and character, but a rhetorical study is necessary to explain more fully the man and his influence.

A key to understanding Chávez's career lies in his unique worldview that privileged public address. Drawing upon his experiences as a youth and later a CSO organizer, and from his interrelated views of God, unions, reform rhetoric, and social movements, Chávez concluded that a divinely ordained plan would send forth rhetors to teach the truth about injustices to a public who, when well informed, would inevitably eliminate those injustices. Thus God's will ensured that social movements would succeed once their righteous case was widely heard. Farm workers, long suffering and constantly mistreated, represented a clear case of injustice. If Chávez could present the themes, arguments, explanations, and facts to enough people, he was convinced that his union would be transformed into a movement that would be part of the history of social movements destined to better the world.

Chávez's millennial interpretation of history and his attendant theory of discourse could scarcely have been better suited for a reform rhetor battling long odds against success. It motivated him to speak, write, fast, march, and otherwise tirelessly communicate his message. His determination could not be dampened by negative reactions of immediate audiences or disappointing setbacks to his movement. He knew that his cause was right and his discourse would ultimately enlist the people needed to reach his goals. Although he would lose much of his early faith in the political process, he never wavered in his faith that people would react positively to a well-presented case for a just cause.

Chávez's millennialism had no relationship to the calendar, for the year 2000 was not a finish line in his lifelong rhetorical tour to remake the world. His was a long-distance race in which only God knew the timetable for the inevitable victory. Hence Chávez's enthusiasm for his rhetorical campaign and movement could not be undone by the passing years or by any other human markers. With optimism and assurance he would stay the course, regardless of the year, the response of audiences, or the progress of his cause.

Chávez's worldview directed him to his characteristic rhetorical strategies and rhetorical profile, a profile that accounted for his surprising effects, his quiet charisma, and to a large degree his accomplishments as a reformer. Dedicated to informing listeners, he crafted extraordinarily well-organized, fact-filled, simply worded messages that contained thoughtful arguments for and explanations of the justice of his cause and the need to join or support his movement. A seasoned instructor, he added impact to his statistics by coupling them with moving examples; he often preceded maxims or sayings that encapsulated his point by telling a story or giving an example to make that point palpable and compelling; and he arranged his words to enliven his ideas and involve listeners, particularly through the use of anaphora and rhetorical questions. His messages reflected his overarching role of teacher; the emphasis was on the substance of his case rather than on himself or on his delivery or style, for his goal was to teach rather than to impress.

Chávez's years of speaking and observing persuasive and reconstitutive rhetoric—including the rhetorical principles he had learned from his parents—also taught him to be an adept and adaptable rhetor. He skillfully adjusted his rhetorical strategies for various audiences and to the issues of the day. When speaking in Spanish to farm workers and others, for example, he employed more of the *dichos* or aphorisms and *cuentos* or stories that were common in Mexican-American discourse, appealed to the Mexican-American values and topics of sacrifice, suffering, family, hard-work, courage, God, and Mexican history, and invoked the powerful image of blood.

Despite Chávez's skills in rhetorical adaptation, his worldview overrode any tendency to elevate immediate success with auditors over his long-range goals. Consequently, he never changed his fundamental message or rhetorical profile of a teacher of truth in a just cause. A powerful union and attendant social movement remained his goal, which sometimes placed him in conflict with Chicano groups, as when he opposed the bracero program and a lax governmental policy on undocumented immigrants, or when he insisted on a multicultural union. Yet the idealistic Chávez also continued to be a pragmatist whose discourse was rhetorically sophisticated as well as morally uncompromising. He often used specific rhetorical techniques to achieve particular purposes; and he converted various occasions such as marches or fasts into rhetorical events in service of his just cause. To put to point another way: In his career Chávez combined the practical art of rhetoric with the idealistic goals of a servant of God.

From his arrival at Delano in 1962 to his death in 1993, Chávez followed his own unique and well-thought-out plan of public communication. Our rhetorical perspective on Chávez not only offers an explanation of his motivation for his unending rhetorical campaign and of his use of the particular rhetorical qualities and strategies that characterized his message, it can help to explain his startling effects on audiences. Remaining consistent in his goals, worldview, and rhetorical characteristics, Chávez repeatedly embodied his millennial message by presenting that message in a way that authenticated his commitment to easily understood and fact-filled arguments. By emphasizing his ideas and not himself, by employing rhetorical means that depicted him as a teacher, while at the same time emphasizing the theme that truth needed to be taught, the man became indistinguishable from his message. Chávez added to his persona by retaining the lifestyle and appearance of a farm worker, and by remaining one with the subject of his speeches and the people in his core audiences. As biographer Winthrop Yinger commented, "He is the archetype, he is a farm worker."[1] Labor historian Cletus E. Daniel described Chávez's embodiment of his union and the effects of this embodiment:

> More than any other labor leader of his time, and perhaps in the whole history of American labor, César Chávez leads a union that is an extension of his own values, experience, and personality. This singular unity of man and movement has found its most forceful and enduring expression in the unprecedented economic and political power that has accrued to the membership of the United Farm Workers (UFW) under Chávez's intense and unrelenting tutelage.[2]

Thus Chávez embodied his message in several ways, first by expressing his ideas in a form, style, and manner appropriate for the worldview he presented, and second through his life and appearance that further projected a persona wholly appropriate to his substantive themes and arguments. This embodiment created the merger of thought and character that allows a rhetor to achieve the kind of potent identification with audiences that can effect persuasion and, in some cases, a reformulation of those audiences. Through his second persona, moreover,

Chávez defined audiences to invest them with the personal qualities needed to carry out his plans—the same qualities he demonstrated in his first persona. Chávez redefined often-fearful farm workers so that they could act out their courage, dignity, idealism, dedication, and willingness to work hard and sacrifice for their cause without expectation of appreciation or material gain. In turn, these reconstituted farm workers would themselves become rhetors who embodied their message as they educated, persuaded, and at times reconstituted audiences. Chávez lifted the character of audiences of college students and others to sacrifice for and serve in a just cause as they became unpaid organizers and workers in his movement. And he liberated in the general public its nascent generosity of spirit, belief in ideals, and commitment to justice, motivating in it allegiance to his boycott and support in various other ways.

The effects of Chávez's career are captured in a comment by one of his close followers upon his death, "He was our teacher and we were his students."[3] Chávez's discourse motivated audiences across a wide spectrum. For example, in 1993, Libby Lindsey, an activist among women in the membership of the United Mine Workers, discussed her long struggle in words that echoed those of Chávez, "We're still saying, 'Si, se puede'—Yes, we can."[4]

Our rhetorical study takes an additional important step further than other biographical studies and personal accounts that consider Chávez and the meaning of his life. Whereas biographer Eugene Nelson attributes the labor leader's striking effects in part to his "personal magnetism" and depicts him as "one of those persons one feels [one] has known all [one's] life," we explain Chávez's remarkable capacity—consciously developed as well as natural—to identify rhetorically with audiences small and large.[5] While Dolores Huerta credits the movement's success in large part to the "younger generation which responds to César's charismatic leadership," we explain much of the design and workings of that charisma.[6]

We also believe that our study complements the recent books by Susan Ferriss and Ricardo Sandoval and by Richard Griswold del Castillo and Richard A. Garcia. We have deepened and broadened Ferriss and Sandoval's study of Chávez considerably by providing an in-depth and thorough rhetorical analysis of a large sample of his discourse across his long career, situating that analysis in the context of Chávez's worldview and experiences and developing a model to explain his rhetorical effectiveness. We have extended Griswold del Castillo and Garcia's observation that Chávez's "hard life gave him strength of character that enabled him to communicate convincingly with field workers," by delineating the elements of that communicated character and explaining the dynamics of its effects on audiences.[7] To develop Griswold del Castillo and Garcia's conclusion that

Chávez "sparked a realistic yet radical belief in people and in the American dream of justice," we show how he planned to, and then did, transform those people in order to reach that dream; to add to the authors' contentions that Chávez was "a man who, for the most part just listened," that "the truth was that Chávez's strength came from his ability to listen to advice," and that he "almost instinctively knew that power lay in changing people, not by theorizing but by doing," we demonstrate that he combined the fruits of his keen ability to listen with a well-thought-out and developed theory and practice of discourse in a massive campaign of speaking, writing, and non-discursive texts that lay at the very heart of his calculated quest to change people.[8]

Our study is the first, we believe, to take Chávez on his own terms. He saw himself as a rhetorical agent in a lifetime campaign of educating audiences. His own orientation has directed our approach to studying him, for we view him as he viewed himself: as a subject, not object in the postmodern sense, who could and did accomplish much through his own efforts—rhetorical and otherwise. As to the question of whether God guided Chávez's rhetorical campaign, we will not speculate here—any more than we can convince all readers of this book of the existence of the God of the Catholic Church. Acknowledging—not discounting—Chávez's understanding of God's overarching place in his rhetorical campaign, we nevertheless account for Chávez's impact not by referring to the power of God but by employing principles of rhetoric. Although no evidence exists that Chávez read the rhetorical scholars who developed these principles, he discovered a very similar set of principles through his experience and studies and applied them masterfully throughout his career.

Our study challenges the boundaries of established approaches to rhetorical and social movement studies. Our model, which should be applicable to rhetors other than Chávez, further develops a method of explaining discourse that redefines its audiences. Our findings may refine the conventional view of charismatic leaders in social movements by showing how charisma can result from a rhetorical embodiment that coheres with one's second persona. Our analysis shows how such ordinary and even prosaic rhetorical elements as clear transitions, frequent summaries, a reliance on facts, and a quiet voice and mild manner while speaking can be sources of charisma rather than attributes of a boring orator. In short, we explain how a persona characterized by seemingly unextraordinary rhetorical and personal qualities, a person without the high-voltage energy and verve of the usual spellbinding orator, can by embodying a message produce electrical effects on audiences and gain a reputation as charismatic.

Chávez's particular upbringing, education, and resulting unusual worldview instilled in him an unbreakable faith that as a rhetor he was in the will of God; he need not doubt his rhetorical means as he executed God's will. Just as Chávez's history cannot be understood without understanding his rhetoric, so his rhetoric cannot be understood without reference to his history and religious beliefs.

In the end, Chávez's conception of and consequent commitment to public address may have contributed to his failures as well as to his successes. He would not moderate his extensive rhetorical campaign even when changing conditions directed him to devote more time to managing and supervising. Instead, he continued to act out his extraordinary faith in the power of his reform rhetoric if presented appropriately; and he stayed his course as an indefatigable campaigner even if it meant neglecting vital needs in his organization. Moreover, Chávez projected his own special relationship with rhetorical discourse onto audiences who in many cases lacked his ideological motivation and emotional makeup. No doubt many people in the materialistic 1980s and early 1990s were unmoved by his claim that following a subsistence life of acting out and speaking up for a righteous cause would bring them the spiritual satisfaction and sense of well-being it had brought him.

That Chávez's worldview as a rhetor led to his failures as well as his successes, that he ineluctably invited his own shortcomings as leader and rhetor, should by now be no surprise if we have accomplished one of our goals for this book: to acquaint readers with Chávez's extensive public discourse and to demonstrate that his views on rhetoric and his practice of public address were at the center of his career and indeed his life. His relationship with rhetoric went far beyond merely using rhetorical theory and practice as tools to advance his union and movement. Matters of a rhetorical nature directed much of his behavior, shaped his fundamental and animating view of the world, and explained a large part of the successes and failures in his career. His truly was a life committed to words, a legacy of devotion to things rhetorical, a story of the deep and lasting influence of a teacher of truth.

Notes

INTRODUCTION

1. César Chávez, "Letter from Delano," in *Pain and Promise: The Chicano Today,* ed. Edward Simmen, 31.
2. Charles Kuralt, narrator, "The State of the Union," CBS television documentary, Summer 1966. A partial transcript of this documentary exists in the San Joaquin Collection, Special Collections Department, Fresno State University Library (hereafter cited as "San Joaquin Collection, Fresno State").
3. For example, Richard Griswold del Castillo and Richard A. Garcia, *César Chávez: A Triumph of Spirit,* 114; Dolores Huerta, quoted ibid., 72; Edward Rucobo Jiménez, "A Critical Analysis of Newspaper Coverage of César Chávez's Death," 39.
4. This volume builds on the authors' previous writings on Chávez. These writings include (in chronological order): "The Rhetorical Worlds of César Chávez and Reies Tijerina," *Western Journal of Speech Communication* 44 (1980): 176–90; "Teaching the 'Truth': The Righteous Rhetoric of César Chávez," in *A War of Words: Chicano Protest in the 1960s and 1970s,* ed. John C. Hammerback, Richard J. Jensen, and José Ángel Gutiérrez (Westport, Conn.: Greenwood Press, 1985), 33–52; "César Chávez," in *American Orators of the Twentieth Century: Critical Studies and Sources,* ed. Bernard K. Duffy and Halford R. Ryan (Westport, Conn.: Greenwood Press, 1987), 55–62; "'A Revolution of Heart and Mind': César Chávez's Rhetorical Crusade," *Journal of the West* 27 (April 1988): 69–74, reprinted in *Western Speakers: Voices of the American Dream,* ed. Susan H. Koester (Manhattan, Kans.: Sunflower University Press, 1988), 69–74; "Ethnic Heritage as Rhetorical Legacy: The Plan of Delano," *Quarterly Journal of Speech* 80 (1994): 53–70; and "César Estrada Chávez," in *Leaders from the 1960s,* ed. David DeLeon (Westport, Conn.: Greenwood Press, 1994), 54–61.
5. Griswold del Castillo and Garcia, *Triumph of Spirit,* 143.
6. Eric Serna, quoted in John Robertson, "Hispanic Leader's Message Transcended Ethnicity, Race," *Albuquerque Journal,* April 24, 1993, A-10.
7. Art Torres, quoted in George Ramos, "President Chávez Was Hero to Millions,'" *Albuquerque Journal,* April 24, 1993, 1; Jerry Brown, quoted in "'Visionary' César Chávez dead at 66," *Las Vegas Review-Journal,* April 24, 1993, 1; Bill Clinton, quoted in "'Visionary' César Chávez dead at 66," 1; Jiménez, "Newspaper Coverage of Chávez's Death," 39; Richard A. Garcia, "César Chávez and the Chicanos: The Presence, the Spirit, and the Fire," unpublished paper in possession of authors. For an extended discussion of the implications of Chávez's death, see Griswold del Castillo and Garcia, *Triumph of Spirit,* 172–78.
8. Griswold del Castillo and Garcia, *Triumph of Spirit,* 143.
9. Ronald B. Taylor, *Chávez and the Farm Workers,* 181; quoted in Winthrop Yinger, *César Chávez: The Rhetoric of Nonviolence,* 20. Peter Matthiessen, *Sal Si Puedes,* 30; Eugene Nelson, *Huelga! The First Hundred Days of the Great Delano Grape Strike,* 51–52; Jeff

Wright, "Farm Workers' Leaders Advocate Boycott," *The Register-Guard* (Eugene, Ore.), April 16, 1991, C–3; Rev. Juan de Leon, quoted in Patricia Sydney Straub, "Workers Recall Strike," The *Bakersfield Californian*, September 10, 1995, B-1; Andrew Young, *An Easy Burden* (New York: HarperCollins, 1996), 445; Thomas E. Hachey and Ralph E. Weber, eds., *American Dissent From Thomas Jefferson to César Chávez: The Rhetoric of Reform and Revolution*, 155; and Senator Robert Kennedy, quoted in "César Chávez, 1927–1993," a synopsis of Chávez's life released by the UFW (photocopy of manuscript in possession of authors).

10. Richard Rodríguez, quoted in Griswold del Castillo and Garcia, *Triumph of Spirit*, 140; ibid.

11. Evan T. Barr, "Sour Grapes: César Chávez Twenty Years Later," *The New Republic*, November 25, 1985, 22.

12. Barr, "Sour Grapes," 20.

13. For example, Griswold del Castillo and Garcia note that in 1991 Mexico awarded Chávez the Águila de Oro, a "prestigious . . . award of merit given to few who are not Mexican citizens" (*Triumph of Spirit*, 169). The award was given in recognition of Chávez's advancement of the welfare of Mexican workers in the United States. In 1992 Chávez received "the award of Premio Benito Juárez," which "honors an individual of international importance who has advanced the cause of justice and peace" (169). The UFW's publication *Food and Justice* details the number of honors Chávez received. See, for example, "Honoring César Chávez's Life," *Food and Justice*, July 1995, 21–22.

14. Chávez, interview at Center for the Study of Democratic Institutions, Santa Barbara, Calif., 1968.

15. John R. Moyer, "A Conversation With César Chávez," in *Readings on La Raza: The Twentieth Century*, ed. Matt S. Meier and Feliciano Rivera, 248.

16. Quoted in Yinger, *Rhetoric of Nonviolence*, 19.

17. Bob Vice of the California Farm Bureau Federation, quoted in "'Visionary' César Chávez Dead at 66," 3A.

18. Chávez, interview by Nancy Padilla, Albuquerque, N.M., December 7, 1981.

19. Matthiessen, *Sal Si Puedes*, 103.

20. Hammerback and Jensen, "Teaching the 'Truth,'" 35.

21. George Boss, "Essential Attributes of the Concept of Charisma," *Southern Speech Communication Journal* 41 (Spring 1976): 305.

22. Yinger, *Rhetoric of Nonviolence*, 21; John Gregory Dunne, *Delano: Story of the California Grape Strike*, 58.

23. Chávez, interview by Padilla; Stan Steiner, *La Raza: The Mexican Americans* (New York: Harper & Row, 1970), 311.

24. Chávez, interview by Padilla.

25. Yinger, *Rhetoric of Nonviolence*, 46–47.

26. Yinger, *Rhetoric of Nonviolence*, 48.

27. Nelson, *Huelga*, 52; Luis A. Solis-Garza, "César Chávez: The Chicano 'Messiah'?" in *Pain and Promise*, ed. Edward Simmen, 304; quoted in Richard A. Garcia, "César Chávez and the Chicanos," 13.

28. Jiménez, "Newspaper Coverage of Chávez's Death," 51–52.

29. For further readings on the history of the Chicano movement, see Manual Serven, ed., *An Awakening Minority: The Mexican Americans* (1970); Stan Steiner, *La Raza: The Mexican Americans* (1970); Wayne Moquin and Charles Van Doren, eds., *Documentary History of the Mexican Americans* (1971); Edward Simmen, ed., *Pain and Promise: The Chicano Today* (1972); Matt S. Meier and Feliciano Rivera, eds., *Readings on La*

Raza: The Twentieth Century (1974); F. Chris García and Rudolph O. de la Garza, *The Chicano Political Experience: Three Perspectives* (1977); Rodolfo Acuña, *Occupied America: A History of Chicanos* (1988); Matt S. Meier and Feliciano Ribera, *Mexican Americans: American Mexicans* (1993); F. Arturo Rosales, *Chicano! The History of the Mexican American Civil Rights Movement* (1996).

30. For a discussion of the "Plan of Delano" as rhetoric, see Hammerback and Jensen, "Ethnic Heritage as Rhetorical Legacy."

31. Marc Grossman, interview by authors, Sacramento, Calif., October 14, 1995. Audiotape of interview in possession of authors.

Grossman came to know Chávez through Grossman's friendship with Chávez's oldest son, Fernando, whom Grossman met as a fellow student at the University of California at Los Angeles. In 1975 Chávez asked the journalism graduate student to assist him. Grossman served with Chávez until early 1981 as the primary and often only full-time press aide, press secretary, media consultant, and general aide. He continued to work with Chávez on speeches and written messages until Chávez's death. (Grossman, interview by authors.)

CHAPTER I. THE MAKING OF A RHETOR AND A MOVEMENT

1. Matthiessen, *Sal Si Puedes,* 8.
2. Chávez, quoted in Taylor, *Chávez and the Farm Workers,* 61.
3. Griswold del Castillo and Garcia, *Triumph of Spirit,* 4.
4. Chávez, quoted in Taylor, *Chávez and the Farm Workers,* 59–60; also Chávez, quoted in Griswold del Castillo and Garcia, 7.
5. ARC 20, KMEX, TC 10:00:00. Archival footage ("ARC") was furnished to the authors from materials collected for a documentary on Chávez's life, "The Fight in the Fields: César Chávez and the Farmworkers Movement." The film's producers, Rick Tejada-Flores and Ray Telles, transcribed tapes and provided the authors with photocopies of the transcriptions. Chávez's words were then translated to English from Spanish by Alicia García, a student at the University of Nevada, Las Vegas. Specific citations to the transcripts are noted as provided to us.
6. Chávez, quoted in Jacques E. Levy, *César Chávez: Autobiography of La Causa,* 42; Chávez, quoted in Taylor, *Chávez and the Farm Workers,* 61–62.
7. Chávez, quoted in Dunne, *Delano,* 5.
8. Chávez, quoted in Taylor, *Chávez and the Farm Workers,* 60.
9. Dunne, *Delano,* 5–6.
10. Yinger, *Rhetoric of Nonviolence,* 23.
11. UFW, "César Chávez, 1927–1993."
12. Chávez, quoted in Levy, *Autobiography of La Causa,* 65.
13. Chávez, quoted in Taylor, *Chávez and the Farm Workers,* 64. Griswold del Castillo and Garcia (*Triumph of Spirit,* 13) quote Chávez as saying that he himself was the student humiliated.
14. Chávez, quoted in Taylor, *Chávez and the Farm Workers,* 62.
15. Chávez, quoted in Griswold del Castillo and Garcia, *Triumph of Spirit,* 13.
16. Cletus E. Daniel, "César Chávez and the Unionization of California Farm Workers," in *Labor Leaders in America,* ed. Melvyn Dubofsky and Warren Van Tine, 354.
17. Chávez, "The Organizer's Tale," in *The Chicanos: Mexican-American Voices,* ed. Ed Ludwig and James Santibáñez, 112.

18. Chávez, quoted in Levy, *Autobiography of La Causa*, 18.
19. Daniel, "Unionization of California Farm Workers," 355.
20. Steiner, *La Raza*, 313.
21. Chávez, quoted in Levy, *Autobiography of La Causa*, 84; Matthiessen, *Sal Si Puedes*, 209; Griswold del Castillo and Garcia, *Triumph of Spirit*, 19; Daniel, "Unionization of California Farm Workers," 356.
22. Chávez, quoted in Levy, *Autobiography of La Causa*, 85.
23. Chávez, quoted in Levy, *Autobiography of La Causa*, 50.
24. ARC 20, KMEX, TC 10:00:00.
25. Chávez, quoted in Nelson, *Huelga*, 49.
26. UFW, "César Chávez, 1927–1993."
27. Fred Ross, *Conquering Goliath: César Chávez at the Beginning*, 1.
28. Chávez, quoted in Levy, *Autobiography of La Causa*, 97, 99.
29. Fred Ross, quoted in Levy, *Autobiography of La Causa*, 102.
30. Chávez, interview at Wayne State University, Detroit, 1980, ARC 1:46. Audiotape in UFW Papers, Archives of Labor History and Urban Affairs, Walter E. Reuther Library, Wayne State University, Detroit (hereafter cited as "UFW Papers, Wayne State"). Chávez, "The Organizer's Tale," 102–103.
31. Chávez, "The Organizer's Tale," 103.
32. Chávez, interview at Wayne State, ARC 2:48.
33. Chávez, quoted in Yinger, *Rhetoric of Nonviolence*, 23, 25.
34. Chávez, interview at Wayne State, ARC 4:20.
35. Levy, *Autobiography of La Causa*, 92.
36. Levy, *Autobiography of La Causa*, 92.
37. Chávez, "The Organizer's Tale," 102; Chávez, quoted in Mark Day, *Forty Acres: César Chávez and the Farm Workers* (New York: Praeger, 1971), 121, 114.
38. Chávez, "The Organizer's Tale," 102.
39. Chávez, quoted in Levy, *Autobiography of La Causa*, 110–11.
40. Dolores Huerta, quoted in Jerald B. Brown, "The United Farm Workers Grape Strike and Boycott, 1965–1970: An Evaluation of the Culture of Poverty Theory," Latin American Studies Program Dissertation Series no. 39 (Ithaca, N.Y.: Cornell University Press, 1972), 149.
41. Chávez, interview at Wayne State, ARC 20:30.
42. Chávez, quoted in Rosales, *Chicano!* 130.
43. Chávez, quoted in Levy, *Autobiography of La Causa*, 109–10.
44. Levy, *Autobiography of La Causa*, 112.
45. Chávez, quoted in Levy, *Autobiography of La Causa*, 115–16.
46. Chávez, quoted in Levy, *Autobiography of La Causa*, 117; Chávez, "The Organizer's Tale," 103.
47. Ross, *Conquering Goliath*, 5.
48. Fred Ross's *Conquering Goliath* detailed Chávez's organizing efforts in Oxnard.
49. Sam Kushner, *Long Road to Delano*, 150.
50. Ross, *Conquering Goliath*, 143.
51. Dunne, *Delano*, 71; Chávez, quoted in Levy, *Autobiography of La Causa*, 3.
52. Chávez, quoted in UFW, "César Chávez, 1927–1993."
53. Griswold del Castillo and Garcia, *Triumph of Spirit*, 32, 38.
54. Griswold del Castillo and Garcia, *Triumph of Spirit*, 14–15.
55. Levy, *Autobiography of La Causa*, 151–52.
56. Griswold del Castillo and Garcia, *Triumph of Spirit*, 14–16.

57. Chávez, quoted in Levy, *Autobiography of La Causa*, 3–4; Rodolfo Acuña, *Occupied America*, 326.

CHAPTER 2. CHÁVEZ'S CONCEPTION OF RHETORICAL COMMUNICATION

1. Hammerback, Jensen, and Gutiérrez, *A War of Words*, 3.
2. Studies of Mexican-American leaders in the 1960s and 1970s usually focus on four major leaders and their organizations: in New Mexico, Reies López Tijerina and the *Alianza Federal de Mercedes Libres*; in Texas, José Ángel Gutiérrez and a variety of organizations including the Chicano political party and *La Raza Unida* (the United Race); in Colorado, Rodolfo "Corky" Gonzales and the Crusade for Justice; and in California, César Chávez and the UFW. For descriptions of these leaders see Hammerback, Jensen, and Gutiérrez, *A War of Words*, 1–100. The term "Chicano" is a difficult one to define. Once derogatory, it was transformed into a term of pride during the 1960s and 1970s by young Mexican Americans who, like members of other minority groups, developed positive symbols for self-identification. In *A War of Words* (p. 5) we described the term this way: "Although the term has carried different meanings to different people, and although extensive discussion and examination of its origins have been inconclusive, for many people 'Chicano' connoted a militant stance, confrontational actions, and intense pride associated with the movement for . . . identity and power." For a more recent treatment see Rosales, *Chicano!*, a companion piece to the 1996 four-part PBS series on the Chicano movement.
3. Hammerback, Jensen, and Gutiérrez, *A War of Words*, 6.
4. Hammerback and Jensen, "Ethnic Heritage as Rhetorical Legacy."
5. José Ángel Gutiérrez, "César Estrada Chávez: The First and Last of the Chicano Leaders," *San Jose Studies* 20 (spring 1994): 35, 37.
6. Chávez, quoted in Steiner, *La Raza*, 319; Yinger, *Rhetoric of Nonviolence*, 30.
7. Chávez, interview by Bill Olson and Dennis Luchetti, August 13, 1967.
8. Frederick J. Antczak, *Thought and Character: The Rhetoric of Democratic Education* (Ames: Iowa State University Press, 1985), 201.
9. Blanca Alvarado, Vice-Mayor of San Jose, Calif., quoted in Josephine Méndez-Negrete, "We Remember César Chávez: A Catalyst for Change," *San Jose Studies* 20 (Spring 1994): 75.
10. Sofía Mendoza, quoted in Méndez-Negrete, "We Remember César Chávez," 79.
11. Yinger, *Rhetoric of Nonviolence*, 28.
12. Chávez, quoted in Moyer, "A Conversation with César Chávez," 250.
13. Chávez, quoted in Levy, *Autobiography of La Causa*, 161.
14. Chávez, quoted in Steiner, *La Raza*, 292.
15. Chávez, quoted in Steiner, *La Raza*, 292.
16. Moyer, "A Conversation with César Chávez," 249.
17. Chávez, quoted in Steiner, *La Raza*, 291–92.
18. Dolores Huerta, quoted in Yinger, *Rhetoric of Nonviolence*, 34.
19. Méndez-Negrete, "We Remember César Chávez," 76.
20. Quoted in "Joe Serna," *3/1/61* (winter 1996): 2. *3/1/61* is a publication of the National Peace Corps Association.
21. Eliseo Medina, quoted in Rosales, *Chicano!*, 130.
22. Chávez, quoted in Levy, *Autobiography of La Causa*, 78.
23. Daniel, "Unionization of California Farm Workers," 355.

24. Yinger, *Rhetoric of Nonviolence*, 57.
25. Chávez, "The Philosophy of César Chávez," *El Malcriado*, December 2, 1966, 29. The article is a translation of the original article in Spanish, which appeared in *El Malcriado*, December 15, 1964.
26. Chávez, quoted in Yinger, *Rhetoric of Nonviolence*, 56–57.
27. Chávez, quoted in Donovan Orman Roberts, "Theory and Practice in the Life and Thought of César E. Chávez: Implications for a Social Ethic," 12. Roberts spent six weeks in California during the summer of 1975 studying with Chávez. He frequently traveled with Chávez on his thousand-mile march, interviewed him, and heard many of his speeches but did not closely analyze any of them. Roberts found "considerable correlation and coherence between Chávez's theoretical principles and his ability to implement them in practice" (vii).
28. Chávez, interview at KQED, San Francisco State University, 1970. ARC 30, 17:03:06. Copy in possession of authors.
29. Chávez, quoted in Steiner, *La Raza*, 250.
30. Chávez, quoted in Matthiessen, *Sal Si Puedes*, 105; Chávez, quoted in Yinger, *Rhetoric of Nonviolence*, 29.
31. Chávez, quoted in Steiner, *La Raza*, 292.
32. César Chávez, "The Mexican American and the Church," 143.
33. Chávez, quoted in Eugene Kennedy, "César Chávez: Powerful Innocent," *The Critic*, 31 (July–August 1973) no. 6, cited in Roberts, "Implications for a Social Ethic," 312.
34. Levy, *Autobiography of La Causa*, 27.
35. Yinger, *Rhetoric of Nonviolence*, 75; Chávez, quoted in ibid.
36. Day, *Forty Acres*, 112.
37. Chávez, interview at Wayne State, ARC 23:11.
38. Chávez, quoted in Day, *Forty Acres*, 58.
39. Yinger, *Rhetoric of Nonviolence*, 31.
40. Fred Ross, quoted in Day, *Forty Acres*, 202–203.
41. Chávez, interview at KQED, ARC 30, 17:04:18.
42. Fred Ross, quoted in "Birth of A Union," ARC 42, 12:04:23, 1966. "Birth of a Union" was a documentary produced by KQED in 1966.
43. Chávez, "Why Delano?" in *Aztlán: An Anthology of Mexican American Literature*, ed. Luis Valdez and Stan Steiner, 202.
44. Chávez, quoted in Dunne, *Delano*, 70.
45. Chávez, quoted in Dunne, *Delano*, 74.
46. Daniel, "Unionization of California Farm Workers," 360.
47. Chávez, quoted in Levy, *Autobiography of La Causa*, 107.
48. Levy, *Autobiography of La Causa*, 105.
49. Chávez, quoted in Dunne, *Delano*, 71.
50. Chávez, quoted in Yinger, *Rhetoric of Nonviolence*, 31; Moyer, "A Conversation with César Chávez," 248.
51. Moyer, "A Conversation With César Chávez," 250.
52. Chávez, "The Organizer's Tale," 103; Chávez, quoted in Levy, *Autobiography of La Causa*, 161.
53. Griswold del Castillo and Garcia, *Triumph of Spirit*, 100, italics in original.
54. Moyer, "A Conversation With César Chávez," 248–50; Chávez, quoted in Levy, *Autobiography of La Causa*, 161.
55. "Bitter Harvest—Chávez Fights On," ARC 5, 5:08:29, 1973. The film was written and directed by Maurice Hatton. Transcript in possession of authors.

56. Moyer, "A Conversation With César Chávez," 249; Chávez, quoted in Matthiessen, *Sal Si Puedes,* 78; Lauro García Jr., quoted in Steiner, *La Raza,* 319.

57. Chávez, quoted in Levy, *Autobiography of La Causa,* 75; Daniel, "Unionization of California Farm Workers," 355.

58. Taylor, *Chávez and the Farm Workers,* 70–71, 180.

59. Chávez, interview by Padilla.

60. Chávez, quoted in Yinger, *Rhetoric of Nonviolence,* 103.

61. Chávez, interview by Padilla; Chávez, quoted in Steiner, *La Raza,* 312, 311.

62. Moyer, "A Conversation With César Chávez," 251.

63. Chávez, interview by Olson and Luchetti; Matthiessen, *Sal Si Puedes,* 106–107.

64. Chávez, quoted in Yinger, *Rhetoric of Nonviolence,* 83.

65. Chávez, quoted in Steiner, *La Raza,* 320; Chávez, quoted in Levy, *Autobiography of La Causa,* 92.

66. Chávez, quoted in Day, *Forty Acres,* 115.

67. Day, *Forty Acres,* 115.

68. Day, *Forty Acres,* 114; Chávez, quoted in Levy, *Autobiography of La Causa,* 196.

69. Chávez, quoted in Levy, *Autobiography of La Causa,* 93, 269.

70. Levy, *Autobiography of La Causa,* 92.

71. Steiner, *La Raza,* 292; Dunne, *Delano,* 174–75.

72. Chávez, quoted in Levy, *Autobiography of La Causa,* 269–70; Chávez, quoted in Yinger, *Rhetoric of Nonviolence,* 45.

73. Chávez, interview at Wayne State, ARC 29:32.

74. Chávez, quoted in Roberts, "Implications for a Social Ethic," 312.

75. Chávez, quoted in Steiner, *La Raza,* 295.

76. Chávez, quoted in Yinger, *Rhetoric of Nonviolence,* 61.

77. Chávez, "César Chávez Talks in New York," *Catholic Worker,* June 1968. An unpaginated copy of this article is in the San Joaquin Collection, Fresno State. Chávez, quoted in "El Malcriado: The Voice of the Farm Worker," in *Aztlán: An Anthology of Mexican American Literature,* ed. Luis Valdez and Stan Steiner, 208.

78. Ricardo Aecio Bomfim, "César Estrada Chávez: Militant Prophet," 109–10. Bomfim, relying largely on secondary sources in his study of Chávez's persuasion, identified four characteristic rhetorical aspects of Chávez's language: his expression of workers' sacrifice and suffering; his own self-sacrifice; identification with families and workers; and justice.

79. Chávez, "Letter from Delano," 31; Interview With César Chávez, "Nonviolence Still Works," *Look,* April 1, 1969, 56–57; Bob Fitch, "Tilting With the System: An Interview with César Chávez," 360.

80. Chávez, quoted in Steiner, *La Raza,* 295.

81. Chávez, "The Organizer's Tale," 107.

82. Chávez, quoted in Steiner, *La Raza,* 292; Chávez, quoted in Yinger, *Rhetoric of Nonviolence,* 57–58.

83. Chávez, quoted in Yinger, *Rhetoric of Nonviolence,* 59; Acuña, *Occupied America,* 325.

84. Hammerback and Jensen, 53–70.

85. Rosales, *Chicano!* 139. The Cursillo movement, which was an attempt to bring non-practicing Catholics back into the church, began in Spain in the 1940s and came to the United States in the 1950s, where it spread broadly throughout the Southwest. It was first offered in California in Stockton in 1961. Run by lay leaders, Cursillo meetings were held in Spanish and used the Mexican culture as a basis for discussion. See Antonio Soto, "The Chicano and the Catholic Church in Northern California, 1846–1978:

A Study of an Ethnic Minority in the Roman Catholic Church" (Ph.D. diss., University of California, 1978).

86. Chávez, quoted in Matthiessen, *Sal Si Puedes,* 35.

87. Chávez, quoted in Ross, *Conquering Goliath,* 50. The book quoted others of Chávez's dichos: "El Mejor torero es él de la barrera" ("The bravest bullfighter of all is he who has the protection of the barrier") (56–57); "Poco, poquito, llena la gallina el buche" ("Little by little, the chicken fills up her craw") (57); "Mientras menos burros, más olotes" ("The fewer the burros, the more corncobs there are for each") (60); "Hacer como hacen no es pecado" ("Doing what is done to you is not a sin") (62); "Al nopal lo van a ver solo cuando tiene tunas" ("The only time they pay any attention to the cactus is when it bears fruit") (66); "Dios dirá" ("God will say") (99); and "No es lo mismo ver morir, como cuando a uno le toca" ("It's not the same to see death as to die"; more freely, "It's easy for us who are not out there to judge the workers in the field!") (103).

88. Chávez, "Peregrinación, Penitencia, Revolución," in *Aztlán: An Anthology of Mexican American Literature,* ed. Luis Valdez and Stan Steiner, 385.

89. Dolores Huerta, quoted in Levy, *Autobiography of La Causa,* 277.

90. Jim Drakes, quoted in Lincoln Richardson, "César Chávez," *Presbyterian Life,* October 1, 1968, 19; Drake, quoted in Roberts, "Implications for a Social Ethic," 297.

91. Chávez, quoted in Levy, *Autobiography of La Causa,* 272; Matthiessen, *Sal Si Puedes,* 166.

CHAPTER 3. THE RHETORICAL CRITICISM OF DECONSTITUTIVE DISCOURSE

1. We discovered only one public speaking book that considered what we are calling reconstitution: Sonia K. Foss and Karen A. Foss, *Inviting Transformation: Presentational Speaking for a Changing World* (Prospect Heights, Ill.: Waveland Press, 1994). Foss and Foss strive to help teachers create an atmosphere where the speaker and audience can grow and change. Foss and Foss do not focus on rhetors identifying with audiences, however; and the four "external conditions" they propose as "particularly critical for the creation of an environment in which self-change may take place—safety, value, freedom, and openness" (5)—are worthy goals but need not be present in reconstitutive discourse.

2. Kenneth Burke, *Permanence and Change,* 2nd rev. ed. (Los Altos, Calif: Hermes, 1954), 7–11.

3. Aristotle, *"On Rhetoric": A Theory of Civic Discourse,* ed. and trans. George Kennedy (New York: Oxford University Press, 1991), 1.2.

4. Antczak, *Thought and Character,* 3. The book was reviewed favorably by communication scholars. See, for example, David Henry, review, *The Quarterly Journal of Speech* 73 (1987): 380–81.

5. Antczak, *Thought and Character,* 201.

6. Ibid., 201.

7. Ibid., 8–11.

8. Kenneth Burke, *A Rhetoric of Motives,* 1950; reprint (Berkeley: University of California Press, 1969), 21, 23, 57.

9. Antczak, *Thought and Character,* 8–11.

10. See part 2, "The Author's Voice in Fiction," of Wayne Booth's *The Rhetoric of Fiction,* 2nd ed. (Chicago: University of Chicago Press) 169–270.

11. Frederick J. Antczak, "Learning to Read Martin Luther King's 'Pilgrimage to Nonviolence': Wayne Booth, Character, and the Ethical Criticism of Public Address," in *Rhetoric*

and *Pluralism: Legacies of Wayne Booth*, Frederick J. Antczak, ed. (Columbus: Ohio State University Press, 1995), 153–63.

12. Antczak, *Thought and Character*, 89–196.
13. Ibid.
14. Antczak, "Pilgrimage to Nonviolence," 153–63.
15. Ibid., 160.
16. Ibid., 161.
17. Ibid., 161.
18. Ibid., 155–56.
19. Frederick J. Antczak, "When 'Silence Is Betrayal': An Ethical Criticism of the Revolution of Values in the Speech at Riverside Church," in *Martin Luther King Jr. and the Sermonic Power of Public Discourse*, ed. Carolyn Calloway-Thomas and John Louis Lucaites (Tuscaloosa: University of Alabama Press, 1993), 145.
20. Frederick J. Antczak, "Differences that Unite Us: John Kennedy's Speech to the Houston Ministerial Association and the Possibility of Ethical Criticism," in *Rhetoric and Ethics: Historical and Theoretical Perspectives*, ed. Victoria Aarons and Willis A. Solomon (Lampeter, Wales: Edwin Mellen Press, 1991), 125.
21. This analysis is condensed from John C. Hammerback, "José Antonio's Rhetoric of Fascism," *Southern Communication Journal* 59 (1994): 181–93.
22. Edwin Black, "The Second Persona," *Quarterly Journal of Speech* 61 (1970): 109–19.
23. Hammerback, "José Antonio," 191.
24. Kenneth Burke introduced and developed his concepts of rhetoric primarily through a series of books spanning several decades: *Counter-Statement*, 1931; *Permanence and Change*, 1935; *Attitudes Toward History*, 1937; *The Philosophy of Literary Form*, 1941; *A Grammar of Motives*, 1945; *A Rhetoric of Motives*, 1950; *Rhetoric of Religion*, 1961; and *Language as Symbolic Action*, 1966.
25. Burke, *A Rhetoric of Motives*, xiv.
26. Burke, *Counter-Statement* (1931; reprint, Los Altos, Calif.: Hermes, 1953), 124–29.
27. Walter R. Fisher, *Human Communication as Narration: Toward a Philosophy of Reason, Value, and Action* (Columbia: University of South Carolina Press, 1987), 64.
28. For an insightful discussion of Freud's influence on Burke, see Stephen D. O'Leary and Mark H. Wright, "Psychoanalysis and Burkeian Rhetorical Criticism," *The Southern Communication Journal* 61 (1995): 104–21.
29. Karlyn Kohrs Campbell and Kathleen Hall Jamieson, *Form, Genre, and the Study of Political Discourse* (Falls Church, Virginia: Speech Communication Association, 1978), 203–25. The study, which discusses enactment in generic discourse, and specifically its place in "reconstituting 'the people' as an audience that can witness the rite of investiture" in presidential inaugural addresses, contains words and concepts that prefigure some of those in Antczak, although Campbell and Jamieson's analysis and conceptual framework lack the depth and detail that Antczak later provided.
30. Martha Solomon, "Ideology as Rhetorical Constraint: The Anarchist Agitation of 'Red Emma' Goldman," *Quarterly Journal of Speech* 74 (1988): 184, 190.
31. Solomon, "Red Emma," 195.
32. Black, "The Second Persona."
33. Hammerback, "José Antonio," 181–93.
34. Maurice Charland, "Constitutive Rhetoric: The Case of the *Peuple Québécois*," *Quarterly Journal of Speech* 73 (1987): 133–50.
35. Ernest G. Bormann, "The Eagleton Affair: A Fantasy Theme Analysis," *Quarterly Journal of Speech* 59 (1973): 143–59.

36. Bormann, "Eagleton Affair," 159.
37. Booth, quoted in Antczak, *Thought and Character,* 8.
38. For exceptions to the conventional approaches, see Michael McGee, "In Search of 'The People': A Rhetorical Alternative," *Quarterly Journal of Speech* 61 (October 1975): 235–49; and Maurice Charland, "Constitutive Rhetoric: The Case of the *Peuple Québéçois*." Study of the rhetoric of social movements began with Leland M. Griffin, "The Rhetoric of Social Movements," *Quarterly Journal of Speech* 38 (1952): 184–88. This celebrated 1952 article defined a movement as occurring when:

> 1. [people] have become dissatisfied with some aspect of their environment;
> 2. They desire change—social, economic, political, religious, intellectual, or otherwise—and desiring change, they make efforts to alter their environment;
> 3. Eventually their efforts result in some degree of success or failure. . . . (185)

Griffin outlined three stages of development in movements:

> 1. A period of inception, a time when the roots of a pre-existing sentiment, nourished by interested rhetoricians, begins to flower into public notice, or when some striking event occurs . . . and is itself sufficient to initiate the movement; 2. A period of rhetorical crisis, a time when one of the opposing groups of rhetoricians . . . succeeds in irrevocably disturbing the balance between the groups which had existed in the minds of the collective audience; and 3. A period of consummation, a time when . . . rhetoricians abandon their efforts, either because they are convinced . . . the cause [is] won, or because they are convinced that perseverance is useless, or merely because they meet the press of new interests. (184)

In "The Minority in the Middle: Asian-American Dissent in the 1960s and 1970s" (*Western Journal of Speech Communication* 51 [Fall 1987]: 402–16), Richard J. Jensen and Cara J. Abeyta attempted to add to Griffin's ideas by proposing that in some groups there is a "pre-inception stage [in which] rhetors had to spend a considerable amount of time and energy creating a sense of awareness in the community before members were willing or able to move to the period of inception" (404). If rhetors are successful, according to Jensen and Abeyta, members of the community go through a process of reconceptualization whereby they become emotionally ready to move to the period of inception. Thus Jensen and Abeyta underscored the value of understanding the internal states of members of a movement as well as the external forces which influence such movements.

Griffin's ideas were a starting point for the study of movements by rhetoricians. Later scholars have expanded on his ideas. An example of a more thorough outline of the cycles of a social movement was offered by Charles J. Stewart, Craig Allen Smith, and Robert E. Denton Jr. in *Persuasion and Social Movements* 3rd ed. (Prospect Heights, Ill.: Waveland Press, 1994). Stewart, Smith, and Denton built on Griffin and other theorists by outlining five stages in a social movement: genesis, social unrest, enthusiastic mobilization, maintenance, and termination (71–88).

39. James R. Andrews, "The Passionate Negation: The Chartist Movement in Rhetorical Perspective," *Quarterly Journal of Speech* 54 (April 1973): 196–97.
40. Herbert W. Simons, "Requirements, Problems, and Strategies: A Theory of Persuasion For Social Movements," *The Quarterly Journal of Speech* 51 (February 1970): 1–11.

41. Ibid., 2–4.

42. Ibid., 7.

43. Kenelem Burridge, quoted in Stewart, Smith, and Denton, 96–101.

44. Max Weber, "The Nature of Charismatic Authority and Its Routinization," in S. N. Eisenstadt, ed., *Max Weber: On Charisma and Institution Building* (Chicago: The University of Chicago Press, 1968), 48.

45. Ibid.

46. Jay A. Conger, quoted in Martha D. Cooper and William L. Nothstine, *Power Persuasion: Moving an Ancient Art Into the Media Age* (Greenwood, Ind.: The Educational Video Group, 1992), 106.

47. Weber, "Charismatic Authority," 52.

48. Boss, "Essential Attributes of Charisma."

CHAPTER 4. FINDING HIS MESSAGE AND FORMING HIS UNION

1. Chávez, interview at Wayne State, ARC 6:11.

2. Chávez, "Why Delano?" 203; Matthiessen, *Sal Si Puedes,* 50–51.

3. Matthiessen, *Sal Si Puedes,* 51; Acuña, *Occupied America,* 325; Dunne, *Delano,* 14; Chávez, interview by Olson and Luchetti.

4. Chávez, interview at Wayne State, ARC 6:11.

5. Chávez, "The Organizer's Tale," 105; ABC News, Reel 207, "César Chávez Stories," ARC 15, 10:25:33. Translated from Spanish by Alicia García.

   For further discussion of the role of women in the UFW, see: "Coleadership: The Strength of Dolores Huerta," in Griswold del Castillo and Garcia, *A Triumph of Spirit,* 59–75; Barbara L. Baer and Glenna Matthews, "The Women in the Boycott," *The Nation,* February 1974, 232–38; Joan M. Jensen, *With These Hands: Women Working on the Land* (Old Westbury, N.Y.: McGraw Hill, 1981).

6. Chávez, quoted in Levy, *Autobiography of La Causa,* 158.

7. Steiner, *La Raza,* 279–80.

8. Chávez, "Why Delano?" 204; Chávez, quoted in Taylor, *Chávez and the Farm Workers,* 113–14; Chávez, quoted in Levy, *Autobiography of La Causa,* 158; Matthiessen, *Sal Si Puedes,* 54–55.

9. Chávez, interview at Wayne State.

10. Chávez, "The Organizer's Tale," 106.

11. Chávez, quoted in Levy, *Autobiography of La Causa,* 176; Chávez, "Why Delano?" 203–204.

12. Chávez, interview at Wayne State.

13. Chávez, quoted in Levy, *Autobiography of La Causa,* 173.

14. Marjorie Fallows, "The Mexican-American Laborers: A Different Drummer?" in *Pain and Promise,* ed. Edward Simmen, 320–21.

15. Chávez, "The Mexican American and the Church," 144; Matthiessen, *Sal Si Puedes,* 13–14; Chávez, quoted in Day, *Forty Acres,* 53.

16. Bert Corona, quoted in Kushner, *Long Road to Delano,* 122.

17. Rosales, *Chicano!* 138.

18. Rosales, *Chicano!* 138.

19. Dunne, *Delano,* 51.

20. Steiner, *La Raza,* 248; Dunne, *Delano,* 22.

21. Nelson, *Huelga,* 18–19.

22. Chávez, quoted in Rosales, *Chicano!* 135.

23. Steiner, *La Raza,* 276; Matthiessen, *Sal Si Puedes,* 59; Solis-Garza, "The Chicano 'Messiah'?" 300.

24. Chávez, quoted in Rosales, *Chicano!* 135.

25. Chávez, quoted in Levy, *Autobiography of La Causa,* 184–85; Yinger, *Rhetoric of Nonviolence,* 27–28; Steiner, *La Raza,* 282–83.

26. Griswold del Castillo and Garcia, *Triumph of Spirit,* 49.

27. Chávez, "An Open Letter," *El Malcriado,* December 8, 1965, 8–9.

28. Dunne, *Delano,* 4.

29. For a discussion of how establishments typically react when challenged, see John W. Bowers, Donovan J. Ochs, and Richard J. Jensen, *The Rhetoric of Agitation and Control,* 2nd ed. (Prospect Heights, Ill.: Waveland Press, 1993), 8–11.

30. Martin Zaninovich, quoted in Levy, *Autobiography of La Causa,* 284; Day, *Forty Acres,* 92–93.

31. Day, *Forty Acres,* 92–93.

32. Bruno Dispoto, quoted in Dunne, *Delano,* 102; Jack Pandol, quoted in Steiner, *La Raza,* 260.

33. Chávez, quoted in Steiner, *La Raza,* 261.

34. Chávez, quoted in Matthiessen, *Sal Si Puedes,* 135.

35. Levy, *Autobiography of La Causa,* 189–90; Dunne, *Delano,* 12.

36. Matthiessen, *Sal Si Puedes,* 120–21.

37. Yinger, *Rhetoric of Nonviolence,* 71–72; Day, *Forty Acres,* 40; Dunne, *Delano,* 111.

38. Dunne, *Delano,* 91–92.

39. Jack Pandol, quoted in Dunne, *Delano,* 106.

40. Chávez, quoted in "Birth of Union," ARC 42, 12:13:34, 1966.

41. Levy, *Autobiography of La Causa,* 222; Dunne, *Delano,* 184.

42. Nelson, *Huelga,* 74, 85.

43. Nelson, *Huelga,* 106.

44. Quoted in "Birth of a Union," ARC 42, 12:17:16, 1966.

45. Chávez, quoted in Rosales, *Chicano!* 136.

46. Nelson, *Huelga,* 85; Matthiessen, *Sal Si Puedes,* 34.

47. Day, *Forty Acres,* 117; Levy, *Autobiography of La Causa,* 227.

48. Dunne, *Delano,* 130–31; Levy, *Autobiography of La Causa,* 141; Chávez, "Peregrinación, Penitencia, Revolución," 386.

49. At the beginning of the march the union issued the "Plan of Delano." For an in-depth study of that plan as rhetoric, see Hammerback and Jensen, "Ethnic Heritage as Rhetorical Legacy."

50. Luis Valdez, quoted in "Huelga!" ARC 67, UFW Rally in Delano, 1:31:14.

51. Rosales, *Chicano!* 138.

52. Chávez, quoted in Rosales, *Chicano!* 141.

53. Rosales, *Chicano!* 140.

54. Chávez, quoted in Griswold del Castillo and Garcia, *Triumph of Spirit,* 51.

55. Chávez, quoted in ABC NEWS, Reel 207, "César Chávez Stories," ARC 15, 10:36:55. Translated from Spanish by Alicia García.

56. Yinger, *Rhetoric of Nonviolence,* 32–33; Levy, *Autobiography of La Causa,* 27.

57. Robert Kennedy, quoted in ARC 18, 1968, ABC News, Reel 210, "César Chávez Stories," 10:25:39, 1968.

58. Robert Kennedy, quoted in "Decision at Delano: 1967," ARC 68, 02:21:15.

59. Yinger, *Rhetoric of Nonviolence,* 51.

60. Kushner, *Long Road to Delano,* 167.
61. Chávez, quoted in Yinger, *Rhetoric of Nonviolence,* 51. After Kennedy's death, a special issue of *El Malcriado* (June 15, 1968) focused on Kennedy's contribution to the union.
62. Griswold del Castillo and Garcia, *Triumph of Spirit,* 88.
63. Steiner, *La Raza,* 322.
64. Day, *Forty Acres,* 71.
65. Ronald Reagan, quoted in ARC 34, 4:18, 2:13.
66. ARC 32, 19:18:14, 19:18:28, 1970.
67. Dunne, *Delano,* 53; Luis Valdez, "The Tale of La Raza," in *The Chicanos: Mexican-American Voices,* ed. Ludwig and Santibáñez, 96.
68. Antczak, 101. Antczak quoted Ralph Waldo Emerson to make this point.
69. Solis-Garza, "The Chicano 'Messiah'?" 298.
70. Yinger, *Rhetoric of Nonviolence,* 21; Matthiessen, *Sal Si Puedes,* 155, 9–10.
71. Rosales, *Chicano!* 130–31.
72. Chávez, interview by Olson and Luchetti; "A Farm-Bred Unionist: César Estrada Chávez," *New York Times,* March 11, 1968, 22.
73. Chávez, "César Chávez Talks in New York," *Catholic Worker,* June, 1968. According to the *Catholic Worker* the speech was given to "an interfaith luncheon of clergy and labor people at Calvary Episcopal Church, Manhattan." Text in San Joaquin Collection, Fresno State.
74. Ibid. Chávez's speech at the AFL-CIO "Solidarity House" contains many of the same ideas.
75. Chávez, quoted in "Huelga!" ARC 67, 1:19:40.
76. Chávez, quoted in "Decision at Delano," ARC 68, 2:04:56, 1967.
77. Chávez, quoted in "ABC, Newsreel #206," ARC 14, 6:13:30, 1970.
78. Chávez, interview by Olson and Luchetti.
79. Chávez, quoted on KQED, San Francisco State University, 1970, ARC 30, 17:00:16.
80. Chávez, quoted in Levy, *Autobiography of La Causa,* 53.
81. Chávez, quoted in Matthiessen, *Sal Si Puedes,* 260–61.
82. Matthiessen, *Sal Si Puedes,* 261.
83. Chávez, quoted in Taylor, *Chávez and the Farm Workers,* 6–7.
84. Chávez, quoted in Taylor, *Chávez and the Farm Workers,* 7.
85. Chávez, quoted in Taylor, *Chávez and the Farm Workers,* 7.
86. Chávez, "Nothing Has Changed," in *Aztlán: An Anthology of Mexican American Literature,* ed. Luis Valdez and Stan Steiner, 205.
87. Chávez, "Letter from Delano," 30.
88. Chávez, quoted in Steiner, *La Raza,* 260; Chávez, quoted in Dunne, *Delano,* 60.
89. Chávez, quoted in Dunne, *Delano,* 59.
90. Chávez, "The Plan of Delano," in *Three Perspectives on Ethnicity in America,* ed. Carlos Cortes, Arlin I. Ginsburg, Alan W. F. Green, and James A. Joseph (New York: Capricorn Books, 1976), 379–80.
91. Chávez, "Letter from Delano," 30.
92. "CBS," ARC 59,16:04:10, 1966. See also, "Birth of a Union," ARC 42, 12:02:37, 1966.
93. Chávez, interview by Olson and Luchetti; Chávez, introduction to *Forty Acres,* by Mark Day, 9–10.
94. César E. Chávez, "Farm Workers Association," *El Malcriado,* May 1966, 20 (an open letter to members of the union in the union newspaper); Chávez, quoted in Levy, *Autobiography of La Causa,* 193–94.
95. Chávez, interview by Olson and Luchetti; Chávez, quoted in Levy, *Autobiography of La Causa,* 190–91.

96. Steiner, *La Raza,* 302; Chávez, quoted in Levy, *Autobiography of La Causa,* 63.

97. Chávez, interview by Olson and Luchetti; Chávez, quoted in Dunne, *Delano,* 153; Chávez, quoted in Matthiessen, *Sal Si Puedes,* 132–33.

98. Chávez, quoted in "California Grape Strike," ARC 7, 7:23:04; Chávez, quoted in Levy, *Autobiography of La Causa,* 92.

99. Chávez, introduction to *Forty Acres,* 12; Chávez, "Plan of Delano," 381; Chávez, "Letter from Delano," 31.

100. Chávez, introduction to *Forty Acres,* 10.

101. Chávez, quoted in "Bitter Harvest—Chávez Fights On," ARC 5, 5:08:29.

102. Chávez, quoted in "KMEX," ARC 20, 10:06:54, 10:08:22. Translated from Spanish by Alicia García.

103. Chávez, quoted in Steiner, *La Raza,* 293.

104. Chávez, interview by Olson and Luchetti; Chávez, quoted in Yinger, *Rhetoric of Nonviolence,* 57–58.

105. Chávez, introduction to *Forty Acres,* 12.

106. Chávez, quoted in "KQED," ARC 29 16:21:20.

107. Chávez, quoted in UFW Public Service Announcement (PSA) "Face to Face," ARC 19, 9:23:09.
    The term "La Raza" ("the people" or "the race") was used in an attempt to unite all Mexican Americans into a group capable of fighting for their rights. The term implied both a positive coming-together as a community and a call for the community to unite to fight a common enemy, the Anglo power structure. Chávez rejected the term when it was used to mean that Mexican Americans should exclude other individuals from their group. He tried to make the union inclusive of all people, rejecting the idea of groups based only on race. See Hammerback, Jensen, and Gutiérrez, *A War of Words,* 88.

108. Levy, *Autobiography of La Causa,* 123; Matthiessen, *Sal Si Puedes,* 103–104.

109. Chávez, speech at the seventh constitutional convention of the AFL-CIO, Miami, Fla., December 12, 1967. The authors would like to thank Eastern Michigan University's library for loan of the manuscript.

110. Levy, *Autobiography of La Causa,* 196; Matthiessen, *Sal Si Puedes,* 103–104.

111. Chávez, quoted in Moyer, "A Conversation With César Chávez," 251.

112. Chávez, introduction to *Forty Acres,* 10–11.

113. Chávez, "The Mexican American and the Church," 144–45.

114. Chávez, "The Mexican American and the Church," 144–45.

115. Chávez, "The Mexican American and the Church," 146, 143.

116. Chávez, "The Mexican American and the Church," 145.

117. "KQED," ARC 32.

118. "KQED," ARC 32, 19:01:31; 19:06:10.

119. Chávez, "Plan of Delano," 380.

120. ARC 2, 2:00:01, 1966.

121. ARC 2, 2:25:17/30.

122. ARC 2, 2:26:25.

123. Chávez, "Testimony Before the Subcommittee on Labor of the Senate Committee on Labor and Public Welfare, April 16, 1969.

124. Chávez, "KQED," ARC 29, 16:27:58–59.

125. Chávez, quoted in UFW PSA "Face to Face" ARC 19, 9:09:29; Chávez, interview at KQED, quoted at ARC 30, KQED interview.

126. Chávez, quoted in Yinger, *Rhetoric of Nonviolence,* 103.

127. Chávez, quoted in "ABC, Newsreel #206," ARC 14, 6:17:38.
128. Chávez, "César Chávez Talks About Organizing."
129. "CBS," ARC 65, 23:08:20. See also ARC 30, 1970 interview.
130. Chávez, quoted in Steiner, *La Raza,* 320; Chávez, "The Organizer's Tale," 104–105.
131. Chávez, quoted on ARC 2, 2:27:14.
132. Chávez, interview by Olson and Luchetti.
133. Chávez, quoted at San Francisco State University, ARC 30, 17:24:51.
134. Outlines for speeches: AFL-CIO luncheon, Denver, Colo., December 21, 1967; seventh constitutional convention of the AFL-CIO, Miami, Fla., December 12, 1967. Copies in possession of authors.
135. Chávez, speech at the seventh constitutional convention of the AFL-CIO, Miami, Fla., December 12, 1967.
136. Chávez, quoted in "CBS News," ARC 43, 1:10:42, 1970.
137. Steiner, *La Raza,* 320.
138. Ibid.
139. Alberto González, "Mexican 'Otherness' in the Rhetoric of Mexican Americans," *Southern Communication Journal* 55 (Spring 1990): 276–91; Alberto González, "Participation at WMEX-FM: Inventional Rhetoric of Ohio Mexican Americans," *Western Journal of Speech Communication* 53 (Fall 1989): 389–410.
140. UFW PSA "Face to Face," ARC 19, 9:12:59.
141. Moyer, "A Conversation With César Chávez," 249.
142. Chávez, "César Chávez Talks About Organizing"; Chávez, quoted in Levy, *Autobiography of La Causa,* 178.
143. Chávez, quoted in Levy, *Autobiography of La Causa,* 178.
144. Chávez, speech ending fast, March 10, 1968.
145. Chávez, "The Plan of Delano," 380–81.
146. Chávez, quoted in Levy, *Autobiography of La Causa,* 198.
147. Chávez, speech at the seventh constitutional convention of the AFL-CIO, Miami, Fla., December 12, 1967.
148. Chávez, notes for speech at the seventh constitutional convention of the AFL-CIO, Miami, Fla., December 12, 1967.
149. Yinger, *Rhetoric of Nonviolence,* 59.
150. Chávez, speech at the seventh constitutional convention of the AFL-CIO, Miami, Fla., December 12, 1967.
151. Moyer, "A Conversation With César Chávez," 253–54; Chávez, quoted in Day, *Forty Acres,* 97.
152. Roberts, "Implications for a Social Ethic," 287.
153. ARC 19, 9:10:42; see also ARC 30, 17:07:36, 1970.
154. Chávez, quoted in Yinger, *Rhetoric of Nonviolence,* 60; Chávez, "Letter from Delano," 31–32.
155. Chávez, "Letter from Delano," 31–32.
156. Chávez, quoted in Yinger, *Rhetoric of Nonviolence,* 46.
157. Chávez, quoted in UFW PSA "Face to Face," ARC 19, 9:16:44.
158. Yinger, *Rhetoric of Nonviolence,* 39; Joel Solkoff, "Can César Chávez Cope with Success?" *The New Republic,* May 22, 1976, 13.
159. Chávez, quoted in Matthiessen, *Sal Si Puedes,* 168–69; Chávez, "Sacramento March Letter," in Yinger, *Rhetoric of Nonviolence,* 106–107. For a discussion of the Mexican cultural orientation as it influences the public address of Mexican-Americans, see González, "Mexican 'Otherness,'" 276–91, and "Participation at WMEX-FM," 389–410.

160. Chávez, "Sacramento March Letter," in Yinger, *Rhetoric of Nonviolence,* 106; Elizabeth Sutherland Martínez and Enriqueta Longeaux y Vasquez, *Viva La Raza!* (Garden City, N.Y.: Doubleday and Company, Inc., 1974), 196–97.

161. Chávez, "Plan of Delano," 379.

162. Chávez, quoted in "KRON-TV," Reels 2–4, ARC 23, 14:30:03.

163. Chávez, speech at Solidarity House, April 1, 1967. Unless otherwise noted, all quotations in our analysis of the speech are drawn from this text.

164. Often Chávez relied heavily on lengthy stories. For example, his 1967 speech to the AFL-CIO's seventh constitutional convention in Miami contained two long stories: his story of Juan García (retold in chapter 6) and a story about the fears he and his wife had about telling their children that they had been in jail. In other regards the speeches are similar.

165. Chávez, quoted in "California Grape Strike," ARC 7 7:02:24.

166. Ibid.

167. "Inspiration, Sí—Administration, No," *Time,* April 22, 1974, 94.

168. Chávez, quoted in "CBS," ARC 59, 16:04.

169. Chávez, quoted in "KQED," ARC 29, 16:27.

170. Griswold del Castillo and Garcia, *Triumph of Spirit,* 49, 88, 44.

171. Griswold del Castillo and Garcia, *Triumph of Spirit,* 76.

172. Acuña, *Occupied America,* 325.

173. "California Grape Strike," ARC 7, 7:01:35.

174. Charles Kuralt, quoted in "CBS," ARC 59, 16:11:23.

CHAPTER 5. RHETORICALLY "WORKING TOWARDS CREATING THE NEW MAN"

1. Chávez, quoted in Roberts, "Implications for a Social Ethic," 533; ibid., 532–33; Griswold del Castillo and Garcia, *Triumph of Spirit,* 119–20.

2. "Inspiration, Sí—Administration, No," 94; Michael Yates, "A Union Is Not A 'Movement,'" *The Nation,* November 19, 1977, 518.

3. Quoted in Margaret Crimmins, "Dinner for Chávez," *Washington Post,* November 5, 1971, B2.

4. Coretta King, quoted in "NYC: Cathedral of St. John the Divine," ARC 82, 01:13:55, 1973.

5. Dennis McDermott, quoted in the *Proceedings: Twenty-Fourth Constitutional Convention of International Union, United Automobile, Aerospace and Agricultural Implement Workers of America, Los Angeles, June 2–6, 1974,* 253. Copy of text in UFW Papers, Wayne State. Photocopy of text in possession of authors.

6. "What Happened to Chávez's Union?" 22.

7. Acuña, *Occupied America,* 272–73.

8. Roberts, "Implications for a Social Ethic."

9. "Chávez vs The Teamsters: Farm Workers' Historic Vote," *U.S. News and World Report,* September 22, 1975, 83.

10. "Can Chávez Survive?" *Time,* September 3, 1973, 73.

11. Chávez, speech at convention of International Union, Automobile, Aerospace, and Agricultural Implement Workers of America, Los Angeles, June, 1974 (hereafter cited as "Chávez, speech to UAW, June, 1974").

12. Chávez, "The Biggest Danger is Running Out of Patience," interview by Vernon Schmid, *Fellowship Magazine,* 1975, 14. Photocopy of text in possession of authors.

13. Jack Pandol, quoted in "CBS," ARC 47, 5:00:47; 5:03:49; 5:13:20, 1973.
14. Chávez, "CBS," ARC 56 13:03:02/6.
15. Edward Roybal, quoted in "Fighting for Our Lives," ARC 64, 1974.
16. "Fighting for Our Lives," ARC 64.
17. "Fighting for Our Lives," ARC 64.
18. J. Craig Jenkins, *The Politics of Insurgency: The Farm Worker Movement in the 1960s* (New York: Columbia University Press, 1985), 195.
19. "Chávez vs The Teamsters," 82; "A Boost for Chávez," *Newsweek,* May 26, 1975, 68.
20. Griswold del Castillo and Garcia, *Triumph of Spirit,* 129.
21. "Sacramento State 2," ARC 66, 03:50.
22. Richard Steven Street, "It's Boycott Time in California," *The Nation,* March 23, 1985, 330.
23. J. Craig Jenkins, *The Politics of Insurgency,* 196.
24. Crimmins, "Dinner for Chávez," B2.
25. Crimmins, "Dinner for Chávez," B2.
26. Chávez, notes for talk to the Council for Community Action, Sheraton-Park Hotel, Washington, D.C., November 4, 1971. Photocopy of text in possession of authors.
27. Dorothy Rensenbrink, "On Chávez, Women, and Faith," *Christian Century,* April 24, 1974, 444–46.
28. Chávez, quoted in "Bitter Harvest (Part Two)," ARC 6, 6:08:17, 6:09:20, 1973.
29. Chávez, "The Biggest Danger is Running Out of Patience."
30. Chávez, "The Biggest Danger is Running Out of Patience."
31. Chávez, letter to members of the United Farm Workers, April 16, 1971. Text in UFW Papers, Wayne State.
32. Chávez, "Dear Friends in the FOR," *Fellowship Magazine,* n.d., 15. Photocopy of text in possession of authors.
33. Chávez, speech at Exposition Park, May 2, 1971.
34. Moyer, "A Conversation With César Chávez," 249–52.
35. Chávez, speech to UAW, June, 1974.
36. Chávez, speech to UAW, June, 1974.
37. Chávez, "Cathedral of St. John the Divine," ARC 82; See also Chávez, speech to UAW, June, 1974.
38. Chávez, "Letter from César Chávez to Friends of the Farm Workers," November 16, 1971. Text in UFW Papers, Wayne State.
39. Chávez, "Statement by César Chávez at the End of His 24-day Fast for Justice," Phoenix, Ariz., June 4, 1972.
40. Chávez, speech to UAW, June, 1974.
41. Chávez, speech to UAW, June, 1974.
42. Roberts, "Implications for a Social Ethic."
43. Chávez, "Eulogy for Juan de la Cruz." The speech was delivered in Arvin, Calif., on August 21, 1973. Copy in UFW Papers, Wayne State. For a similar conversion of death into reconstitution, see "Statement by César Chávez on the Occasion of a Funeral Mass for 19 Farm Workers Killed in a Bus Accident in Blythe, California, January 15, 1974." In that statement Chávez speaks of the specifics of the deaths, blaming the company that transported the workers for not treating them like humans, but he also asks, "How can we give meaning to their lives and their sacrifices?" As part of his answer he promises that "the pain that today fills our hearts with mourning also unifies our spirits and strengthens our determination to defend the rights of every worker. Let the labor contractors and the growers know that our union will never stop work-

ing and struggling until there is an end to the inhuman treatment of all farm workers."

44. Chávez, Eulogy for Juan de la Cruz.

45. Chávez, quoted in "ABC News, Reel 202: 'César Chávez Stories,'" ARC 10, 1975.

46. Chávez, speech to Greater Washington Central Labor Council, September 9, 1974. Text in UFW Papers, Wayne State.

47. Chávez, labor news conference, Mutual Broadcasting System, September 17, 1974. Text in UFW Papers, Wayne State.

48. Chávez, "Letter to the National Council of Churches," in Yinger, *Rhetoric of Nonviolence,* 108–109; press release for meeting with 200 religious leaders in Delano, June 6, 1970 (copy in possession of authors).

49. Chávez, "Letter from César Chávez to Friends of the Farm Workers."

50. Chávez, "César Chávez on Money and Organizing," transcription from a talk by Chávez at UFW headquarters at La Paz in Keene, Calif., October 4, 1971. Text in UFW Papers, Wayne State.

51. Chávez, notes for speech to CHD Meeting, October 3, 1979. Copy in UFW Papers, Wayne State.

52. Chávez, speech at Lattimore, September 10, 1972. Copy in UFW Papers, Wayne State. "Don't waste any time mourning—organize!" wrote labor martyr Joe Hill in a letter the night before his execution. Chávez's paraphrase is particularly well chosen because Hill's organization, the Industrial Workers of the World (IWW; the "Wobblies"), was active in attempting to organize farm workers in the early part of the twentieth century.

53. Chávez, "Bitter Harvest (Part Two)," ARC 6.

54. Chávez, speech to UAW, June, 1974.

55. Chávez, speech at California State University, Sacramento, January 18, 1971; Chávez, speech to UAW, June, 1974.

56. Chávez, speech to UAW, June, 1974.

57. Chávez, speech to UAW, June, 1974; Chávez, labor news conference, September 17, 1974.

58. Chávez, speech at California State University, Sacramento, January 18, 1971.

59. Chávez, speech at University of Santa Clara, Santa Clara, Calif., October 26, 1972.

60. Chávez, speech at University of Santa Clara, October 26, 1972; Chávez, speech to Greater Washington Central Labor Council, September 9, 1974; Chávez, speech to UAW, June, 1974. For a discussion of how establishments traditionally attempt to downplay agitators and their movements, see Bowers, Ochs, and Jensen, *The Rhetoric of Agitation and Control,* 8–11.

61. Chávez, speech to UAW, June, 1974.

62. Chávez, speech at University of Santa Clara, October 26, 1972.

63. Chávez, "Bitter Harvest (Part 2)," ARC 6, 6:19:30.

64. Chávez, labor news conference, September 17, 1974.

65. Chávez, labor news conference, September 17, 1974.

66. Chávez, speech to UAW, June, 1974.

67. Chávez, speech to Greater Washington Central Labor Council, 1974.

68. Chávez, nomination address by César Chávez to Democratic National Convention, July 14, 1976. Copy of transcript in UFW Papers, Wayne State.

69. Chávez, speech at California State University, Sacramento, January 18, 1971.

70. Chávez, speech at California State University, Sacramento, January 18, 1971.

71. Chávez, quoted in Yinger, *Rhetoric of Nonviolence,* 60, 76.

72. Chávez, speech ending fast, March 10, 1968, quoted in Yinger, *Rhetoric of Nonviolence,* 46–47.

73. Chávez, text of Chicano Report of speech to American Citizens' Club, March 7, 1971, Brawley, Ca., edited by William Hensey Jr. and Larry Lyons. This article summarizes the speech by Chávez in Brawley, a speech primarily in English but with a conclusion in Spanish. Here Chávez noted that audience was mainly composed of affluent Chicanos. Photocopies of transcripts in possession of authors.

74. Chávez, notes for speech at San Jose, Calif., on the fifth anniversary of community organizing, November 17, 1972. Copy in UFW Papers, Wayne State.

75. Chávez, speech at California State University, Sacramento, January 18, 1971.

76. Frederick J. Antczak, *Thought and Character,* 201.

77. Chávez, "The Biggest Danger is Running Out of Patience."

78. Chávez, speech to UAW, June, 1974.

79. Ibid.

80. Chávez, speech to Greater Washington Central Labor Council.

81. Chávez, speech at California State University, Sacramento, January 18, 1971.

82. Ibid.

83. Chávez, interview by Padilla.

84. "Chávez in Austin, Texas, February 6, 1971." The speech was translated from Spanish by Robert Tice. A discussion of the speech appears in Hammerback, Jensen, and Gutiérrez, *A War of Words,* 41–44. Unless otherwise noted, all quotations in our analysis of the speech are drawn from this text.

85. Chávez, speech notes for Oxnard rally, October 5, 1972. Translated from Spanish by Alicia García. Photocopy of text in possession of authors.

86. Chávez, speech notes for Oxnard rally, October 5, 1972.

87. Chávez's comments to Jacques Levy, in Griswold del Castillo and Garcia, *Triumph of Spirit,* 121.

88. Jack Pandol, quoted on ARC 45, 1973.

89. "ABC News, Reel 209: 'César Chávez Stories,'" ARC 17, 9:12:02.

90. Chávez, "Sacramento State 2," ARC 66, 13:25.

91. Chávez, notes for speech at Stockton rally, Stockton, Calif., February 28, 1971. Photocopies of texts in possession of authors. Text in UFW Papers, Wayne State.

92. Acuña, *Occupied America,* 370; "Can Chávez Survive?" 73–74.

93. Daniel, "Unionization of California Farm Workers," 372; Acuña, *Occupied America,* 272–275.

94. "Inspiration, Sí—Administration, No," 94.

95. Herbert W. Simons, "Requirements, Problems, and Strategies," 7.

CHAPTER 6. THE MERGER
OF MAN AND MESSAGE

1. Grossman, interview by authors.

2. Chávez, notes for speech at Stockton rally, February 28, 1971; Chávez, notes for speech in Brawley, Brawley, Calif., February 27, 1971. See also the Text of Chicano Report, March 7, 1971.

3. Chávez, interview by Padilla.

4. Yinger, *Rhetoric of Nonviolence,* 48.

5. Kushner, *Long Road to Delano,* 192.

6. Gutiérrez, "The First and Last of the Chicano Leaders," 35.

7. Griswold del Castillo and Garcia, *Triumph of Spirit,* 49.

8. Grossman, interview by authors; Chávez, interview by Padilla.

9. Pat Hoffman, "'The More Trouble We Get the More Religious We Get': An Interview With César Chávez," *Sojourners,* October, 1977, 25.
10. Chávez, interview by Padilla.
11. Chávez, letter to Latin American Fiesta, May 1, 1971. Copy in UFW Papers, Wayne State.
12. Chávez, interview by Padilla; Grossman, interview by authors. Grossman recalled Chávez speaking 30–40 minutes at rallies for farm workers on a tour in the 1970s.
13. Chávez, interview by Padilla.
14. Grossman, interview by authors.
15. Chávez, interview by Padilla.
16. Yinger, *Rhetoric of Nonviolence,* 48.
17. Grossman, interview by authors. The authors possess many of Chávez's outlines for speeches he delivered. Those outlines indicate that he used a similar speech numerous times during a tour or a given period of time.
18. Grossman, interview by authors. Grossman remembers that Chávez was well-prepared for all his addresses, working many hours on major speeches and taking a serious approach to all his public address.
19. Chávez, interview by Padilla.
20. Grossman, interview by authors.
21. Yinger, *Rhetoric of Nonviolence,* 20, 47–48.
22. See, for example: Chávez, notes for a talk to the Council for Community Action, November 4, 1971; Chávez, outline for HEW address on money and organizing, Washington, D.C., March 21, 1978; Chávez, notes for speech at a school, Brawley, Calif., February 27, 1971. Photocopies in possession of authors.
23. See, for example, Chávez, notes for speech, Fresno, Calif., October 25, 1971; Chávez, Calexico rally, Calexico, Calif., January 16, 1971; Chávez, OIC Address, San Jose, Calif., November 17, 1972; Chávez, Lattimore address, Lattimore, Pa., September 10, 1972. Photocopies in possession of authors.
24. Quoted in Yinger, *Rhetoric of Nonviolence,* 20, 84, 47, 14.
25. Chávez, speech at University of Santa Clara, October 26, 1972.
26. Chávez, speech to UAW, June, 1974.
27. Grossman, interview by authors. Copies of Chávez's speeches usually have the names of those he wanted to recognize written on the text.
28. Grossman, interview by authors.
29. Testimony before the subcommittee on labor of the Senate committee on labor and public welfare, April 16, 1969.
30. Chávez, speech at California State University, Sacramento, January 18, 1971.
31. Chávez, speech to UAW, June, 1974.
32. Testimony before the subcommittee on labor of the Senate committee on labor and public welfare, April 16, 1969.
33. Chávez, speech at University of Santa Clara, October 26, 1972.
34. Chávez, "Letter to Members of UFW," April 16, 1971.
35. Chávez, speech at University of Santa Clara, October 26, 1972.
36. Chávez, testimony before subcommittee on migratory labor, September 29, 1969, 3390–93.
37. An audiotape of this speech in the Latin American Library of the Oakland Public Library, Oakland, Calif. The speech is also discussed in Hammerback, Jensen, and Gutiérrez, *A War of Words,* 38–41.
38. Chávez, "Chávez in Austin, Texas," in Robert Tice, "The Rhetoric of La Raza," 41–44.

39. One example is Chávez's speech before the migratory labor subcommittee of the Senate committee on labor and public welfare, September 29, 1969, which simply ends; there is no conclusion at all.
40. Chávez, speech at University of Santa Clara, October 26, 1972.
41. Chávez, "Wrath of Grapes" boycott speech, 1986.
42. Chávez, interview by Padilla.
43. Chávez, "César Chávez Talks About Organizing."
44. Chávez at California State University, Sacramento, January 18, 1971.
45. Chávez, "The Mexican American and the Church," 146.
46. Chávez, speech at Lattimore, September 10, 1972.
47. Chávez, speech to UAW, June, 1974.
48. Chávez, quoted in "CBS," ARC 55, 12:00, 1970.
49. Chávez, speech to UAW, June, 1974.
50. Chávez, notes for speech to AFL-CIO luncheon, Denver, Colo., December 21, 1967 (photocopy of text in possession of authors); Chávez, notes for speech at Stockton rally, February 28, 1971.
51. Chávez, notes for speech to AFL-CIO luncheon, Denver, Colo., December 21, 1967.
52. Chávez, "César Chávez Talks About Organizing."
53. Richard A. Garcia, "César Chávez and the Chicanos."
54. Chávez, interview by Olson and Luchetti.
55. Chávez, hearings before the Senate subcommittee on migratory labor of the committee on labor and public welfare, *Congressional Record,* September 29, 1969, 3397–98.
56. Ibid.
57. Ibid., 3399. His testimony on that day listed numerous other similar examples.
58. See, for example, notes for speech at the seventh constitutional convention of the AFL-CIO, Miami, Fla., December 12, 1967. Photocopies of texts in possession of authors.
59. Chávez, speech at Lattimore, September 10, 1972; Chávez, notes for speech at Stockton rally, February 28, 1971.
60. Chávez, speech to UAW, June, 1974.
61. Chávez, speech to UAW, June, 1974.
62. Chávez, speech at California State University, Sacramento, January 18, 1971.
63. Chávez, testimony before the subcommittee of labor of the Senate subcommittee on labor and public welfare, April 16, 1969.
64. Chávez, speech at Exposition Park, May 2, 1971.
65. For a discussion of Mexican-American public address, see Hammerback and Jensen, "Ethnic Heritage as Rhetorical Legacy."
66. Chávez, quoted in Levy, *Autobiography of La Causa,* 18–19.
67. The story is detailed in Hammerback, Jensen, and Gutiérrez, *A War of Words,* 39–40. The story also appears on the audiotape of Chávez's speech at the seventh constitutional convention of the AFL-CIO, Miami, Fla., December 12, 1967.
68. Yinger, *Rhetoric of Nonviolence,* 52, 72; Chávez, quoted in ibid., 46–47.
69. Chávez, quoted in Day, *Forty Acres,* 116.
70. Chávez, speech at California State University, Sacramento, January 18, 1971.
71. Chávez, "Chávez in Austin, Texas," in Robert Tice, "The Rhetoric of La Raza," 41–44.
72. Grossman, interview by authors.

CHAPTER 7. TRIUMPHS AND DEFEATS IN THE ONGOING QUEST

1. Patrick H. Mooney and Theo J. Majka, *Farmers' and Farm Workers' Movements: Social Protest in American Agriculture* (New York: Twayne, 1995), 176–77.
2. Richard Steven Street, "It's Boycott Time in California," 330; Acuña, *Occupied America*, 370. Patrick H. Mooney and Theo J. Majka outline the effects of the action in *Farmers' and Farm Workers' Movements*, 176–78.
3. Griswold del Castillo and Garcia, *Triumph of Spirit*, 129–30.
4. Daniel, "Unionization of California Farm Workers," 379. The pact was signed for a five-year period in 1977 and was renewed in 1982.
5. Yates, "A Union is Not a 'Movement,'" 518–19.
6. Barr, "Sour Grapes," 22–23.
7. Ibid., 23; "What Happened to Chávez's Union?" 22.
8. Yates, "A Union is Not a 'Movement,'" 519.
9. Acuña, *Occupied America*, 429; Judith Cummings, "Dispute Intensifies Over Chávez's Leadership of Farm Workers," *New York Times,* January 3, 1983, A-8.
10. Mooney and Majka, *Farmers' and Farm Workers' Movements,* 186.
11. Ibid., 186–87.
12. Ibid., 187.
13. Barr, "Sour Grapes," 23.
14. Robert Lindsey, "Chávez and Farm Workers Adapt Tactics to the Times," *New York Times,* July 31, 1983, 20.
15. Robert Lindsey, "César Chávez Tries New Directions for United Farm Workers," *New York Times,* September 16, 1983, A-16.; Lindsey, "Chávez and the Farm Workers Adapt Tactics to the Times," 20.
16. Chávez, "Chávez: Farm Worker Initiative is Needed to Guard Against Abuse," *Los Angeles Times,* April 8, 1976, 5.
17. Chávez, "He Showed Us the Way," *Maryknoll,* April 1978, 52.
18. Ibid., 52–54.
19. Chávez, report to fourth constitutional convention of UFW, September 1–3, 1979. Photocopy of text in possession of authors.
20. Ibid.
21. Ibid.
22. Ibid.
23. Ibid.
24. Chávez, HEW address, March 21, 1978. Copy in possession of authors. Both his manuscript outline and notes were used in this analysis.
25. Ibid. We are using upper- and lowercase letters, but Chávez's notes are in all capital letters.
26. Ibid.
27. Ibid.
28. Ibid.
29. Ibid.
30. Ibid.
31. Chávez, president's address to Texas organizing convocation, Pharr, Tex., February 25, 1979. Photocopy of text in possession of authors.
32. Ibid.
33. Ibid.

34. Ibid.
35. Chávez, speech to United Church of Christ, October 1981. Copy in possession of authors.
36. Ibid.
37. Chávez, speech to UFW graduating negotiations class, 1982. Copy in possession of authors.
38. Ibid.
39. Chávez, personal letter to friends of UFW. This letter was a fund-raising letter. Photocopy of text in possession of authors.
40. Ibid.; emphasis in original.
41. Ibid.
42. Ibid.

CHAPTER 8. THE DIFFICULT LAST DECADE

1. Griswold del Castillo and Garcia, *Triumph of Spirit,* 172.
2. Mooney and Majka, *Farmers' and Farm Workers' Movements,* 186.
3. Catherine Wilson, "UFW's Chávez Announces New Grape Boycott," *The Sacramento Bee,* July 12, 1984, A-3. The United Farm Workers distributed copies of Wilson's article throughout the country in its public mailings.
4. Matt S. Meier and Feliciano Ribera, *Mexican Americans: American Mexicans* (New York: Hill and Wang, 1993), 211.
5. Meier and Ribera, *Mexican Americans: American Mexicans,* 211.
6. Chávez, quoted in Griswold del Castillo and Garcia, *Triumph of Spirit,* 135.
7. Lindsey, "Chávez and the Farm Workers Adapt Tactics to the Times," 20.
8. Wright, "Farm Workers' Leaders Advocate Boycott," C-3.
9. Meier and Ribera, *Mexican Americans: American Mexicans,* 211.
10. Chávez, quoted in Griswold del Castillo and Garcia, *Triumph of Spirit,* 137–38.
11. "UFW Pressure Prompts Stores to Pull Grapes; United Farm Workers; Vons Companies Inc. and Other Supermarket Chains," *Supermarket News,* July 3, 1989, 1.
12. Frank Bardacke, "César's Ghost: Decline and Fall of the UFW," *The Nation,* July 26, 1993.
13. Daniel, "Unionization of California Farm Workers," 380.
14. Ibid.
15. Ibid., 381.
16. Chávez, address to UFW's seventh constitutional convention, Bakersfield, Calif., September, 1984. Photocopy of text in possession of authors.
17. Ibid.
18. Ibid.
19. Chávez, address to the Commonwealth Club of San Francisco, November 9, 1984. Copy in possession of authors; Grossman, interview by authors.
20. "César Chávez Warns Rural Democrats Against Siding With Big Agriculture," *Los Angeles Times,* June 24, 1984, Sec. 4: 1–2.
21. Chávez, address to Commonwealth Club, November 9, 1984.
22. Ibid.
23. Ibid.
24. Ibid.
25. Ibid.
26. Ibid.
27. Ibid.

28. Ibid.
29. Ibid.
30. Ibid.
31. Ibid.
32. Ibid.
33. Ibid.
34. Chávez, outline for breakfast speech, September 26, 1984. Copy in possession of authors.
35. Chávez, "Solidarity," October 7, 1984. Translated from Spanish by Alicia García. Photocopy of text in possession of authors.
36. Ibid.
37. Ibid.
38. Ibid.
39. Chávez, speech to Los Angeles County Chicano Employee Association, October 25, 1985. Copy in possession of authors.
40. Chávez, personal letter to friends of the UFW. This was a fund-raising letter. Photocopy of text in possession of authors.
41. Ibid.
42. Ibid.; Henry Weinstein, "Farm Worker Death Stirs Chávez's Anger," *Los Angeles Times,* September 24, 1983, 1, 8. Copy of the article was included in Chávez's personal letter to friends of the UFW.
43. Chávez, personal letter to friends of the UFW.
44. Ibid.
45. Ibid.
46. Chávez, "Wrath of Grapes" boycott speech, 1986.
47. Ibid.
48. Ibid.
49. Ibid.
50. Ibid.
51. Ibid. A slightly altered version of this address is a copy labeled CWA, April 23, 1986, where the opening phase "the court of last resort" is "the American labor movement" rather than "the American people"; the demand for "good faith bargaining" is not made; the word "build" has been replaced by "bind" in front of "foundation" (9); and a final plea for support contains the word "I" instead of "we." (9) Other differences are in underlining and paragraph form and in punctuation such as exchanging an exclamation point for a comma, or a question mark for a period; placement of commas; and the numbering of several points in the "America" version.
52. Chávez, address at Boatt Law School, May 24, 1986. Photocopy of text in possession of authors.
53. Ibid.
54. Chávez, pecan workers strike speech, 1987. The authors have texts of the speech in both English and Spanish.
55. Ibid.
56. Chávez, interviewed on "Between the Lines," Public Access Television, November 9, 1987. Photocopy of text in possession of authors.
57. Griswold del Castillo and Garcia, *Triumph of Spirit,* 137–38.
58. Bridget Flanagan, quoted in Wright, "Farm Workers' Leaders Advocate Boycott," C-3; David S. Wilson, "Despite Boycott, Grape Sales are Up," *The New York Times,* November 27, 1988, 30.
59. Griswold del Castillo and Garcia, *Triumph of Spirit,* 173.

60. Chávez, "Statement From César Chávez, President, United Farm Workers, Sacramento, April 3, 1991." Photocopy of text in possession of authors.

61. Chávez, "Statement by César Chávez, School Dedication, Coachella, October 19, 1990. Photocopy of text in possession of authors.

62. Chávez, "Statement from César Chávez, President, United Farm Workers on Earlimart Cancer Clusters, September 14, 1989." Photocopy of text in possession of authors.

63. Chávez, "Statement from César Chávez, President, United Farm Workers of America, AFL-CIO, September 1992, Hong Kong"; "Statement By César Chávez, President, United Farm Workers, June 18, 1992, Mecca, California"; "Statement By César Chávez, President, United Farm Workers, Lamont, California, July 15, 1992." Photocopies of texts in possession of authors.

64. Chávez, statement in Hong Kong; Chávez, "Statement From César Chávez, President, United Farm Workers, Sacramento, December 18, 1989; Chávez, statement in Lamont, July 15, 1992.

65. Chávez, "Statement by César Chávez, President, United Farm Workers, Santa Monica, March 13, 1990." Photocopy of text in possession of authors.

66. Chávez, statement in Hong Kong, 1992.

67. Chávez, statement in Sacramento, April 3, 1991.

68. Chávez, statement in Coachella, October 19, 1990.

69. Chávez, statement in Mecca, June 18, 1992.

70. Chávez, statement in Mecca, June 18, 1992; Statement in Lamont, July 15, 1992; Chávez, "Statement from César Chávez, President, United Farm Workers, Coachella Valley, October 10, 1991."

71. Chávez, op-ed piece for the Bakersfield *Californian,* October, 1990. Photocopy of text in possession of authors.

72. Chávez, statement in Coachella, October 19, 1990.

73. Chávez, statement in Sacramento, April 3, 1991.

74. Chávez, op-ed piece for the Bakersfield *Californian.*

75. Chávez, statement on Earlimart Cancer Cluster, September 14, 1989.

76. Chávez, statement at Pacific Lutheran University, Tacoma, Wash., March, 1989. Photocopy of text in possession of authors.

77. Chávez, statement at Pacific Lutheran University.

78. Chávez, "Statement from César Chávez, President, United Farm Workers Calling for a Case-Control Study on Cancer and Pesticides, Bakersfield, Calif., October 24, 1991." Photocopy of text in possession of authors.

79. Chávez, statement in Hong Kong, 1992; Chávez, statement in Sacramento, April 3, 1991; Chávez, statement in Mecca, June 18, 1992.

80. Chávez, statement in Hong Kong, 1992.

81. Chávez, statement in Sacramento, April 3, 1991.

82. Chávez, statement on Earlimart Cancer Cluster, September 14, 1989.

83. Chávez, statement in Santa Monica, March 13, 1990.

84. Chávez, statement in Hong Kong, 1992.

85. Chávez, statement on Earlimart Cancer Cluster, September 14, 1989; Chávez, statement in Sacramento, December 18, 1989.

86. Chávez, statement in Santa Monica, March 13, 1990.

87. Chávez, statement in Sacramento, April 3, 1991.

88. Chávez, statement on Earlimart Cancer Cluster, September 14, 1989.

89. Chávez, "My Anger and Sadness Over Pesticides," *Sacramento Bee,* April 16, 1989, 6; Chávez, "Statement By César Chávez, Delano, California, August 1988."

90. Chávez, speech at Pacific Lutheran University, March 1989.
91. Ibid.
92. Ibid.
93. Ibid.
94. Ibid.
95. Ibid.
96. Ibid.
97. Ibid.
98. Chávez, "'Public Policy or Public Action': An Address By César Chávez, Washington, D.C., October 27, 1991." Photocopy of text in possession of authors.
99. Ibid.
100. Ibid.
101. Ibid.
102. Ibid.
103. Ibid.
104. Ibid.
105. On September 12, 1991, Chávez had delivered an earlier version of the BIA address to an audience in San Francisco, with the only change being his introduction that related his now-common theme of Hispanic growth to the need for housing. See: Chávez, "Address by César Chávez, President United Farm Workers of America, AFL-CIO," San Francisco, September 12, 1991.
106. Gary W. Hambly, "Chávez's Appeal Touched Homebuilders," *BIA News,* April 1994, 17, 11.
107. Chávez, "Address by César Chávez, President, United Farm Workers of America, AFL-CIO Before Building Industry Assn. of Northern Calif., San Jose, November 21, 1991." Photocopy of text in possession of authors.
108. Ibid.
109. Ibid.
110. Ibid.
111. S. Reid Gustafson, quoted in Hambly, "Chávez's Appeal Touched Homebuilders," 17.
112. Chávez, "César Chávez's Statement on the Fast, Delano, California, July 19, 1988." Photocopy of text in possession of authors.
113. Ibid.
114. Chávez, "Statement By César Chávez, Delano, California, August 1988." Photocopy of text in possession of authors.

CHAPTER 9. CONCLUSION

1. Yinger, *Rhetoric of Nonviolence,* 21.
2. Daniel, "Unionization of California Farm Workers," 351.
3. Quoted in Jiménez, "Newspaper Coverage of Chávez's Death," 28.
4. Quoted in Marat Moore, "Women Go Underground," in *The United Mine Workers of America: A Model of Industrial Solidarity?* ed. John H. M. Laslett (University Park, Pa.: Pennsylvania State University Press, 1996), 512.
5. Eugene Nelson, quoted in Griswold del Castillo and Garcia, *Triumph of Spirit,* 147.
6. Dolores Huerta, quoted in Griswold del Castillo and Garcia, *Triumph of Spirit,* 72.
7. Griswold del Castillo and Garcia, *Triumph of Spirit,* 157.
8. Ibid., 100.

Selected Bibliography

I. BIBLIOGRAPHIES, COLLECTIONS OF PAPERS, AND WEB SITES

Fodell, Beverly. *César Chávez and the United Farm Workers: A Selective Bibliography.* Detroit: Wayne State University Press, 1974.

Meier, Matt S. *Bibliography of Mexican-American History.* Westport, Conn.: Greenwood Press, 1984.

———. *Mexican-American Biographies: A Historical Dictionary, 1836–1987,* 55–57. New York: Greenwood Press, 1988.

Meier, Matt S., and Feliciano Rivera. *Dictionary of Mexican-American History.* Westport, Conn.: Greenwood Press, 1981.

San Joaquin Valley Farm Workers Collection. Special Collections Department. Fresno State University Library, Fresno, Calif. (hereafter cited as "San Joaquin Collection, Fresno State").

United Farm Workers Papers. Archives of Labor History and Urban Affairs. Walter E. Reuther Library. Wayne State University, Detroit (hereafter cited as "UFW Papers, Wayne State").

Web site of the César E. Chávez Institute for Public Policy Studies, San Francisco State University, San Francisco, Calif. Address: http://thecity.sfsu.edu/~ccipp/. Resources on Chávez and the UFW, including sound and video clips, pictures, documents, texts of speeches, and links to related web sites.

Yinger, Winthrop, ed. *César Chávez and El Malcriado—1965–1970 Compilation.* Delano, Calif.: Farm Workers Press, 1970. Listing of all references to Chávez in the farm workers' newspaper. Copy of text in San Joaquin Collection, Fresno State.

II. CHÁVEZ'S WORKS
A. Speeches by Chávez (in chronological order)

Speech at Robert Young Auditorium, n.d. Copy in UFW Papers, Wayne State.

"César Chávez Talks About Organizing and the History of the NFWA," *Movement,* December 1965, 3–6. A nearly full text of a speech Chávez gave in Fresno, Calif., in November of 1965. Text in San Joaquin Collection, Fresno State. Photocopy of text in possession of authors. Reprinted as "César Chávez: Grass-Roots Organizer," in *Aztecas Del Norte: The Chicanos of Aztlán,* ed. Jack D. Forbes (Greenwich, Conn.: Fawcett Publications, 1973).

"UAW Western Region Pledges New Support." *El Malcriado,* March 29, 1967, 15. Contains speech at United Auto Workers gathering.

Speech at Solidarity House, Lansing, Mich., April 1, 1967. Audiotape and transcript in UFW Papers, Wayne State. Copy of speech in possession of authors.

Speech to Seventh Constitutional Convention of AFL-CIO, December 12, 1967. Audiotape at Eastern Michigan University, Ypsilanti. Audiotape in possession of authors.

Speech ending 1968 fast, March 10, 1968, Delano, Calif. *Ahora!* 3, no. 3 (January 28, 1972): 1. Reprinted in *César Chávez: The Rhetoric of Nonviolence,* by Winthrop Yinger, 46–47.

Speech at City College of New York, May 1968. Audiotape in the Latin American Library, Oakland Public Library, Oakland Calif.

"La Migra Shapes Up . . . We Hope." *El Malcriado,* May 15, 1968, 3–4. Chávez speech on the border patrol.

"César Chávez Talks in New York." *Catholic Worker,* June 1968, 4. Speech to a religious conference in Manhattan. Photocopy of text in possession of authors.

Testimony Before Congressional Labor and Education Subcommittee Hearings in Delano, Calif., August 15, 1968. Text in San Joaquin Collection, Fresno State.

Statement of César E. Chávez Before the Subcommittee on Labor and the Senate Committee on Labor and Public Welfare, Washington, D.C., April 16, 1969. Text in San Joaquin Collection, Fresno State.

Speech at Lamont, Calif., Community Center, July 13. 1969. *El Malcriado,* July 15–31, 1969, 12–13.

Statement on Medical Plan, August 1, 1969. Audiotape in UFW Papers, Wayne State.

Testimony Before Subcommittee on Migratory Labor, September, 29, 1969. San Joaquin Collection, Fresno State.

Speech to AFL-CIO Eighth Constitutional Convention, Atlantic City, N.J., October 1969. Text in UFW Papers, Wayne State.

A Dialogue With Congress. Washington, D.C.: National Campaign for Agricultural Democracy, 1969. Transcript of a public hearing before the Education and Labor Committee, House of Representatives, October 1, 1969.

Speech at First Unitarian Church, Philadelphia, Pa., October 6, 1969.

Speech to rally in front of Food and Drug Administration Headquarters, Washington, D.C., October 11, 1969.

"César Chávez at City College of New York," 1969. Pacifica Tape Library. Audiotape in possession of authors.

César Chávez Gives Talk on California Grape Boycott, n.d. (circa 1970). Copy at University of Washington, Seattle.

"California Labor Backs Boycott 100 Percent." *El Malcriado,* April 1970, 5.

"Press Release," Delano, Calif., June 6, 1970. Mimeographed document containing excerpts of a speech by Chávez. Text in San Joaquin Collection, Fresno State. Photocopy of text in possession of authors.

Address to students at LeMoyne College, Syracuse, N.Y., December 2, 1970. Audiotape at UFW Papers, Wayne State.

Speech at California State University, Sacramento, January 18, 1971. Audiotape and transcript in possession of authors.

"Chávez in Austin, Texas, February 6, 1971." The text in English and Spanish appears in Robert Tice, "The Rhetoric of La Raza," an unpublished manuscript housed in the Chicano Studies Collection, Hayden Library, Arizona State University, Tempe, Ariz. Photocopy of text of speech in possession of authors.

Speech on Vietnam in Exposition Park, May 2, 1971. Text in UFW Papers, Wayne State. Photocopy of text in possession of authors.

Speech at Economy Furniture Strike, Austin, Texas, August 1971. Audiotape in possession of authors.

Address to the Twenty-Third Constitutional Convention of the UAW, April 1972. Text in UFW Papers, Wayne State.

"Statement by César Chávez at the End of His 24-day Fast for Justice," Phoenix, Ariz., June 4, 1972. Text in UFW Papers, Wayne State.

Meeting with White River Farm Strikers, October 10, 1972. Audiotape in UFW Papers, Wayne State.

Speech at the University of California at Los Angeles, October 11, 1972. Text in UFW Papers, Wayne State.

Speech at Rabbi's Luncheon, ELA College, October 24, 1972. Audiotape in UFW Papers, Wayne State.

Speech at University of Santa Clara, Calif., October 26, 1972. Audiotape and transcript in possession of authors.

Lincoln Park Rally, Los Angeles, Calif., October 27, 1972. Audiotape in UFW Papers, Wayne State.

Talk to farm workers on Proposition 22, Lincoln Park, Los Angeles, November 4, 1972. Audiotape in UFW Papers, Wayne State.

San Francisco Labor March, November 4, 1972. Audiotape in UFW Papers, Wayne State.

Speech at St. Paul, Minn., 1973. Audiotape at University of Wisconsin, Oshkosh.

Speech at meeting in Coachella Auditorium, April 12, 1973. Audiotape in UFW Papers, Wayne State.

Speech at the National Press Club, Washington, D.C., May 11, 1973. Text in UFW Papers, Wayne State.

Eulogy for Juan de la Cruz (shot on a UFW picket line), August 21, 1973, Arvin, Calif. Text in UFW Papers, Wayne State.

Speech in Livingston, September 12, 1973. Audiotape in UFW Papers, Wayne State.

Speech at First Farm Workers Convention, Fresno, Calif., September 23, 1973. Audiotape in UFW Papers, Wayne State.

"Statement by César Chávez on the Occasion of a Funeral Mass for 19 Farm Workers Killed in a Bus Accident in Blythe, California, January 15, 1974." Text in UFW Papers, Wayne State. Reprinted in an article in the *Los Angeles Times,* February 11, 1974; and in *American Dissent,* ed. Thomas E. Hachey and Ralph E. Weber, 160–61.

Speech at park in Colexico, Calif., February 18, 1974. Audiotape in UFW Papers, Wayne State.

Address to opening session of National Federation of Priests' Councils, March 1974. Text in UFW Papers, Wayne State.

Chávez talking to Coachella farm workers, March 20, 1974. Audiotape in UFW Papers, Wayne State.

Tour of Ohio, April 5–10, 1974. April 5: clergy meeting, Cuyahoga Community College, Oberlin. April 6: rally at public square, Cleveland; supporters' meeting, Cleveland. April 7: coffee hour speech after Palm Sunday mass, St. Patrick's Church, Youngstown; labor breakfast, Youngstown; labor breakfast, Case Western Reserve, Cleveland; questions and answers, Hiram College, Kent; speech at Kent State University, Kent; speech at Wooster College, Wooster; supporters' potluck dinner, Wooster. April 8: evening banquet, Dayton; supporters meeting, Dayton. April 9: labor meeting, Columbus; media interview at Bishop Watterson High School, Columbus; seder at Hillel Foundation and interviews with Ohio State University *Lantern* and *Columbus Free Press,* Columbus; airport press conference, Columbus; evening rally, Columbus. April 10: ecumenical service and luncheon, Cincinnati; discussion in Channel 9 TV studio before talk show, University of Cincinnati; TV talk show, Channel 9, Cincinnati. Audiotape in UFW Papers, Wayne State.

Speech at convention of International Union, Automobile, Aerospace, and Agricultural Implement Workers of America, Los Angeles, June 1974. Text in UFW Papers, Wayne State. Photocopy of text in possession of authors.

"César's Speech at a Rally in Oxnard," Oxnard, Calif., June 1, 1974. Photocopy of text in possession of authors.

Transcript of remarks at a Greater Washington Central Labor Council luncheon, September 9, 1974. Transcript in UFW Papers, Wayne State. Copy in possession of authors.

Statement for David Crosby/Graham Nash Concert, San Francisco, December 14, 1974. Text in UFW Papers, Wayne State. Photocopy of text in possession of authors.

Speech at Wheeler Auditorium, the University of California, Berkeley, May 2, 1975. Audiotape at the Bancroft Library, University of California, Berkeley.

Speech at organizing conference, La Paz, Calif., June 6, 1976. Audiotape in UFW Papers, Wayne State.

Rally, Garrison Theatre, Claremont College, Claremont, Calif., June 25, 1976. Audiotape in UFW Papers, Wayne State.

Nominating Speech for Jerry Brown for President, Democratic National Convention, July 14, 1976. Audiotape and transcript in UFW Papers, Wayne State.

Address to Texas Organizing Convocation, February 25, 1979. Text in UFW Papers, Wayne State.

Speech to California Association of Bilingual Educators, Sacramento, Calif., February 18, 1980. Photocopy of text in possession of authors.

Speech to the United Church Board for Homeland Ministries, United Church of Christ dinner meeting, October 24, 1981. Text in UFW Papers, Wayne State.

Speech, no other identification, 1982. (The speech begins with this sentence: "After thirty years organizing poor people I have become convinced that the two greatest aspirations of humankind are equality and participation.") Text in UFW Papers, Wayne State.

Speech made to a graduating negotiations class, 1982. Text in UFW Papers, Wayne State.

Address to the Commonwealth Club of San Francisco, November 9, 1984. Copy in UFW Papers, Wayne State. Audiotape and transcript in possession of authors.

Speech at Southern Methodist University, Dallas, Tex.: [c. 1985]. Videocassette at SMU Central Library.

Speech in Canada, October 9, 1985. Photocopy of text in possession of authors.

Speech at Toronto, Labor Luncheon, October 1985. Audiotape in UFW Papers, Wayne State.

Speech to Los Angeles County Chicano Employee Association, November 25, 1985. Photocopy of text in possession of authors.

"Wrath of Grapes Boycott," 1986. Photocopy of speech text in possession of authors.

Speech to Communication Workers, April 23, 1986. Photocopy of text in possession of authors.

Speech at Boalt Law School, University of California at Berkeley, May 24, 1986. Photocopy of text in possession of authors.

Speech at Courtland College, Courtland, N.Y., October 30, 1986. Videocassette at State University of New York, Courtland.

"Wrath of Grapes," 1987. Audiotape recorded at East Lansing, Mich. Audiotape at Eastern Michigan University, Ypsilanti.

"César Chávez Talks About Farm Workers," shown on "Between the Lines" on public access television, November 9, 1987. Audiotape at Eastern Michigan University, Ypsilanti.

United Farm Workers of America, Pecan Workers Speech, Ariz., 1987. Texts in both English and Spanish. Photocopy of text in possession of authors.

Statement at end of fast, August 1988. Copy in UFW Papers, Wayne State.

Speech at Pacific Lutheran University, Tacoma, Wash., March 1989. Text in UFW Papers, Wayne State.

Statement from César Chávez, President, United Farm Workers on Earlimart Cancer Cluster, September 14, 1989. Text in UFW Papers, Wayne State.

Statement at headquarters of the California Food and Agricultural Department, Sacramento, Calif., December 18, 1989. Text in UFW Papers, Wayne State.

"Pesticides Speech," January 9, 1990. Reprinted in *Contemporary American Speeches,* 7th ed., ed. Richard L. Johannesen, R. R. Allen, and Wil A. Linkugel (Dubuque, Iowa: Kendall/

Hunt, 1992), 210–13. The text was furnished to the editors by the United Farm Workers.

"Lessons of Dr. Martin Luther King Jr.," January 12, 1990. Taken from the César E. Chávez Institute for Public Policy at San Francisco State University's web site at (http://thecity.sfsu.edu/~ccipp/cesarmlk.html). Transcript in possession of authors.

Statement by César Chávez, President, United Farm Workers, Santa Monica, Calif., March 13, 1990. Photocopy of text in UFW Papers, Wayne State. Copy in possession of authors.

Statement From César Chávez, President, United Farm Workers, Los Angeles, Apr. 23, 1990. Text in UFW Papers, Wayne State. Photocopy of text in possession of authors.

Statement by César Chávez, School Dedication, October 19, 1990, Coachella. Text in UFW Papers, Wayne State. Photocopy of text in possession of authors.

Statement from César Chávez, President, United Farm Workers, Sacramento, Calif., April 3, 1991. Text in UFW Papers, Wayne State. Photocopy of text in possession of authors.

Address, San Francisco, September 12, 1991. Copy in UFW Papers, Wayne State.

Statement From César Chávez, President, United Farm Workers, Coachella Valley, October 10, 1991. Photocopy of text in UFW Papers, Wayne State. Copy in possession of authors.

Statement from César Chávez, President, United Farm Workers Calling for a Case-Control Study on Cancer and Pesticides, Bakersfield, Calif., October 24, 1991. Text in UFW Papers, Wayne State. Photocopy of text in possession of authors.

"Public Policy or Public Action," an address by César Chávez, President, United Farm Workers of America, Washington, D.C., October 27, 1991. Text in UFW Papers, Wayne State. Photocopy of text in possession of authors.

Address by César Chávez before Building Industry Association of Northern California, San Jose, Calif., November 21, 1991. Text in UFW Papers, Wayne State. The speech was discussed in *BIA News*, April 1994, 11, 17.

Statement by César Chávez, President, United Farm Workers, Grape Workers' Rally, Mecca, Coachella Valley, Calif., June 18, 1992. Text in UFW Papers, Wayne State. Photocopy of text in possession of authors.

Statement by César Chávez, President, United Farm Workers, Lamont, Calif., July 15, 1992. Text in UFW Papers, Wayne State. Photocopy of text in possession of authors.

Statement from César Chávez, President, United Farm Workers, Hong Kong, September 12, 1992. Text in UFW Papers, Wayne State. Photocopy of text in possession of authors.

B. Writings by Chávez (and selected responses)

"Creative Nonviolence." *Center Magazine*, March 1969, 27.

"Effective Protest Doesn't Require a Majority." *Los Angeles Times*, January 2, 1991, B-5.

"Farm Union Is Alive." *Los Angeles Times*, January 2, 1975. Reprinted in *American Dissent*, ed. Thomas E. Hachey and Ralph E. Weber, 156–59.

"Farm Workers." *Los Angeles Times*, February 11, 1974. Reprinted in *American Dissent*, ed. Thomas E. Hachey and Ralph E. Weber, 159–65.

"The Farm Workers' Next Battle." *Nation*, March 25, 1978. Reprinted in *American Dissent*, ed. Thomas E. Hachey and Ralph E. Weber, 165–70.

"Good Friday Letter." *National Catholic Reporter*, April 23, 1969, 4. An open letter to growers.

"Huelga! Tales of the Delano Revolution: The Organizer's Task." *Ramparts*, July 1966.

Introduction to *Forty Acres: César Chávez and the Farm Workers,* by Mark Day. New York: Praeger, 1971, 9–13.

"Letter from Delano." In *Pain and Promise: The Chicano Today,* ed. Edward Simmen, 29–32. Also in *César Chávez,* by Winthrop Yinger, 106–107. This public letter was originally published in *Christian Century*, April 23, 1969, 539–40, addressed to E. L. Barr Jr., President of the California Grape and Tree Fruit League. Barr and his successor R. K. Sanderson responded in a letter titled "Why Grape Growers Do Not 'Render unto César,'" *Christian Century,* June 11, 1968, 810–11. Winthrop Yinger responded to Barr and Sanderson in "Viva La Causa!" *Christian Century,* August 27, 1969, 115–16.

"Letter to Members of UFW," April 16, 1971. Copy in possession of authors.

"The Mexican American and the Church." In *La Causa Política: A Chicano Politics Reader,* ed. F. Chris García, 143–46. Also reprinted in *Voices: Readings From El Grito,* ed. Octavio I. Romano V (Berkeley: Quinto Sol Publications, 1971), 215–18; and *Chicano Politics: Readings,* ed. F. Chris García, 97–100. Paper presented to the Second Annual Mexican American Conference in Sacramento, March 8–10, 1968; originally published in *El Grito,* Summer 1968, 9–12.

"Nonviolence Still Works." *Look,* April 1, 1969, 52.

"The Organizer's Tale." In *The Chicanos: Mexican-American Voices,* ed. Ed Ludwig and James Santibáñez, 101–12. Also reprinted in *Chicano: The Evolution of a People,* ed. Renato Rosaldo, Robert A. Calvert, and Gustav L. Seligmann Jr., 273–78. Originally published in *Ramparts,* July 1966, 43–50.

"Peregrinación, Penitencia, Revolución," in *Aztlán: An Anthology of Mexican-American Literature,* ed. Luis Valdez and Stan Steiner, 385.

"The Philosophy of César Chávez." *El Malcriado,* December 1966, 29. Translated from *El Malcriado,* December 15, 1964.

"El Plan de Delano." *El Malcriado,* March 17, 1966, 11–14. Reprinted in *The Chicanos,* ed. Gilberto López y Rivas (New York: Monthly Review Press, 1974), 107–10. Also reprinted in *Justica al Obrero del Campo!* by José Gallego (Chicago: Fabet Press Service, 1967).

"Plan for the Liberation of the Farm Workers of the U.S. of North America," September 4, 1972. Texts (in English and Spanish) in UFW Papers, Wayne State.

Right to Work Laws—A Trap for America's Minorities. New York: A. Philip Randolph Institute, 1968. With Bayard Rustin. Pamphlet in English and Spanish. Photocopy of text in possession of authors.

"Sharing the Wealth." *Playboy,* January 1970, 127.

"Strike Notes." *Farm Labor,* October 1965, 4. A letter from Chávez to members of the Student Nonviolent Coordination Committee (SNCC) at the University of California.

"Telegram to Mrs. Martin Luther King." *El Malcriado,* April 15, 1968. Telegram sent after the death of Dr. Martin Luther King Jr. It reaffirms Chávez's nonviolent principles.

"Why Delano?" In *Aztlán: An Anthology of Mexican-American Literature,* ed. Luis Valdez and Stan Steiner, 202–204. Originally distributed as a mimeographed, undated document.

C. Interviews with Chávez (in chronological order)

Goepel, Wendy. "Viva La Causa!" *Farm Labor,* April 1964, 23–28.

Interview at the Agriculture College, Michigan State University, April 1967. Text in UFW Papers, Wayne State.

"Marcher: Interview," *New Yorker,* May 1967, 28.

Interview by Bill Olson and Dennis Luchetti, August 13, 1967, for "Kaleidoscope," a show on KUNM radio (University of New Mexico, Albuquerque). Audiotape and transcript in possession of authors.

Interview. *Farm Labor Problems (The Anguish of Delano).* Fresno, Calif.: *Central California Register,* 1968. This pamphlet also contains several articles and an interview with a grower representative, in English and in Spanish.

Interview at the Center for the Study of Democratic Institutions, Santa Barbara, Calif., 1968. Audiotape in possession of authors.

"Nonviolence Still Works: UFWOC During the Grape Pickers Strike," *Look,* April 1, 1969, 52. Reply by C. G. Adamy, *Look,* June 10, 1969, 52.

Cabell, Paul. "A *Free Press* Interview With César Chávez." *Los Angeles Free Press,* August 22, 1969.

"An Interview with César Chávez," with Alexander Hoffman, Pacifica Tape Library, 1970.

Fitch, Bob "Tilting With the System." *Christian Century,* February 18, 1970, 204–207. Reprinted in *Chicano Politics: Readings,* ed. F. Chris García, 97–100; and *La Causa Política: A Chicano Politics Reader,* ed. F. Chris García, 360–65.

Moyer, John R., "A Conversation With César Chávez." In *Readings on La Raza: The Twentieth Century,* ed. Matt S. Meier and Feliciano Rivera, 248–54. First published in *Journal of Current Social Issues,* November–December 1970, 3–9.

Moyer, John R., "A Continuing Conversation With César Chávez." *Journal of Current Social Issues,* Spring 1971, 30–31.

Labor News Conference, Washington, D.C. November 17, 1973. Text in UFW Papers, Wayne State.

"Farm Workers Lettuce and Grape Boycott." Labor News Conference, September 17, 1974. Text in UFW Papers, Wayne State.

"Interview: César Chávez: The Undefeated Leader of the Migrant Farm Workers." *Penthouse,* July 1975, 64–66, 99, 108, 110.

Hoffman, Pat. "The More Trouble We Get the More Religious We Get": An Interview With César Chávez." *Sojourners* 6 (October 1977): 21–25.

"Farm Workers' Problems Today." Labor News Conference (AFL-CIO), May 1, 1979. Text in UFW Papers, Wayne State.

Interview by Nancy Padilla, December 7, 1981, Albuquerque, N.M. Audiotape and transcript in possession authors.

III. WRITINGS ABOUT CHÁVEZ AND THE UFW

"A Boost for Chávez." *Newsweek,* May 26, 1975, 68.

Acuña, Rodolfo. *Occupied America: The Chicano's Struggle toward Liberation.* San Francisco: Canfield Press, 1972.

———. *Occupied America: A History of Chicanos.* 3rd ed. New York: Harper & Row, 1988.

Adair, Doug. "César Chávez's Biggest Battle." *Nation,* December 11, 1967, 627–28.

"After Chávez, Farm Workers Struggle." *New York Times,* July 19, 1993, A12.

Allen, Gary. "The Grapes: Communist Wrath in Delano." *American Opinion,* June 1966, 1–14.

Allen, Steve. *The Ground Is Our Table.* New York: Doubleday and Co., 1966.

"Ambiguity of Awards." *Christian Century,* November 4, 1970, 1308.

Axford, Roger. *Spanish-Speaking Heroes.* Midland, Mich.: Pendell, 1973.

Backus, Bertha Rhodes. "A Communicator for La Causa: A Burkeian Analysis of the Rhetoric of César Chávez." Master's thesis, University of California, Santa Barbara, 1970.

Bacon, Jack. "Farm Labor Leader's Fasting Gets Spotlight." *National Catholic Reporter,* March 10, 1968.

Baer, Barbara L., and Glenna Matthews. "The Women in the Boycott." *Nation,* February 1974, 232–38.

Ballis, George. *Basta! La Historia de Nuestra Lucha.* Delano, Calif.: Farm Workers Press, 1966.

Bardacke, Frank. "César's Ghost: Decline and Fall of the UFW." *Nation,* July 26/August 2, 1993, 130–35.

Barnes, Peter. "The Future of the United Farm Workers: Chávez Against the Wall." *New Republic,* December 7, 1974, 13.

Barr, Evan T. "Sour Grapes." *New Republic,* November 25, 1985, 20.

Berman, J. J., and J. Hightower. "Chávez and the Teamsters." *Nation,* November 2, 1970, 427–31.

Bernstein, Aaron, and Jonathan Tsini. "Chávez Tries a Computerized Grape Boycott." *Business Week,* September 9, 1985, 35, 38.

Bernstein, Harry. "General Counsel of State Farm Labor Board Quits." *Los Angeles Times,* April 17, 1976, 4.

———. "Hymn-Singing Farm Workers Support Fasting Union Leader." *Los Angeles Times,* February 28, 1968.

———. "Judge Fears for Chávez's Health, Delays Hearing." *Los Angeles Times,* February 28, 1968.

Bishop, Katherine. "Fast by Chávez Over Pesticides Passes Twenty-Ninth Day." *New York Times,* August 16, 1988, A18.

"Black Eagle Wins." *Time,* August 10, 1970, 10–11.

Bomfim, Ricardo Aecio. "César Estrada Chávez: Militant Prophet." Master's thesis, University of Georgia, 1982.

Bonham, Frank. *Viva Chicano.* New York: Dell, 1971.

"Breakthrough Agreement in Coachella Valley." *Christian Century,* April 22, 1970, 469.

Breakthrough for La Huelga." *Time,* June 27, 1969, 18.

Buckley, William F., Jr. "Chávez Machine." *National Review,* August 10, 1971, 888–89. A negative view of Chávez by a noted conservative writer.

———. "Don't Eat Grapes Along With Me." *National Review,* July 15, 1969, 715.

———. "Victory of César Chávez." *National Review,* September 8, 1970, 965.

"California Compromise." *Time,* May 19, 1975.

"California Grape Boycott." *Trans-Action,* February 1969, 6.

"Can Chávez Survive?" *Time,* September 3, 1973, 73.

"Can They Pull Off a Nationwide Boycott?" *Nation's Business,* October 1968, 46–48.

Castro, Tony. "César Chávez: Father, Son, and Holy Ghost." In *Chicano Power: The Emergence of Mexican America,* 79–96.

———. *Chicano Power: The Emergence of Mexican America.* New York: Saturday Review Press, 1974.

"César Chávez: Fall From Grace." *This World, San Francisco Examiner and Chronicle,* October 21, 1984.

"César Chávez: 'La Causa' and the Man." *American Labor* (February 1971): 20–30.

Chandler, David. *Huelga!* New York: Simon & Schuster, 1970.

"César Chávez—The Shy Mobilizer of American Farm Workers." *Life,* April 29, 1966.

"César's War." *Time,* March 22, 1968, 23.

Cedeno, María E. *César Chávez: Labor Leader.* Brookfield, Conn.: Hispanic Heritage, The Millbrook Press, 1993. A children's book for grades 3–4.

"Chance for Chávez." *Economist,* September 6, 1975, 74.

"Chávez." *San Diego Free Press,* November 1–14, 1968, 7.

"Chávez: Again the Boycott." *America,* May 5, 1973, 402.

"Chávez Blight Spreads East." *Nation's Business,* May 1972, 32–35.

"Chávez, César Estrada." *Current Biography,* February 1969, 8–10.

"Chávez Ends Fast Over Pesticide Use." *New York Times,* August 22, 1988, A12.

"Chávez Escalates His Attack on Gallo." *Business Week,* January 27, 1975, 53–54.

"Chávez's Fast for Nonviolence." *CMM Newsletter,* May 15, 1968, 5.

"Chávez: One Battle Ends, Another Begins." *U.S. News and World Report,* August 10, 1970, 49–51.

"Chávez Strikes Again; Suit Against the Defense Department." *Newsweek,* January 25, 1971, 64.

"Chávez vs. The Teamsters: Farm Workers' Historic Vote." *U.S. News and World Report,* September 22, 1975, 32–33.

"The Chicanos Campaign for a Better Deal." *Business Week,* May 29, 1971, 48.

Cleath, R. L. "Rendering Unto César." *Christianity Today,* July 3, 1970, 32–33.

Cohen, Irving J. "La Huelga! Delano and After." *Monthly Labor Review,* June 1968, 13–16.

Collins, David R. *Farm Workers' Friend: The Story of César Chávez.* Minneapolis: Carolrhoda Books, 1996.

Copeland, Jeff B. "Wooing the Migrant Farmer." *Newsweek,* June 29, 1987, 47.

Coyne, J. R., Jr. "Doctored Grapes?" *National Review,* July 1, 1969, 639.

————. "Grapes of Wrath." *National Review,* July 1, 1969, 639.

Daniel, Cletus E. *Bitter Harvest: A History of California Farm Workers, 1870–1941.* Ithaca, N.Y.: Cornell University Press, 1981.

————. "César Chávez and the Unionization of California Farm Workers." In *Labor Leaders in America,* ed. Melvyn Dubofsky and Warren Van Tine. Urbana: University of Illinois Press, 1987.

Day, Mark. *Forty Acres: César Chávez and the Farm Workers.* New York: Praeger, 1971.

De Ruiz, Dana Catherine, and Richard Larios. *La Causa: The Migrant Farm Workers' Story.* Austin, TX: Steck-Vaughn Publishers, 1993. A children's book for grades 3–5.

De Toledano, Ralph. *Little César.* New York: Anthem Books, 1970. Negative portrayal from National Right to Work Committee.

Degnan, P. "Monopoly in the Vineyards: Grapes of Wrath Strike." *Nation,* February 7, 1966, 151–54.

"The Delano Proclamation." *IUD Agenda,* July 1966, 14.

"Down on the Farm: Court Injunction by Bud Antle, Inc. Against the UFWOC's Picketing." *New Republic,* December 12, 1970, 8.

Drake, J., and G. Gersmehl. "Salad Days at the Pentagon." *Commonweal,* February 19, 1971, 485–86.

Dunne, John Gregory. *Delano: Story of the California Grape Strike.* New York: Farrar, Straus, and Giroux, 1967.

————. "Strike." *Saturday Evening Post,* May 6, 1967, 32–36.

————. "To Die Standing: César Chávez and the Chicanos." *Atlantic,* June 1971, 39–45.

Erenburg, Mark. "Obreros Unidos in Wisconsin; Migrant Farm Worker Unionization." *Monthly Labor Review,* June 1968, 17–23.

Faivre, Lynn. *Chávez: One New Answer.* New York: Praeger, 1970.

"A Farm-Bred Unionist: César Estrada Chávez." *New York Times,* March 11, 1968, 22.

Farm Labor Organizing 1905–1967: A Brief History. New York: National Advisory Committee on Farm Labor, 1967.

"Farm Union Reaps First California Victory." *Business Week,* April 16, 1966, 158.

"Farm Workers Choose a Union; and Now the Southwest." *America,* September 17, 1966, 270.

"Farm Workers Drop Boycott Weapon." *U.S. News and World Report,* April 17, 1972, 89.

"Farm Workers: Grapes of Wrath." *Economist,* August 20, 1988, 25.

Ferriss, Susan, and Ricardo Sandoval. *The Fight in the Fields: César Chávez and the Farmworkers Movement.* New York: Harcourt Brace, 1997.

Flynn, Julie. "A Lawsuit Could Ruin the Farm Workers' Union." *Business Week,* March 23, 1987, 42.

"For a Vote in the Vineyards." *America,* November 22, 1969, 482.

"Four-Year Strike, Two-Year Boycott: Showdown." *U.S. News and World Report*, July 14, 1969, 83–84.

Franchere, Ruth. *César Chávez*. New York: Crowell, 1970.

"From Fruit Bowl to Salad Bowl." *Time*, September 14, 1970, 18.

Gaines, Judith. "César Chávez and the United Farm Workers." *Nuestro*, November 1985.

García, F. Chris, ed. *Chicano Politics: Readings*. New York: MSS Information Corp., 1973.

García, F. Chris. *La Causa Política: A Chicano Politics Reader*. Notre Dame, Ind.: University of Notre Dame Press, 1974.

García, F. Chris, and Rudolph O. de la Garza. *The Chicano Political Experience: Three Perspectives*. North Scituate, Mass.: Duxbury Press, 1977.

Garza, Ernesto. *Spiders in the House and Workers in the Field*. Notre Dame: University of Notre Dame Press, 1970).

Gómez, Rudolf. *The Changing Mexican American*. El Paso: University of Texas, El Paso, 1972. A children's book.

Gozales, Doreen. *César Chávez: Leader for Migrant Farm Workers*. Springfield, NY: Enslow Publishers, 1996.

Gonzales, Raymond J. "A Surprise Chicano View of César Chávez." *California Journal*, April 1977, 110.

"Grape Boycott Round 3." *Time*, August 19, 1985, 36.

"Grape Pickers Win Contract." *America*, April 18, 1970, 400.

"Grapes of Wrath." *Economist*, August 20, 1988, 25.

Griffith, Winthrop. "Is Chávez Beaten?" *New York Times Magazine*, Sept 15, 1974, 18–35.

Griswold del Castillo, Richard, and Richard A. Garcia. *César Chávez: A Triumph of Spirit*. Norman: University of Oklahoma Press, 1995.

Gutiérrez, José Ángel. "César Estrada Chávez: The First and Last of the Chicano Leaders." *San Jose Studies* 20 (Spring 1994): 35, 37.

Hachey, Thomas E., and Ralph E. Weber, eds. *American Dissent from Thomas Jefferson to César Chávez: The Rhetoric of Reform and Revolution*. Huntington, N.Y.: Robert E. Krieger Publishing Co., 1981.

Hallet, D. L. "Bitter Fruit in the Vineyards." *Nation's Business*, February 1970, 80–83.

Hammerback, John C. "The Words of César Chávez, Teacher of Truth." *San Jose Studies* 20 (1994): 10–14.

Hammerback, John C., and Richard J. Jensen. "César Chávez." In *American Orators of the Twentieth Century: Critical Studies and Sources*, ed. Bernard K. Duffy and Halford R. Ryan, 55–62. Westport, Conn.: Greenwood Press, 1987.

———. "César Estrada Chávez." In *Leaders From the 1960s: A Biographical Sourcebook of American Activism*, ed. David DeLeon, 54–61. Westport, Conn.: Greenwood Press, 1994.

———. "Ethnic Heritage as Rhetorical Legacy: The Plan of Delano." *Quarterly Journal of Speech* 80 (1994): 53–70.

———. "'A Revolution of Heart and Mind': César Chávez's Rhetorical Crusade" *Journal of the West* 27 (April 1988): 69–74. Reprinted as "César Chávez" in *Western Speakers: Voices of the American Dream*, ed. Susan H. Koester (Manhattan, Kans.: Sunflower University Press, 1988), 69–74.

———. "The Rhetorical Worlds of César Chávez and Reies Tijerina." *Western Journal of Speech Communication* 44 (1980): 176–90.

———. "Teaching the 'Truth': The Righteous Rhetoric of César Chávez." in *A War of Words*, ed. John C. Hammerback, Richard J. Jensen, and José Ángel Gutiérrez, 33–52.

Hammerback, John C., Richard J. Jensen, and José Ángel Gutiérrez, eds. *A War of Words: Chicano Protest in the 1960s and 1970s*. Westport, Conn.: Greenwood Press, 1985.

Hannula, Don. "Chávez Welcomed at McNeil." *Seattle Times,* December 19, 1969.

———. "From Chávez: A Spiritual Note." *Seattle Times,* December 21, 1969.

"Harvest Nears for César Chávez." *Business Week,* June 27, 1970, 62.

Henninger, D. "And Now Lettuce." *New Republic,* October 10, 1970, 9–11.

Higgins, George C. "César Chávez: 'New Breed' Labor Leader?" *National Catholic News,* April 18, 1966.

———. "La Causa: The Rank and File in Step." *America,* July 5, 1975, 11–12. Review of Ronald Taylor's *Chávez and the Farm Workers.*

Hoffman, Pat. "Gaining Justice Ground." *Sojourners* 6 (October 1977): 18–20.

Howell, L. "Dear César Chávez." *Christianity and Crisis,* September 19, 1977, 194–95.

Hribar, Paul Anthony. "The Social Fasts of César Chávez: A Critical Study of Nonverbal Communication, Nonviolence, and Public Opinion." Ph.D. diss., University of Southern California, 1978.

Hubner, John. "The God of the Movement." *San Jose Mercury News,* August 19, 1984.

"Huelga! Tales of the Delano Revolution." *Ramparts,* July 1966, 12–15.

Huerta, Dolores. "Reflections of the UFW Experience." *The Center Magazine,* July August 1985, 2–8.

———. "Dolores Huerta Talks About Republicans, César, Children, and Her Home Town." In *An Awakening Minority: The Mexican Americans,* ed. Manual E. Serven, 289.

"Inspiration, Sí—Administration, No." *Time,* April 22, 1974, 94.

Jeffs, William George. "The Roots of the Delano Grape Strike." Master's thesis, California State University, Fullerton, 1969.

Jenkins, J. Craig. *The Politics of Insurgency: The Farm Worker Movement of the 1960s.* New York: Columbia University Press, 1985.

Jensen, Joan M. *With These Hands: Women Working on the Land.* Old Westbury, N.Y.: McGraw Hill, 1981.

Jiménez, Edward Rucobo. "A Critical Analysis of Newspaper Coverage of César Chávez's Death." Master's thesis, Fresno State University, 1995.

Kanten, Ron. "Grape Wars." *Progressive,* July 1992, 14.

Keerdoja, E., and others. "What Happened to Chávez's Union?" *Newsweek,* December 14, 1981, 22.

Knowlton, Clark S. "The Neglected Chapters in Mexican-American History." In *Mexican-Americans Tomorrow,* ed. Gus Tyler. Albuquerque: University of New Mexico Press, 1967.

Kopkind, A. "Grape Pickers Strike." *New Republic,* January 29, 1966, 12.

Krebs, A. V. "César Chávez: Final Hope for Farm Workers." *St. Anthony,* August 1968, 17–22.

———. "César Chávez: Huelga!" *U.S. Catholic,* September 1966.

Kushner, Sam. "César Chávez: Far From Defeated." *Christian Century,* November 13, 1974, 1070.

———. *Long Road to Delano.* New York: International Publishers, 1975.

"Labor, 1970." *Nation,* September 7, 1970, 162.

Lamb, Ruth S. *Mexican Americans: Sons of the Southwest.* Claremont, Calif.: Ocelot Press, 1970.

Levy, Jacques E. *César Chávez: Autobiography of La Causa.* New York: Norton, 1975.

Lindsey, Robert. "Chávez and Farm Workers Adapt Tactics to the Times." *New York Times,* July 31, 1983, 20.

———. "César Chávez Tries New Direction for United Farm Workers." *New York Times,* September 16, 1983, A16.

———. "Little Strike that Grew to La Causa." *Time,* July 4, 1969, 19. Same article abridged under title "Battle of the Grapes," *Readers Digest,* October 1969, 33.

———. "Glory Days Are Fading For Chávez and UFW." *New York Times,* December 23, 1984, 4E.

Logsdon, G. "Wrath of Grapes." *Farm Journal,* February 1969, 33.

London, Joan, and Henry Anderson. *So Shall Ye Reap.* New York: Crowell, 1970.

Ludwig, Ed, and James Santibáñez, eds. *The Chicanos: Mexican-American Voices.* Baltimore: Penguin Books, Inc., 1971.

Machado, Manuel A., Jr. *Listen Chicano!* Chicago: Nelson Hall, 1978.

Madera, Corte. "An Organizer's Organizer." *Progressive,* December 1988, 12.

"March of the Migrants." *Life,* April 29, 1966, 93–94.

Matthiessen, Peter. "Profiles: César Chávez." *New Yorker,* June 21, 1969, 42–44; and June 28, 1969, 43.

———. *Sal Si Puedes: César Chávez and the New American Revolution.* New York: Random House, 1969. Reviews by M. H. Gavin, *America,* April 11, 1970, 396; R. De Toledano, *National Review,* March 24, 1970, 313.

McCall, C. "Lettuce Rots and a Man Dies as César Chávez's Dream Strike Turns Nightmare." *People,* March 12, 1979, 24–27.

Meier, Matt S., and Feliciano Rivera. *The Chicanos: A History of Mexican Americans.* New York: Hill and Wang, 1972.

———. *Mexican Americans: American Mexicans.* New York: Hill and Wang, 1993. This book is a revision of *The Chicanos: A History of Mexican Americans.*

Meier, Matt S., and Feliciano Rivera, eds. *Readings on La Raza: The Twentieth Century.* New York: Hill and Wang, 1974.

Meister, D. "La Huelga Becomes La Causa." *New York Times Magazine,* November 17, 1968, 52–53.

Meister, Dick and Anne Loftis. *A Long Time Coming: The Struggle to Unionize America's Farm Workers.* New York: Macmillan, 1977.

Miller, Michael V. "Grape Pickers in California." In *Poverty: Views from the Left,* ed. Jeremy Larner and Irving Hower. New York: William Morrow and Co., 1968.

Mills, Nicolaus C. "Eagle Over the Lettuce Fields." *Commonweal,* November 6, 1970, 140–41.

———. "Workers on the Farms: Agreement With the Western Conference of Teamsters." *New Republic,* September 23, 1967, 9.

Mooney, Patrick H., and Theo J. Majka. *Farmers' and Farm Workers' Movements: Social Protest in American Agriculture.* New York: Twayne, 1995.

Moquin, Wayne, and Charles Van Doren, eds. *A Documentary History of the Mexican Americans.* New York: Praeger, 1971.

Navarro, Joseph. "La Causa and the History of Its Opposition." *Probe,* April 1969, 10.

Nelson, Eugene. *Huelga! The First Hundred Days of the Great Delano Grape Strike.* Delano, Calif.: Farm Workers Press, 1966.

Nelson, Eugene, Jr. "Huelga: New Goals for Labor." *Nation,* June 5, 1967.

"New Boycotts, New Troubles." *New Republic,* April 8, 1972, 6.

"Newcomer Wins on the Farm." *Business Week,* September 10, 1966, 158.

Nicholson, Tom, and William J. Cook. "César's Triumph." *Newsweek,* March 21, 1977, 70.

O'Connell, T. J. "Lettuce Boycott Reaches New York: First of Lawsuits Against the Pentagon." *America,* February 13, 1971, 148–49.

Palmer, L. M. "Grape Fight Spreads to Other Crops." *Farm Journal,* September 1970, 22.

"Pentagon Scabs." *Ramparts Magazine,* November 30, 1968, 12.

Perez, Jean M. *Viva La Huelga: The Struggle of the Farm Workers.* New York: Pathfinder Press, 1973.

"Perseverance and Purity Pay Off For Chávez." *Christian Century,* August 12, 1970, 956.

Pitrone, Jean M. *Chávez: Man of the Migrants.* New York: Pyramid Communications, 1970. A pro-Chávez juvenile text.

Politzer, J. "César's Salad." *Christianity Today,* January 1, 1971, 38.

"Put Politicians 'On Spot' Grape-Strike Leader Says." *Harvard Crimson,* December 19, 1967, 1.

"Render Unto César?" *Economist,* May 5, 1973, 53.

"Rendering to César." *Time,* September 22, 1975, 32.

Rensenbrink, Dorothy. "On Chávez, Women, and Faith." *Christian Century,* April 24, 1974, 444–46.

Richardson, Lincoln. "César Chávez." *Presbyterian Life,* October 1, 1968.

Rivera, Feliciano. "César E. Chávez: Farm Labor Leader." In *A Mexican-American Source Book With Study Guideline.* Menlo Park, Calif.: Educational Consulting Associates, 1970, 120.

Roberts, Donovan O. "Theory and Practice in the Life and Thought of César Estrada Chávez: Implications for a Social Ethic." Ph.D. diss., Boston University, 1978.

Roberts, Maurice. *César Chávez and La Causa.* Chicago: Children's Press, 1986. A children's book.

Rodríguez, Consuelo. *César Chávez.* New York: Chelsea House Publishers, 1995.

Rolle, Andrew F. *California: A History.* 3rd ed. Arlington Heights, Ill.: AHM Publishing Corp., 1978.

Rosaldo, Renato, Robert A. Calvert, and Gustav L. Seligmann Jr., eds. *Chicano: The Evolution of a People.* Malabar, Fla.: Robert E. Krieger Publishing Co., 1982.

Rosales, F. Arturo. *Chicano! The History of the Mexican-American Civil Rights Movement.* Houston: Arte Público Press, 1996.

Ross, Fred. *Conquering Goliath: César Chávez at the Beginning.* Keene, Calif.: El Taller Grafico Press, 1989.

Salandini, Victor. "Breakthrough in Coachella Valley." *America,* May 2, 1970, 470–71. Reply by C. C. Crawford, *America,* June 13, 1970, 619.

———. "Decision at DiGiorgio." *America,* October 17, 1970, 415.

———. "Lessons of the Grape Strike." *America,* October 17, 1970, 285–87.

———. "More Grapes of Wrath." *America,* August 17, 1968, 104–105.

Samora, Julian, and Patricia Vandel Simon. "César Chávez and the Farm Workers." In *A History of the Mexican-American People,* ed. Julian Samora and Patricia Vandel Simon. Notre Dame, Indiana: University of Notre Dame Press, 1977, 189–90.

Sanderson, R. K., and E. L. Barr. "Why Grape Growers Do Not 'Render Unto César,'" *Christian Century,* June 11, 1969, 810–11. A letter to the editor in response to Chávez's "Letter From Delano."

"Seething Vineyards." *Newsweek,* July 8, 1968, 62.

Serven, Manual E. *An Awakening Minority: The Mexican Americans.* 2nd ed. Beverly Hills: Glencoe Press, 1970.

Sherry, Gerald E. "Chávez's Fast in Cause of Nonviolent Action." *Central California Register,* March 7, 1968.

Simmen, Edward, ed. *Pain and Promise: The Chicano Today.* New York: Mentor, 1972.

Solis-Garza, Luis A. "César Chávez, The Chicano Messiah?" In *Pain and Promise,* ed. Edward Simmen, 297–305.

Solkoff, Joel. "Can César Chávez Cope With Success?" *New Republic,* May 22, 1976, 13–17.

Staples, Paul W. "César Chávez is Throwback to Pioneer Labor Leader." *Seattle Times,* December 14, 1969.

Steiner, Stan. *La Raza: The Mexican Americans.* New York: Harper & Row, 1970.

Stine, Annie. "Farm Workers Out on the Line Again." *Sierra,* July-August 1987, 14.

Stoddard, Ellwyn R. *Mexican Americans.* New York: Random House, 1973.

Street, Richard Steven. "It's Boycott Time in California." *Nation,* March 23, 1985, 330–33.

Taylor, Ronald B. *Chávez and the Farm Workers.* Boston: Beacon Press, 1975.

———. "Chávez and the NLRA: Something is in the Wind." *Nation,* February 22, 1975, 206–209.

———. "Chicanos on the Move." *Fresno Bee,* April 19, 1967, 1–2D.

———. "Huelga! The Boycott That Worked." *Nation,* September 7, 1970, 167–69.

———. "Nerve Gas in the Orchards." *Nation,* June 22, 1970.

———. "NFWA Claims Ethnic Ties, Clergy Support." *Fresno Bee,* November 21, 1965.

———. "Why Chávez Spurns the Labor Act." *Nation,* April 12, 1971, 254–56.

Terzian, James P., and Kathryn Cramer. *Mighty Hard Road: The Story of César Chávez.* Garden City, New York: Doubleday and Company, 1970. Book for high-school students.

Thomas More Bertels, Sister. "Why Chávez Fell Back on Boycotts." *Farm Journal* (April 1976): 19–20.

Tobin, Richard L. "The Revolution Is Not Coming, It is Here." *Saturday Review,* August 17, 1968, 12–15.

"Trial Date Is Set for Farm Labor Leader." *Fresno Bee,* November 21, 1965, 1.

Turner, Wallace. "Head of Farm Workers Union Ends 25-Day Fast in California." *New York Times,* March 11, 1968, 22.

"The UFW Targets Boycotts." *American Demographics* (October 1986): 22.

"Unionizing the Farm: DiGiorgio Signs an AFL-CIO Contract." *Business Week,* April 22, 1967, 164.

Valdez, Luis. "The Tale of La Raza." *Ramparts,* July 1966, 40.

Valdez, Luis, and Stan Steiner, eds. *Aztlán: An Anthology of Mexican-American Literature.* New York: Vintage, 1972.

"Victory for César Chávez." *Newsweek,* August 10, 1970, 56.

Vizzard, James L., S.J. "The Extraordinary César Chávez." *Progressive,* July 1966, 16–20.

"Viva La Causa!" *IUD Agenda,* II (July 1966). The entire issue is devoted to the Mexican-American farm workers.

Watson, M. L. "Boycott Seeks to Aid Grape Workers." *Christian Century,* June 5, 1968, 769–70.

Weinstein, Henry Elliott. "New Rows to Hoe." *Wall Street Journal,* July 31, 1970, 1, 15. Reprinted in *La Causa Política: A Chicano Politics Reader,* ed. F. Chris García, 366–71.

"What Happened to Chávez's Union." *Newsweek,* December 14, 1981, 22–23

"Whatever Happened to the Grape Strike and Boycott?" *U.S. News and World Report,* April 6, 1970, 58.

White, Florence M. *César Chávez: Man of Courage.* New Caanan, Conn.: Garrard Publishing Co., 1973. For juvenile audience.

"Will Mr. Chávez Finally Prevail?" *America,* March 23, 1968, 366.

Wilson, David S. "Despite Boycott, Grape Sales Are Up." *New York Times,* December 27, 1988, 30.

"Wooing the Migrant Farmer." *Newsweek,* June 29, 1987, 47.

Yates, Michael. "A Union Is Not A 'Movement.'" *Nation,* November 19, 1977, 518–20.

Yinger, Winthrop. *César Chávez, The Rhetoric of Nonviolence.* Hicksville, New York: Exposition Press, 1975.

Young, Jan. *The Migrant Workers and César Chávez.* New York: Julian Messner, 1972.

Zermeno, Andy, and the staff of *El Malcriado. Don Sotaco: Cartoons From the Delano Strike.* Delano, Calif.: Farm Workers Press, 1966.

Index